taste of home
GRAND PRIZE
WINNERS

taste of home
GRAND PRIZE
WINNERS

Senior Vice President, Editor in Chief	**Catherine Cassidy**
Vice President, Executive Editor/Books	**Heidi Reuter Lloyd**
Creative Director	**Ardyth Cope**
Food Director	**Diane Werner RD**
Senior Editor/Books	**Mark Hagen**
Editor	**Krista Lanphier**
Art Director	**Edwin Robles, Jr.**
Content Production Supervisor	**Julie Wagner**
Project Art Director	**Catherine Fletcher**
Layout Designer	**Nancy Novak**
Proofreaders	**Linne Bruskewitz, Amy Glander, Victoria Soukup Jensen**
Recipe Asset Management System	**Coleen Martin**
Premedia Supervisor	**Scott Berger**
Recipe Testing and Editing	**Taste of Home Test Kitchen**
Food Photography	**Taste of Home Photo Studio**
Administrative Assistant	**Barb Czysz**
U.S. Chief Marketing Officer	**Lisa Karpinski**
Vice President/Book Marketing	**Dan Fink**
Creative Director/Creative Marketing	**Jim Palmen**

The Reader's Digest Association, Inc.

President and Chief Executive Officer	**Mary G. Berner**
President, U.S. Affinities	**Suzanne M. Grimes**
SVP, Global Chief Marketing Officer	**Amy J. Radin**

Taste of Home is a registered trademark
of The Reader's Digest Association, Inc.

COVER PHOTOGRAPHY
Photographer **Lori Foy**
Food Stylist **Kaitlyn Besasie**
Set Stylist **Melissa Haberman**

FRONT COVER PHOTO
White Chocolate Mousse Cherry Pie (p. 196)

BACK COVER PHOTOS
Gone-All-Day Stew (p. 47)
Sour Cream-Lemon Pie (p. 201)
Fresh Broccoli and Mandarin Salad (p. 26)

International Standard Book Number (10):
0-89821-770-9
International Standard Book Number (13):
978-0-89821-770-4
Library of Congress Control Number:
2009935070

For other Taste of Home books and products,
visit **ShopTasteofHome.com**.

For more Reader's Digest
products and information,
visit **rd.com** (in the United States)
or see **rd.ca** (in Canada).

Printed in U.S.A.
3 5 7 9 10 8 6 4

table of contents

73

154

186

Blue-Ribbon Recipes All Year Long!

Cooking with confidence has never been easier with the Grand Prize Winners Cookbook, because every recipe within these pages has been judged to be the best of the best! This exciting new book is jam-packed with over 350 delicious, blue-ribbon dishes and helpful kitchen tips. And every recipe has taken top prize in a national recipe contest held by either *Taste of Home* magazine or one of its sister publications, such as *Simple and Delicious, Healthy Cooking, Country* and *Country Woman*. That's **the best** from five different publications, all in **one cookbook!**

"Most of all, every single recipe in this beautiful cookbook withstood a rigorous process to win the top prize!"

How a Recipe Takes Top Prize

A Grand Prize winner from the *Taste of Home* family of magazines isn't just a yummy dish; it's a reliable recipe, made from easy-to-find ingredients, that looks as great as it tastes. Most of all, every single recipe in this beautiful cookbook withstood a rigorous process to win the top prize.

Home cooks just like you read our request for contest entries and sent in their best must-have dishes, the ones family and friends ask for time and again. Our expert home economists sorted through thousands of recipes, looking for ones that had interesting flavors, accurate measurements, easy cooking techniques and a creative use of ingredients. The most promising ones were prepared by the Test Kitchen team for a judging panel made up of experienced food editors and home economists with a knack for picking winners. After much deliberating and sampling, the panel decided which recipes were the absolute best, and declared which ones deserved to be called Grand Prize winners.

A Variety of Fabulous Dishes to Choose From

This one is a winner!

The Grand Prize Winners Cookbook showcases a variety of recipes from dozens and dozens of contests. These dishes include appetizers, salads, side dishes, soups, stews, breakfast items, main courses, casseroles, breads, cookies, bars, candies, cakes, pies and delectable desserts. No matter what type of recipe you're looking for, you're sure to find it in this one-of-a-kind collection.

Every recipe features easy-to-follow directions and a full-color photograph. And each one has been tasted and approved by our Test Kitchen professionals, so you can be sure that you are serving your family the absolute best-tasting dishes. When you choose from the celebrated favorites in Grand Prize Winners Cookbook, everyone comes out a winner!

broccoli chicken cups, p. 10

Rich, flavorful dips, delicious, savory snacks and smooth, creamy spreads create some of the most tongue-tingling bites perfect for any occasion.

appetizers

1. In a large saucepan over medium heat, bring water and butter to a boil. Add flours, parsley, garlic powder and salt all at once; stir until a smooth ball forms. Remove from the heat; let stand for 5 minutes. Beat in eggs, one at a time. Beat until smooth.

2. Drop batter by rounded teaspoonfuls 2 in. apart onto greased baking sheets. Sprinkle with caraway. Bake at 400° for 18-20 minutes or until golden brown. Remove to wire racks. Immediately cut a slit in each puff to allow steam to escape; cool.

3. In a large bowl, combine the first eight filling ingredients. Stir in olives. Split puffs; add filling. Refrigerate.

Chunky Blue Cheese Dip

PREP/TOTAL TIME: 10 MIN. YIELD: 1-3/4 CUPS

SANDY SCHNEIDER NAPERVILLE, ILLINOIS

Every time I make this quick dip, someone asks for the recipe. It only requires a few items, so it's a snap to put together. I often prepare the thick spread with Gorgonzola cheese and serve it with toasted pecans.

- 1 package (8 ounces) cream cheese, softened
- 1/3 cup sour cream
- 1/2 teaspoon white pepper
- 1/4 to 1/2 teaspoon salt
- 1 cup (4 ounces) crumbled blue cheese
- 1/3 cup minced chives

Apple and pear slices *and/or* toasted pecan halves

1. In a small bowl, beat the cream cheese, sour cream, pepper and salt until blended. Fold in the blue cheese and chives. Serve with apple and pear slices and/or pecan halves.

Rye Party Puffs

PREP: 30 MIN. BAKE: 20 MIN. + COOLING YIELD: 4-1/2 DOZEN

KELLY WILLIAMS MORGANVILLE, NEW JERSEY

I can't go anywhere without taking along my party puffs. They're pretty enough for a wedding reception yet also hearty enough to snack on while watching football on television. A platterful of these will disappear.

- 1 cup water
- 1/2 cup butter, cubed
- 1/2 cup all-purpose flour
- 1/2 cup rye flour
- 2 teaspoons dried parsley flakes
- 1/2 teaspoon garlic powder
- 1/4 teaspoon salt
- 4 eggs

Caraway seeds

CORNED BEEF FILLING:

- 2 packages (8 ounces *each*) cream cheese, softened
- 2 packages (2 ounces *each*) thinly sliced deli corned beef, chopped
- 1/2 cup mayonnaise
- 1/4 cup sour cream
- 2 tablespoons minced chives
- 2 tablespoons diced onion
- 1 teaspoon spicy brown *or* horseradish mustard
- 1/8 teaspoon garlic powder
- 10 small pimiento-stuffed olives, chopped

Yummy Mummy Dip With Veggies

PREP: 25 MIN. BAKE: 20 MIN. + COOLING
YIELD: 16 SERVINGS (2 CUPS DIP)

HEATHER SNOW SALT LAKE CITY, UTAH

I came up with this idea for dressing up a veggie tray for our annual Halloween party, and everyone got really "wrapped up" in it. Frozen bread dough and dip mix make this a simple and easy appetizer that's as much fun to display as to eat!

1 loaf (1 pound) frozen bread dough, thawed

3 pieces string cheese

2 cups (16 ounces) sour cream

1 envelope fiesta ranch dip mix

1 pitted ripe olive

Assorted crackers, fresh vegetables and reserved bread

1 Let dough rise according to package directions. Place dough on a greased baking sheet. For mummy, roll out dough into a 12-in. oval that is narrower at the bottom. For the head, make an indentation about 1 in. from the top. Let rise in a warm place for 20 minutes.

2 Bake at 350° for 20-25 minutes or until golden brown. Arrange strips of string cheese over bread; bake 1-2 minutes longer or until cheese is melted. Remove from pan to a wire rack to cool.

3 Meanwhile, in a small bowl, combine sour cream and dip mix. Chill until serving.

4 Cut mummy in half horizontally. Hollow out bottom half, leaving a 3/4-in. shell. Cut removed bread into cubes; set aside. Place bread bottom on a serving plate. Spoon dip into shell. Replace top. For eyes, cut olive and position on head. Serve with crackers, vegetables and reserved bread.

Buffalo Wing Poppers

PREP: 20 MIN. BAKE: 20 MIN. YIELD: 40 APPETIZERS

BARBARA NOWAKOWSKI MESA, ARIZONA

The taste of buffalo wings and pepper poppers pair up in this appealing appetizer. It will disappear fast, so make a double batch, and have copies of the recipe handy.

20 jalapeno peppers

1 package (8 ounces) cream cheese, softened

1-1/2 cups (6 ounces) shredded part-skim mozzarella cheese

1 cup diced cooked chicken

1/2 cup blue cheese salad dressing

1/2 cup buffalo wing sauce

1 Cut peppers in half lengthwise, leaving stems intact; discard seeds. In a small bowl, combine the remaining ingredients. Pipe or stuff into pepper halves.

2 Place in a greased 15-in. x 10-in. x 1-in. baking pan. Bake, uncovered, at 325° for 20 minutes for spicy flavor, 30 minutes for medium spicy and 40 minutes for mild.

Editor's Note: When cutting hot peppers, disposable gloves are recommended. Avoid touching your face.

Broccoli Chicken Cups

PREP: 15 MIN. BAKE: 25 MIN. YIELD: 1 DOZEN

MARTY KINGERY POINT PLEASANT, WEST VIRGINIA

Frozen puff pastry makes these unique and tasty appetizers a snap to prepare. Sometimes, instead of chopping the tomatoes, I put a slice on top of each cup before popping them in the oven.

> 2-1/2 cups diced cooked chicken breast
> 1 can (10-3/4 ounces) reduced-fat reduced-sodium condensed cream of chicken soup, undiluted
> 1 cup frozen chopped broccoli, thawed and drained
> 2 small plum tomatoes, seeded and chopped
> 1 small carrot, grated
> 1 tablespoon Dijon mustard
> 1 garlic clove, minced
> 1/4 teaspoon pepper
> 1 sheet frozen puff pastry, thawed
> 1/4 cup grated Parmesan cheese

1 In a large bowl, combine the first eight ingredients; set aside. On a lightly floured surface, roll pastry into a 12-in. x 9-in. rectangle. Cut lengthwise into four strips and widthwise into three strips. Gently press puff pastry squares into muffin cups coated with cooking spray.

2 Spoon chicken mixture into pastry cups. Sprinkle with Parmesan. Bake at 375° for 25-30 minutes or until golden brown. Serve warm.

Terrific Tomato Tart

PREP: 15 MIN. BAKE: 20 MIN. YIELD: 8 SERVINGS

DIANE HALFERTY CORPUS CHRISTI, TEXAS

This recipe is fabulous! Fresh, colorful tomatoes, feta cheese and prepared pesto perfectly complement the crispy phyllo dough crust.

> 12 sheets phyllo dough (14 inches x 9 inches)
> 2 tablespoons olive oil
> 2 tablespoons dry bread crumbs
> 2 tablespoons prepared pesto
> 3/4 cup crumbled feta cheese, *divided*
> 1 medium tomato, cut into 1/4-inch slices
> 1 large yellow tomato, cut into 1/4-inch slices
> 1/4 teaspoon pepper
> 5 to 6 fresh basil leaves, thinly sliced

1 Place one sheet of phyllo dough on a baking sheet lined with parchment paper; brush with 1/2 teaspoon oil and sprinkle with 1/2 teaspoon bread crumbs. (Keep remaining phyllo covered with plastic wrap and a damp towel to prevent it from drying out.) Repeat layers, being careful to brush oil all the way to edges.

2 Fold each side 3/4 in. toward center to form a rim. Spread with the pesto and sprinkle with half of the feta cheese. Alternately arrange the red and yellow tomato slices over the cheese. Sprinkle with pepper and remaining feta.

3 Bake at 400° for 20-25 minutes or until crust is golden brown and crispy. Cool on a wire rack for 5 minutes. Remove parchment paper before cutting. Garnish with basil.

Marinated Shrimp

PREP: 10 MIN. + MARINATING YIELD: 14 SERVINGS

MARGARET DELONG LAKE BUTLER, FLORIDA

Seafood is a staple here in Florida. These shrimp are quick and easy to make and can be prepared well in advance. I always seem to get a lot of requests for the recipe when I make it for a party or special occasion.

- 2 pounds cooked medium shrimp, peeled and deveined
- 1 medium red onion, sliced and separated into rings
- 2 medium lemons, cut into slices
- 1 cup pitted ripe olives, drained
- 1/2 cup olive oil
- 1/3 cup minced fresh parsley
- 3 tablespoons lemon juice
- 3 tablespoons red wine vinegar
- 1 garlic clove, minced
- 1 bay leaf
- 1 tablespoon minced fresh basil *or* 1 teaspoon dried basil
- 1 teaspoon salt
- 1 teaspoon ground mustard
- 1/4 teaspoon pepper

1 In a 3-qt. glass serving bowl, combine the shrimp, onion, lemons and olives. In a jar with a tight-fitting lid, combine the remaining ingredients; shake well. Pour over shrimp mixture and stir gently to coat. Cover and refrigerate for 24 hours, stirring occasionally. Discard bay leaf before serving.

Chocolate Caramel Fondue

PREP/TOTAL TIME: 10 MIN. YIELD: 2-1/2 CUPS

CHERYL ARNOLD LAKE ZURICH, ILLINOIS

It's best to keep the ingredients for this wonderfully rich fondue on hand in case unexpected company drops by. I serve the thick sauce in punch cups, so guests can carry it on a dessert plate alongside their choice of fruit, pretzels and other dippers.

- 1 can (14 ounces) sweetened condensed milk
- 1 jar (12 ounces) caramel ice cream topping
- 3 ounces unsweetened chocolate, chopped

Assorted fresh fruit *and/or* pretzels

1 In a large saucepan, combine the milk, caramel topping and chocolate. Cook over low heat until chocolate is melted. Transfer to a fondue pot and keep warm. Serve with fruit and/or pretzels.

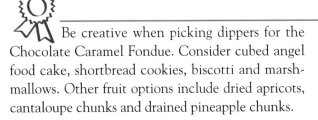

Be creative when picking dippers for the Chocolate Caramel Fondue. Consider cubed angel food cake, shortbread cookies, biscotti and marshmallows. Other fruit options include dried apricots, cantaloupe chunks and drained pineapple chunks.

3   For the sauce, in a large saucepan, combine the cranberry sauce, chili sauce, picante sauce, brown sugar and lemon juice. Cook and stir until cranberry sauce is melted and mixture is heated through. Pour over meatballs.

4   Cover and bake at 350° for 30-35 minutes or until meat is no longer pink. Serve with noodles if desired.

Deviled Crab Dip

PREP: 15 MIN. + CHILLING   YIELD: ABOUT 2 CUPS

DEBBIE JONES CALIFORNIA, MARYLAND

Because blue crabs are so plentiful in Maryland, we're always looking for new ways to enjoy them. This recipe is easy, elegant and delectable!

  1   cup mayonnaise
  2   tablespoons *each* finely chopped celery, green pepper and onion
  2   to 3 teaspoons lemon juice
  1   teaspoon ground mustard
  1   teaspoon Worcestershire sauce
1/4   teaspoon salt
1/8   teaspoon lemon-pepper seasoning
1/8   to 1/4 teaspoon hot pepper sauce
1-1/2   cups crabmeat, drained, flaked and cartilage removed

Assorted fresh vegetables *or* assorted crackers

1   In a large bowl, combine the mayonnaise, celery, green pepper, onion, lemon juice, mustard, Worcestershire sauce, salt, lemon-pepper and pepper sauce. Stir in crab. Cover and refrigerate for at least 1 hour. Serve with vegetables or crackers.

Picante Cranberry Meatballs

PREP: 20 MIN.   BAKE: 30 MIN.   YIELD: 8 SERVINGS

MARGE WYSE WINFIELD, BRITISH COLUMBIA

These zippy ground beef meatballs are my favorite, and the recipe is so easy. Cranberry, chili and picante sauce may sound like an unusual combination, but the sweet and spicy flavors blend deliciously. Our nine grandchildren request these meatballs often.

  2   eggs, lightly beaten
1/3   cup ketchup
1/3   cup minced fresh parsley
  2   tablespoons soy sauce
  2   tablespoons dried minced onion
1/2   teaspoon garlic powder
1/4   teaspoon pepper
  1   cup crushed saltines (about 30 crackers)
  2   pounds lean ground beef

SAUCE:
  1   can (14 ounces) jellied cranberry sauce
  1   cup chili sauce
1/4   cup picante sauce
  2   tablespoons brown sugar
  1   tablespoon lemon juice

Hot cooked noodles, optional

1   In a large bowl, combine the eggs, ketchup, parsley, soy sauce, onion, garlic powder and pepper. Add cracker crumbs. Crumble beef over mixture and mix well. Shape into 1-1/2-in. balls.

2   In a skillet, brown meatballs over medium heat. Transfer to a greased 13-in. x 9-in. baking dish.

CAREN ADAMS
FONTANA, CALIFORNIA

I've been making this recipe ever since I can remember. It's simple to fix, doesn't take a lot of ingredients or time, and is always a favorite with my guests. You can change up the recipe for different crowds by varying the amount of seasoning, from mild to an extra-spicy kick.

Grilled Jerk Chicken Wings

PREP/TOTAL TIME: 30 MIN. YIELD: 6 SERVINGS

1/2 cup Caribbean jerk seasoning

18 fresh chicken wingettes (2 to 3 pounds)

2 cups honey barbecue sauce

1/3 cup packed brown sugar

2 teaspoons prepared mustard

1 teaspoon ground ginger

1   Coat grill rack with cooking spray before starting the grill. Place jerk seasoning in a large resealable plastic bag; add chicken wings, a few at a time, and shake to coat. In a small bowl, combine the barbecue sauce, brown sugar, mustard and ginger; set aside.

2   Grill chicken wings, covered, over medium heat for 12-16 minutes, turning occasionally. Brush with sauce. Grill, uncovered, 8-10 minutes longer or until juices run clear, basting and turning several times.

Festive Appetizer Spread

PREP: 20 MIN. + COOLING   YIELD: ABOUT 3 CUPS

EDITH HOWE WOBURN, MASSACHUSETTS

Our state is known for its cranberries, and there are many bogs in our area. This recipe is as delicious as it is easy. I make it ahead for convenience.

- 1 cup water
- 1 cup sugar
- 1 package (12 ounces) fresh *or* frozen cranberries
- 1/2 cup apricot preserves
- 2 tablespoons lemon juice
- 1/3 cup slivered almonds, toasted
- 1 package (8 ounces) cream cheese

Assorted crackers

1 In a large saucepan over medium heat, bring water and sugar to a boil without stirring; boil for 5 minutes. Add cranberries, cook until berries pop and sauce is thickened, about 10 minutes. Remove from the heat.

2 Cut the apricots in the preserves into small pieces; add to the cranberry mixture. Stir in lemon juice. Cool. Add the toasted almonds.

3 Spoon over cream cheese; serve with crackers. Store leftovers in the refrigerator.

Editor's Note: This sauce may also be served as an accompaniment to poultry or pork.

Pineapple Pecan Cheese Ball

PREP: 10 MIN. + CHILLING   YIELD: 3-1/3 CUPS

JUNE STONE BREWTON, ALABAMA

This festive cheese ball will keep for several days in the refrigerator. It's delicious! I've found it's very popular at a party or get-together.

- 2 packages (8 ounces *each*) cream cheese, softened
- 1 can (8 ounces) crushed pineapple, well drained
- 1/2 cup chopped green pepper
- 1/2 cup chopped green onions
- 1 teaspoon lemon-pepper seasoning
- 1 teaspoon seasoned salt
- 2 cups chopped pecans, *divided*

Assorted crackers

1 In a large bowl, beat cream cheese until smooth. Stir in the pineapple, green pepper, onions, seasonings and 1/2 cup pecans. Place on a sheet of plastic wrap; shape into a ball. Refrigerate overnight.

2 Just before serving, roll cheese ball in remaining pecans. Serve with crackers.

California Fresh Fruit Dip

PREP/TOTAL TIME: 10 MIN. YIELD: ABOUT 1 CUP

NANCY CUTRIGHT SAN JOSE, CALIFORNIA

I tried this dip at a potluck lunch and loved it. Try it with vanilla cookie wafers for dippers, too. My family especially enjoys it as a refreshing snack on hot summer afternoons.

- 1 cup plain low-fat yogurt
- 2 tablespoons honey
- 2 tablespoons lime juice
- 1 teaspoon grated lime peel
- 1/4 teaspoon ground ginger

1   In a small bowl, combine all ingredients. Serve with fresh fruit. Cover and refrigerate leftovers.

Veggie Shrimp Egg Rolls

PREP: 45 MIN. + STANDING   COOK: 10 MIN./BATCH
YIELD: 38 EGG ROLLS

CAROLE RESNICK CLEVELAND, OHIO

These wonderful appetizers will be the hit of your next cocktail party. They're so versatile that you can replace the shrimp with cooked crab, lobster or chicken. The tangy apricot dipping sauce comes together in a pinch.

- 2 teaspoons minced fresh gingerroot
- 1 garlic clove, minced
- 3 tablespoons olive oil, *divided*
- 1/2 pound uncooked medium shrimp, peeled, deveined and chopped
- 2 green onions, finely chopped
- 1 medium carrot, finely chopped
- 1 medium sweet red pepper, finely chopped
- 1 cup canned bean sprouts, rinsed and finely chopped
- 2 tablespoons water
- 2 tablespoons reduced-sodium soy sauce
- 38 wonton wrappers

APRICOT-MUSTARD DIPPING SAUCE:
- 3/4 cup apricot spreadable fruit
- 1 tablespoon water
- 1 tablespoon lime juice
- 1 tablespoon reduced-sodium soy sauce
- 1-1/2 teaspoons Dijon mustard
- 1/4 teaspoon minced fresh gingerroot

1   In a large skillet, saute ginger and garlic in 1 tablespoon oil over medium heat until tender. Add shrimp, onions, carrot, red pepper, bean sprouts, water and soy sauce; cook and stir for 2-3 minutes or until vegetables are crisp-tender and shrimp turn pink. Reduce heat to low; cook for 4-5 minutes or until most of the liquid has evaporated. Remove from the heat; let stand for 15 minutes.

2   Place a tablespoonful of shrimp mixture in the center of a wonton wrapper. (Keep wrappers covered with a damp paper towel until ready to use.) Fold bottom corner over filling. Fold sides toward center over filling. Moisten remaining corner with water; roll up tightly to seal.

3   In a large skillet over medium heat, cook egg rolls, a few at a time, in remaining oil for 5-7 minutes on each side or until golden brown. Drain on paper towels.

4   In a blender, combine the sauce ingredients; cover and process until smooth. Serve with egg rolls.

Gorgonzola Figs with Balsamic Glaze

PREP: 30 MIN. BAKE: 10 MIN. YIELD: 16 APPETIZERS

SARAH VASQUES MILFORD, NEW HAMPSHIRE

I got this recipe from another couple and tweaked it slightly to suit my family's tastes. It's absolutely wonderful, and everyone loves it.

>   1   cup balsamic vinegar
> 16   dried figs
> 1/2 cup crumbled Gorgonzola cheese
>   8   thin slices prosciutto, halved widthwise
>   2   teaspoons minced fresh rosemary
> 1/4 teaspoon pepper

1   For glaze, in a small saucepan, bring the vinegar to a boil over medium heat; cook until reduced to about 1/4 cup.

2   Cut a lengthwise slit down the center of each fig; fill with 1-1/2 teaspoons cheese. Wrap each with a piece of prosciutto; place on a baking sheet. Sprinkle with rosemary and pepper.

3   Bake at 425° for 10-12 minutes or until prosciutto is crisp. Serve warm with glaze.

Editor's Note: Amber-colored dried figs (labeled Turkish or Calimyrna) are recommended for this recipe. Mission figs, which are black, are smaller and hold less cheese. If large stems are present, remove them before stuffing figs.

Bacon-Cheese Appetizer Pie

PREP: 15 MIN. BAKE: 50 MIN. + COOLING
YIELD: 16-20 APPETIZER SERVINGS

JOANIE ELBOURN GARDNER, MASSACHUSETTS

I first made this for an open house once and everybody liked it. It's very easy to make and tastes delicious. Cheesecake is always popular. It's fun to have it for an appetizer instead of dessert for a change.

Pastry for a single-crust pie

>   3   packages (8 ounces *each*) cream cheese, softened
>   4   eggs, lightly beaten
> 1/4 cup milk
>   1   cup (4 ounces) shredded Swiss cheese
> 1/2 cup sliced green onions
>   6   bacon strips, cooked and crumbled
> 1/2 teaspoon salt
> 1/8 teaspoon pepper
> 1/8 teaspoon cayenne pepper

1   Roll the pastry into a 13-1/2 in. circle. Fit into the bottom and up the sides of an ungreased 9-in. springform pan. Lightly prick the bottom. Bake at 450° for 8-10 minutes or until lightly browned. Cool slightly.

2   In a large bowl, beat cream cheese until fluffy. Add eggs and milk; beat until smooth. Add cheese, onions, bacon, salt, pepper and cayenne; mix well. Pour into the crust.

3   Bake at 350° for 40-45 minutes or until a knife inserted near the center comes out clean. Cool 20 minutes. Remove sides of pan. Cut into thin slices; serve warm.

Beef 'n' Cheese Dip

PREP: 10 MIN. BAKE: 1 HOUR YIELD: 3 CUPS

HEATHER MELNICK MACEDON, NEW YORK

I combined two favorite recipes and trimmed them down to create this yummy low-fat cheese dip. It's great for receptions, parties and get-togethers. It was a hit with the guys at our house last Christmas!

- 1 package (8 ounces) reduced-fat cream cheese
- 1-1/2 cups (6 ounces) shredded reduced-fat cheddar cheese
- 1/2 cup fat-free sour cream
- 2 packages (2-1/2 ounces *each*) thinly sliced dried beef
- 1/2 cup chopped green onions
- 1/2 cup mild pepper rings, drained and chopped
- 2 teaspoons Worcestershire sauce
- 1 loaf (1 pound) unsliced round rye bread

Assorted fresh vegetables

1   In a large bowl, combine the cream cheese, cheddar cheese and sour cream. Stir in the beef, onions, peppers and Worcestershire sauce.

2   Cut the top fourth off the loaf of bread; carefully hollow out bottom, leaving a 1-in. shell. Cube removed bread and top of loaf; set aside.

3   Fill bread shell with beef mixture. Wrap in foil; place on baking sheet. Bake at 350° for 60-70 minutes or until heated through. Serve with vegetables and reserved bread cubes.

Editor's Note: Mild pepper rings come in jars and can be found in the pickle and olive aisle of most grocery stores.

Bacon Cheeseburger Balls

PREP: 25 MIN. COOK: 10 MIN. YIELD: 3 DOZEN

CATHY LENDVOY BOHARM, SASKATCHEWAN

When I serve these, my husband and sons are often fooled into thinking we're having plain meatballs until they cut into the flavorful filling inside.

- 1 egg
- 1 envelope onion soup mix
- 1 pound ground beef
- 2 tablespoons all-purpose flour
- 2 tablespoons milk
- 1 cup (4 ounces) shredded cheddar cheese
- 4 bacon strips, cooked and crumbled

COATING:

- 2 eggs
- 1 cup crushed saltines (about 30 crackers)
- 5 tablespoons canola oil

1   In a large bowl, combine egg and soup mix. Crumble beef over mixture and mix well. Divide into 36 portions; set aside. In another large bowl, combine the flour and milk until smooth. Add cheese and bacon; mix well.

2   Shape cheese mixture into 36 balls. Shape one beef portion around each cheese ball. In a shallow bowl, beat the eggs. Place cracker crumbs in another bowl. Dip meatballs into egg, then coat with crumbs.

3   In a large skillet, cook meatballs over medium heat in oil for 10-12 minutes or until the meat is no longer pink and coating is golden brown.

Tempura Chicken Wings

PREP: 40 MIN. BAKE: 25 MIN. YIELD: 2-1/2 DOZEN

SUSAN WUCKOWITSCH LENEXA, KANSAS

When I moved to Kansas City from Texas, I brought many of my mom's recipes with me, including these saucy wings.

> 15 whole chicken wings (about 3 pounds)
> 1 cup cornstarch
> 3 eggs, lightly beaten
> Oil for deep-fat frying
> 1/2 cup sugar
> 1/2 cup white vinegar
> 1/2 cup currant jelly
> 1/4 cup soy sauce
> 3 tablespoons ketchup
> 2 tablespoons lemon juice

1 Cut chicken wings into three sections; discard wing tip section. Place cornstarch in a large resealable plastic bag; add chicken wings, a few at a time, and shake to coat evenly. Dip wings in eggs.

2 In an electric skillet or deep-fat fryer, heat oil to 375°. Fry wings for 8 minutes or until golden brown and juices run clear, turning occasionally. Drain on paper towels.

3 In a small saucepan, combine the sugar, vinegar, jelly, soy sauce, ketchup and lemon juice. Bring to a boil. Reduce heat; simmer, uncovered, for 10 minutes.

4 Place chicken wings in a greased 15-in. x 10-in. x 1-in. baking pan. Pour half of the sauce over wings. Bake, uncovered, at 350° for 15 minutes. Turn wings; top with remaining sauce. Bake 10-15 minutes longer or until chicken juices run clear and coating is set.

Cornmeal Onion Rings

PREP/TOTAL TIME: 30 MIN. YIELD: 8 SERVINGS

MILA BRYNING ALEXANDRIA, VIRGINIA

My husband says these onion rings are the best he's ever eaten, and I would have to agree with him. The cornmeal and chopped pecans in the coating give them an irresistible, special crunch. I like to serve them with chunky ketchup that has a little mayonnaise and hot sauce added to it. There's nothing quite like crispy, homemade onion rings—they really hit the spot!

> 2 pounds onions
> 2 eggs
> 1 cup buttermilk
> 2 cups all-purpose flour
> 1 cup cornmeal
> 1/2 cup chopped pecans
> 1 to 1-1/2 teaspoons salt
> 1/2 teaspoon pepper
> Oil for deep-fat frying

1 Cut the onions into 1/2-in. slices; separate the slices into rings. In a shallow bowl, whisk the eggs and buttermilk until blended. In another shallow bowl, combine the flour, cornmeal, chopped pecans, salt and pepper. Dip the onion rings in egg mixture, then coat with flour mixture.

2 In an electric skillet or deep-fat fryer, heat 1 in. of the oil to 375°. Fry the batter-coated onion rings, a few at a time, for 1 to 1-1/2 minutes on each side or until golden brown. (Avoid overcrowding in deep-fat fryer to prevent greasiness.) Drain on paper towels.

filling across the center of each rectangle. Wet edges of pastry with water and roll pastry around filling. Crimp ends with a fork to seal. Repeat with remaining pastry and filling.

3 Place seam side down on a lightly greased baking sheet. Refrigerate until ready to heat. Bake at 425° for 20-25 minutes or until golden brown. Serve warm with guacamole and salsa.

Picnic Stuffed Eggs
PREP/TOTAL TIME: 15 MIN. YIELD: 2 DOZEN

REBECCA REGISTER TALLAHASSEE, FLORIDA
My dad loves these deviled eggs, which are a Southern favorite. I've been cooking since I became a teenager, and this is one of my original recipes.

    12 hard-cooked eggs
    1/2 cup mayonnaise
    1/4 cup sweet pickle relish, drained
      1 tablespoon honey mustard
      1 teaspoon garlic salt
    1/2 teaspoon Worcestershire sauce
    1/4 teaspoon pepper
Fresh parsley sprigs, optional

1 Slice eggs in half lengthwise; remove yolks and set whites aside. In a small bowl, mash yolks with a fork. Add the mayonnaise, pickle relish, mustard, garlic salt, Worcestershire sauce and pepper; mix well.

2 Stuff or pipe into the egg whites. Refrigerate until serving. Garnish with parsley if desired.

Chickaritos
PREP: 30 MIN. BAKE: 20 MIN. YIELD: 1-1/2 DOZEN

NANCY COATES ORO VALLEY, ARIZONA
This recipe is one I created, substituting chicken for beef and omitting the frying, when our son grew fond of a fast-food restaurant's "junior burritos." They've been a big hit with our whole family ever since!

      3 cups finely chopped cooked chicken
  1-1/2 cups (6 ounces) shredded sharp cheddar cheese
      1 can (4 ounces) chopped green chilies
    1/2 cup finely chopped green onions
      1 teaspoon hot pepper sauce
      1 teaspoon garlic salt
    1/4 teaspoon pepper
    1/4 teaspoon ground cumin
    1/4 teaspoon paprika
      1 package (17-1/4 ounces) frozen puff pastry sheets, thawed *or* pie pastry for double-crust 10-inch pie
Guacamole
Salsa

1 In a large bowl, combine the chicken, cheese, chilies, onions and seasonings. Chill until serving.

2 Remove half of the pastry from the refrigerator. On a lightly floured surface, roll to a 12-in. x 9-in. rectangle. Cut into nine small rectangles. Place 2 tablespoons of

fiery chicken spinach salad, p. 24

Cool, refreshing salads full of good things, hearty, robust side dishes and savory or sweet condiments make delicious additions to any meal.

salads, sides & such

1. Place the first eight ingredients in a blender. Cover and process until blended; set aside. Divide the lettuce, cucumber, avocado, nuts, onion and cilantro between two serving plates.

2. In a small bowl, combine oil and jerk seasoning. Thread shrimp and scallops onto two metal or soaked wooden skewers; brush with oil mixture.

3. Grill, covered, over medium heat for 2-3 minutes on each side or until shrimp turn pink and scallops are firm and opaque. Place on salads; drizzle with dressing.

Tangy Potato Salad

PREP: 15 MIN. + CHILLING   YIELD: 10-12 SERVINGS

MARILYN VAN SCYOC CARTHAGE, INDIANA

My potato salad is so easy, I can quickly put it together in the kitchen of our trailer home on the lake. I've shared the recipe with our three daughters, and it's become a signature dish with all of them. Our grandchildren eat it up.

 8 **cups cubed peeled cooked potatoes (about 11 medium)**
 10 **bacon strips, cooked and crumbled**
 3 **hard-cooked eggs, chopped**
 1 **carton (8 ounces) French onion dip**
 1/2 **cup dill pickle relish**
 1/2 **teaspoon salt**
 1/2 **teaspoon pepper**
Leaf lettuce, optional

1. In a large bowl, combine the potatoes, bacon and eggs. In a small bowl, combine the dip, relish, salt and pepper. Stir into potato mixture. Cover and refrigerate for at least 2 hours. Serve in a lettuce-lined bowl if desired.

Shrimp 'n' Scallops Tropical Salad

PREP: 35 MIN. COOK: 5 MIN. YIELD: 2 SERVINGS

JACKIE PRESSINGER STUART, FLORIDA

A fruity dressing drapes this zippy salad. Served on a bed of greens, the scrumptious combination of grilled seafood, veggies and macadamia nuts is the perfect way to celebrate a special summer occasion.

 2 **tablespoons diced peeled mango**
 1 **tablespoon diced fresh pineapple**
 1-1/2 **teaspoons mango chutney**
 1-1/2 **teaspoons olive oil**
 1 **teaspoon rice vinegar**
 3/4 **teaspoon lime juice**
Dash salt
Dash crushed red pepper flakes
 3 **cups torn Bibb *or* Boston lettuce**
 1 **cup chopped peeled cucumber**
 1/2 **medium ripe avocado, peeled and sliced**
 2 **tablespoons coarsely chopped macadamia nuts, toasted**
 1 **tablespoon finely chopped red onion**
 1 **tablespoon minced fresh cilantro**
 2 **tablespoons canola oil**
 1-1/2 **teaspoons Caribbean jerk seasoning**
 6 **uncooked large shrimp, peeled and deveined**
 6 **sea scallops, halved**

Special Summer Berry Medley

PREP/TOTAL TIME: 25 MIN. YIELD: 12 SERVINGS

NANCY WHITFORD EDWARDS, NEW YORK

No matter how big the meal, folks always find room for this delightfully "special" dessert. With its hint of citrus and mint, this medley makes a light pretty side dish at casual cookouts or potlucks. Best of all, it's as fast and simple to make as it is to clean up!

- 1 cup sparkling wine *or* white grape juice
- 1/2 cup sugar
- 1 tablespoon lemon juice
- 1-1/2 teaspoons grated lemon peel
- 1/2 teaspoon vanilla extract
- 1/8 teaspoon salt
- 3 cups sliced fresh strawberries
- 2 cups fresh blueberries
- 1 cup fresh raspberries
- 1 cup fresh blackberries
- 1 tablespoon minced fresh mint

1 In a small heavy saucepan, bring wine or grape juice and sugar to a boil. Cook, uncovered, for about 15 minutes or until reduced to 1/2 cup, stirring occasionally. Cool slightly. Stir in the lemon juice and peel, vanilla and salt.

2 In a large bowl, combine berries and mint. Add syrup and toss gently to coat. Cover and refrigerate until serving.

Christmas Jam

PREP: 25 MIN. PROCESS: 10 MIN. YIELD: ABOUT 14 HALF-PINTS

JO TALVACCHIA LANOKA HARBOR, NEW JERSEY

I have a passion for cooking, and it's my grandmother I can thank for it. She was a marvelous cook who could really stretch a food dollar. All the same, I've had my share of trial and error over the years. Shortly after we were married, my husband and I were invited to a family picnic. I made the prettiest potato salad you'd ever hope to see. There was only one problem—I hadn't cooked the potatoes!

- 2 packages (20 ounces *each*) frozen whole strawberries *or* 2-1/2 quarts fresh strawberries
- 1 pound fresh *or* frozen cranberries
- 5 pounds sugar
- 2 pouches (3 ounces *each*) liquid fruit pectin

1 Grind the strawberries and cranberries in a food processor or grinder; place in a Dutch oven. Add sugar. Bring to a full rolling boil; boil for 1 minute. Remove from the heat; stir in pectin and return to a full rolling boil. Boil for 1 minute, stirring constantly. Remove from the heat.

2 Cool for 5 minutes; skim off foam. Carefully ladle hot mixture into hot half-pint jars, leaving 1/4-in. headspace. Remove air bubbles; wipe rims and adjust lids. Process for 10 minutes in a boiling-water canner.

Editor's Note: The processing time listed is for altitudes of 1,000 feet or less. Add 1 minute to the processing time for each 1,000 feet of additional altitude.

Sesame Cucumber Salad

PREP: 15 MIN. + STANDING YIELD: 8-10 SERVINGS

LINDA HODGE KANNAPOLIS, NORTH CAROLINA

I learned to cook at an early age and have collected many recipes. Whenever I take this salad to a church supper, it's the first one to disappear!

        8 cups thinly sliced cucumbers
        1 tablespoon salt
        2 green onions, sliced
        1 garlic clove, minced
        2 to 3 tablespoons soy sauce
        2 tablespoons white vinegar
        1 tablespoon canola oil
        1 tablespoon sesame seeds, toasted
     1/8 teaspoon cayenne pepper

1   Place cucumbers in a colander. Set the colander on a plate; sprinkle cucumbers with salt and toss. Let stand for 30 minutes. Rinse and drain well.

2   In a bowl, combine the onions, garlic, soy sauce, vinegar, oil, sesame seeds and cayenne. Add cucumbers and toss to coat. Cover and refrigerate until serving.

Fiery Chicken Spinach Salad

PREP/TOTAL TIME: 10 MIN. YIELD: 6 SERVINGS

KATI SPENCER TAYLORSVILLE, UTAH

This hearty and colorful main-course salad is easy to throw together when I get home from work, because it uses canned black beans and Mexicorn and packaged chicken breast strips. I sometimes add a can of ripe olives and fresh cherry tomatoes from our garden.

        6 frozen breaded spicy chicken breast strips, thawed
        1 package (6 ounces) fresh baby spinach
        1 medium tomato, cut into 12 wedges
     1/2 cup chopped green pepper
     1/2 cup fresh baby carrots
        1 can (15 ounces) black beans, rinsed and drained
        1 can (11 ounces) Mexicorn, drained
        3 tablespoons salsa
        3 tablespoons barbecue sauce
        3 tablespoons prepared ranch salad dressing
        2 tablespoons shredded Mexican cheese blend

1   Heat chicken strips in a microwave according to package directions. Meanwhile, arrange the spinach on individual plates; top with tomato, green pepper, carrots, beans and corn.

2   In a small bowl, combine the salsa, barbecue sauce and ranch dressing. Place chicken over salads. Drizzle with dressing; sprinkle with cheese.

Wild Rice Seafood Salad

PREP: 10 MIN. + CHILLING YIELD: 4-5 SERVINGS

KATHLEEN ZUSAN SCANDIA, MINNESOTA

With the rich Native American heritage of our state, this Minnesota wild rice recipe is popular. Wild rice grows naturally in our shallow lakes.

- 3 cups cooked wild rice
- 2 packages (5 ounces *each*) frozen cooked salad shrimp, thawed
- 2 cups flaked imitation crabmeat
- 1/2 cup *each* chopped sweet yellow, green and red peppers
- 1/2 cup chopped onion
- 1/2 cup red wine vinegar
- 1/4 cup olive oil
- 2 teaspoons minced fresh marjoram *or* 1/2 teaspoon dried marjoram
- 2 teaspoons minced fresh tarragon *or* 1/2 teaspoon dried tarragon
- 2 teaspoons minced fresh thyme *or* 1/2 teaspoon dried thyme
- 1 teaspoon salt
- 1/4 teaspoon pepper

1 In a large serving bowl, combine the rice, shrimp, crab, peppers and onion.

2 In a jar with a tight-fitting lid, combine the remaining ingredients; shake well. Pour over rice mixture and toss to coat. Cover and refrigerate for at least 2 hours before serving.

Creamy Chive Mashed Potatoes

PREP: 15 MIN. COOK: 25 MIN. YIELD: 4-5 SERVINGS

BONNIE THOMPSON RATHDRUM, IDAHO

Buttermilk and cream cheese lend a rich sour cream-like flavor to these wonderful whipped potatoes. The addition of chives makes this dish so attractive, you'll want to serve it at every special-occasion dinner.

- 5 medium potatoes, peeled
- 1-1/2 teaspoons salt, *divided*
- 4 ounces cream cheese, softened
- 2 tablespoons butter, softened
- 2 tablespoons minced chives
- 1/4 teaspoon pepper
- 1/4 to 1/2 cup buttermilk

1 Place the potatoes in a large saucepan and cover with water; add 1 teaspoon salt. Bring to a boil; reduce the heat. Cover and cook for 15-20 minutes or until tender; drain.

2 In a large bowl, mash the potatoes with the cream cheese, butter, chives, pepper and remaining salt; gradually beat in buttermilk.

Fresh Broccoli and Mandarin Salad

PREP: 30 MIN. + CHILLING YIELD: 10-12 SERVINGS

CONNIE BLOMMERS PELLA, IOWA

I write a food column for a local newspaper, and consider myself a pretty good judge of recipes. But I'll admit I was surprised by this one—I didn't think the ingredients would go together as well as they do. I enjoy all kinds of cooking, especially recipes like this.

DRESSING:
- 1/2 cup sugar
- 1-1/2 teaspoons cornstarch
- 1 teaspoon ground mustard
- 1/4 cup white vinegar
- 1/4 cup water
- 1 egg plus 1 egg yolk, lightly beaten
- 1/2 cup mayonnaise
- 3 tablespoons butter, softened

SALAD:
- 4 cups fresh broccoli florets, 1-inch cuts
- 1/2 cup golden raisins
- 6 slices bacon, cooked and crumbled
- 2 cups sliced fresh mushrooms
- 1/2 cup slivered almonds, toasted
- 1 can (11 ounces) mandarin oranges, drained
- 1/2 medium red onion, sliced in 1/8-inch-thick rings

1 In a large saucepan, combine the sugar, cornstarch and mustard. Combine vinegar and water. Stir into sugar mixture until smooth. Cook and stir over medium-high heat until thickened and bubbly. Reduce heat; cook and stir 2 minutes longer. Remove from the heat. Stir a small amount of hot filling into egg and yolk; return all to pan, stirring constantly. Bring to a gentle boil; cook and stir 2 minutes longer. Remove from the heat. Gently stir in mayonnaise and butter. Cool to room temperature without stirring. Chill.

2 In a large salad bowl, combine the broccoli, raisins, bacon, mushrooms, almonds, mandarin oranges and onion. Pour the dressing over the salad; toss to coat. Store in the refrigerator.

Cranberry Orange Vinaigrette

PREP/TOTAL TIME: 10 MIN. YIELD: 1 CUP

TONI SERPE DANIA, FLORIDA

I eat a lot of salad, and this is one of my favorite dressings. Living in Florida, I like using orange products that have been produced in our state.

- 1/4 cup thawed cranberry juice concentrate
- 1/4 cup thawed orange juice concentrate
- 1/4 cup red wine vinegar
- 1/4 cup olive oil
- 1 teaspoon Dijon mustard
- 1/2 teaspoon salt
- 1/2 teaspoon pepper

Torn salad greens

Sliced radishes and sweet yellow and orange peppers *or* vegetables of your choice

1 In a jar with a tight-fitting lid, combine the first seven ingredients; shake well. Serve over greens and vegetables. Store in the refrigerator.

JOAN MCCULLOCH
ABBOTSFORD,
BRITISH COLUMBIA

I made this creamy and comforting potato dish for Thanksgiving and it was a winner with my family. They said to be sure to include it at every holiday dinner. It's a keeper!

Duo Tater Bake

PREP: 40 MIN. BAKE: 20 MIN. + CHILLING YIELD: 2 CASSEROLES (10 SERVINGS EACH)

- 4 **pounds russet *or* Yukon Gold potatoes, peeled and cubed**
- 3 **pounds sweet potatoes, peeled and cubed**
- 2 **cartons (8 ounces *each*) spreadable chive and onion cream cheese**
- 1 **cup (8 ounces) sour cream**
- 1/4 **cup shredded Colby-Monterey Jack cheese**
- 1/3 **cup milk**
- 1/4 **cup shredded Parmesan cheese**
- 1/2 **teaspoon salt**
- 1/2 **teaspoon pepper**

TOPPING:
- 1 **cup (4 ounces) shredded Colby-Monterey Jack cheese**
- 1/2 **cup chopped green onions**
- 1/4 **cup shredded Parmesan cheese**

1 Place russet potatoes in a Dutch oven and cover with water. Bring to a boil. Reduce heat; cover and cook for 10-15 minutes or until tender.

2 Meanwhile, place sweet potatoes in a large saucepan; cover with water. Bring to a boil. Reduce heat; cover and cook for 10-15 minutes or until tender. Drain; mash with half of the cream cheese and sour cream and all of Colby cheese.

3 Drain russet potatoes; mash with the remaining cream cheese and sour cream. Stir in the milk, Parmesan cheese, salt and pepper.

4 Spread 2-2/3 cups russet potato mixture into each of two greased 11-in. x 7-in. baking dishes. Layer with 4 cups sweet potato mixture. Repeat layers. Spread with remaining russet potato mixture.

5 Bake, uncovered, at 350° for 15 minutes or until heated through. Combine topping ingredients; sprinkle over casseroles. Bake 2-3 minutes longer or until cheese is melted.

Summer Salad with Citrus Vinaigrette

PREP/TOTAL TIME: 20 MIN. YIELD: 4 SERVINGS

CAROLYN WILLIAMS COSTA MESA, CALIFORNIA

I live in Orange County and, as you might guess by our county's name, there are plenty of orange trees here. This salad is one of my favorite ways to use this delightful fruit. It makes a nice light supper on a hot day.

VINAIGRETTE:
- 3 tablespoons orange juice
- 3 tablespoons red wine vinegar
- 2 teaspoons honey
- 1-1/2 teaspoons Dijon mustard
- 1 teaspoon olive oil

SALAD:
- 1 pound boneless beef sirloin steak, cut into thin strips
- 1 tablespoon canola oil
- 1/2 teaspoon salt, optional
- 4 cups torn romaine
- 2 large oranges, peeled and sectioned
- 1/2 cup sliced fresh strawberries
- 1/4 cup chopped walnuts, toasted, optional

1 In a small bowl, whisk the vinaigrette ingredients together; set aside.

2 In a large skillet, stir-fry steak in oil for 1-2 minutes. Sprinkle with salt if desired.

3 In a large bowl, toss romaine, oranges, strawberries and steak. Add vinaigrette toss to coat. Top with walnuts if desired.

Tomato Corn Salad

PREP/TOTAL TIME: 30 MIN. YIELD: 7 SERVINGS

CARRIE COMPONILE ROSELLE PARK, NEW JERSEY

Warm and colorful, this tantalizing side dish bursts with refreshing vegetable flavor. Fresh herbs and Dijon mustard add the pizzazz.

- 3 large tomatoes, chopped
- 1 small red onion, halved and thinly sliced
- 1/3 cup chopped green onions
- 1/4 cup balsamic vinegar
- 3 tablespoons minced fresh basil
- 1 tablespoon minced fresh cilantro
- 1 teaspoon salt
- 1/2 teaspoon pepper
- 4 cups fresh corn (about 9 ears of corn)
- 3 garlic cloves, peeled and thinly sliced
- 2 tablespoons olive oil
- 1 tablespoon Dijon mustard

1 In a large bowl, combine the first eight ingredients. In a large skillet, saute corn and garlic in oil until tender; stir in mustard. Add to vegetable mixture; toss to coat. Serve with a slotted spoon.

Spinach-Topped Tomatoes

PREP: 20 MIN. BAKE: 15 MIN. YIELD: 6 SERVINGS

ILA MAE ALDERMAN GALAX, VIRGINIA

The perfect taste of summer, this delicate side dish is sure to please. The spinach and tomato, combined with the Parmesan cheese, give it a fabulous fresh flavor. My daughter especially loves this dish, which I make often.

 1 package (10 ounces) frozen chopped spinach
 2 chicken bouillon cubes
Salt
 3 large tomatoes, halved
 1 cup soft bread crumbs
 1/2 cup grated Parmesan cheese
 1/2 cup chopped onion
 1/2 cup butter, melted
 1 egg, beaten
 1 garlic clove, minced
 1/4 teaspoon pepper
 1/8 teaspoon cayenne pepper
Shredded Parmesan cheese, optional

1 In a saucepan, cook spinach according to package directions with bouillon; drain well. Cool slightly; press out excess liquid.

2 Lightly salt tomato halves; place with cut side down on a paper towel for 15 minutes to absorb excess moisture.

3 Meanwhile, in a small bowl, combine spinach with bread crumbs, Parmesan cheese, onion, butter, egg, garlic, pepper and cayenne pepper. Mix well.

4 Place the tomato halves, cut side up, in a shallow baking dish. Divide the spinach mixture over the tomatoes. Sprinkle with shredded Parmesan cheese if desired. Bake at 350° for about 15 minutes or until heated through.

Paradise Cran-Applesauce

PREP: 15 MIN. COOK: 1 HOUR YIELD: 8-10 SERVINGS

SALLIE MCQUAY SAYRE, PENNSYLVANIA

Appealing apple slices peek through a tangy ruby-red cranberry sauce in this simple but extraordinary side dish. Whether I use this recipe for a holiday dinner or to spark up a Sunday supper, it wouldn't be a feast without a bowl of this beautiful and delicious applesauce!

 4 cups fresh *or* frozen cranberries
 1/4 cup water
 8 cups sliced peeled cooking apples
 2 cups sugar

1 In a covered saucepan, simmer cranberries and water for 20-25 minutes or until tender. Press through a sieve or food mill; return to the saucepan.

2 Add apples; covered and simmer for 35-40 minutes or until apples are tender but retain their shape. Add sugar. Simmer for 5 minutes, stirring occasionally.

Sweet Potato Fries

PREP: 15 MIN. BAKE: 25 MIN. YIELD: 2 SERVINGS

KELLY MCWHERTER HOUSTON, TEXAS

Nutritious sweet potatoes add subtle flavor to these extra-crunchy fries. With the tasty mayo-chutney dip, this super side could double as a party appetizer!

- 2 tablespoons beaten egg
- 1 tablespoon water
- 1/3 cup dry bread crumbs
- 2 tablespoons grated Parmesan cheese
- 1/4 teaspoon cayenne pepper
- 1/4 teaspoon pepper
- 1 large sweet potato (14 ounces), peeled
- 2 teaspoons olive oil

MANGO CHUTNEY MAYONNAISE:
- 1/4 cup mayonnaise
- 2 tablespoons mango chutney
- 1/4 teaspoon curry powder

Dash salt
- 2 teaspoons minced fresh parsley, optional

1 In a shallow bowl, whisk egg and water. In a resealable plastic bag, combine the bread crumbs, cheese, cayenne and pepper. Cut sweet potato into 1/4-in. strips. Add to egg mixture, a few at a time, and toss to coat. Add to the crumb mixture, a few at a time; seal bag and shake to coat.

2 Arrange potato strips in a single layer on a baking sheet coated with cooking spray; drizzle with oil. Bake at 450° for 25-30 minutes or until golden brown and crisp, turning occasionally.

3 In a small bowl, combine the mayonnaise, chutney, curry powder and salt. If desired, sprinkle parsley over fries. Serve with mango chutney mayonnaise.

Cranberry Rice with Caramelized Onions

PREP: 5 MIN. COOK: 55 MIN. YIELD: 4 SERVINGS

TOMMI ROYLANCE CHARLO, MONTANA

Rice provides so many options to a creative cook, because the stir-in ideas are endless. In this recipe, dried cranberries star. Their sweet-tart flavor accents my rice combination and gives a festive feel to everyday meals.

- 2-1/2 cups chicken *or* vegetable broth
- 1/2 cup uncooked wild rice
- 1/2 cup uncooked brown rice
- 3 medium onions, cut into wedges
- 2 teaspoons brown sugar
- 3 tablespoons butter
- 1 cup dried cranberries
- 1/2 teaspoon grated orange peel

1 In a large saucepan, bring broth to a boil. Add the wild rice. Reduce heat; cover and simmer for 10 minutes. Add the brown rice; cover and simmer for 45-50 minutes or until rice is tender and liquid is absorbed.

2 In a large skillet over medium heat, cook the onions and brown sugar in butter until golden brown, stirring frequently. Add the cranberries, orange peel and rice; heat through.

Curried Chicken
Salad Sandwiches

PREP/TOTAL TIME: 20 MIN. YIELD: 6 SERVINGS

CAROLE MARTIN COFFEEVILLE, MISSISSIPPI

This sandwich is perfect to serve when you want to "show off" a little. It features an interesting blend of chicken, nuts, cranberries, curry and other ingredients. I mix it up the night before so the flavors meld.

    2 cups cubed cooked chicken breast
  3/4 cup chopped apple
  3/4 cup dried cranberries
  3/4 cup mayonnaise
  1/2 cup chopped walnuts
  1/2 cup chopped celery
    2 teaspoons lemon juice
    1 tablespoon chopped green onion
    1 teaspoon curry powder
    6 lettuce leaves
    6 croissants, split

1 In a large bowl, combine the chicken, apple, cranberries, mayonnaise, walnuts, celery, lemon juice, onion and curry powder. Place lettuce on croissants. Top with chicken salad mixture.

Fresh Corn Salad

PREP: 20 MIN. + CHILLING YIELD: 10 SERVINGS

CAROL SHAFFER CAPE GIRARDEAU, MISSOURI

People who prefer food with some tang find this corn salad particularly appealing. It's a pretty dish besides–and very economical. If you're like me and enjoy growing your own ingredients, you won't have to pick up much at the store.

      8 ears fresh corn, husked and cleaned
    1/2 cup canola oil
    1/4 cup cider vinegar
  1-1/2 teaspoons lemon juice
    1/4 cup minced fresh parsley
      2 teaspoons sugar
      1 teaspoon salt
    1/2 teaspoon dried basil
    1/8 to 1/4 teaspoon cayenne pepper
      2 large tomatoes, seeded and coarsely chopped
    1/2 cup chopped onion
    1/3 cup chopped green pepper
    1/3 cup chopped sweet red pepper

1 In a large saucepan, cook corn in enough boiling water to cover for 5-7 minutes or until tender. Drain, cool and set aside.

2 In a large bowl, mix the oil, vinegar, lemon juice, parsley, sugar, salt if desired, basil and cayenne pepper. Cut cooled corn off the cob (should measure 4 cups).

3 Add the corn, tomatoes, onion and peppers to the oil mixture. Mix well. Cover and chill for several hours or overnight.

1. Discard seasoning packet from ramen noodles or save for another use. Break noodles into small pieces. In a small skillet, saute noodles and walnuts in butter for 8-10 minutes or until golden; cool.

2. For dressing, in a jar with a tight-fitting lid, combine the oil, sugar, vinegar and soy sauce; shake well. Just before serving combine the romaine, onions, strawberries and noodle mixture in a large bowl. Drizzle with dressing and toss gently.

Sweet Potatoes and Apples au Gratin
PREP: 25 MIN. BAKE: 45 MIN. YIELD: 12 SERVINGS

ERIKA VICKERMAN HOPKINS, MINNESOTA

This is a favorite of ours that we make every year. People on both sides of the family rave about it! My mother-in-law drove over to my house to tell me to enter the contest when she read about it. I'm glad she did!

- 3 cups thinly sliced tart apples (about 3 large)
- 1 teaspoon lemon juice
- 3 pounds sweet potatoes (about 5 medium), peeled and thinly sliced

Crunchy Romaine Strawberry Salad
PREP/TOTAL TIME: 30 MIN. YIELD: 12 SERVINGS

LESLIE LANCASTER ZACHARY, LOUISIANA

This is such an impressive salad! It's been a hit with people of all ages at every get-together we've ever brought it to. In addition to being pretty and colorful, it's a snap to make. And the mouthwatering combination of tastes and textures seems to please every palate.

- 1 package (3 ounces) ramen noodles
- 1 cup chopped walnuts
- 1/4 cup butter
- 1/4 cup canola oil
- 1/4 cup sugar
- 2 tablespoons red wine vinegar
- 1/2 teaspoon soy sauce
- 8 cups torn romaine
- 1/2 cup chopped green onions
- 2 cups fresh strawberries, sliced

1/4 cup maple syrup

1 tablespoon butter, melted

1/2 teaspoon salt

1/4 teaspoon pepper

1 cup soft bread crumbs

2 teaspoons olive oil

1/4 teaspoon ground cinnamon

1/4 teaspoon ground nutmeg

1/4 teaspoon cider vinegar

1 Place apples in a large bowl; sprinkle with lemon juice. Add the sweet potatoes, syrup, butter, salt and pepper; toss to coat.

2 Transfer to a 3-qt. baking dish coated with cooking spray. Bake, uncovered, at 400° for 35-40 minutes or until apples are tender, stirring once.

3 In a small bowl, combine the bread crumbs, oil, cinnamon, nutmeg and vinegar; sprinkle over potato mixture. Bake 10-15 minutes longer or until topping is golden brown.

Spicy Pork Tenderloin Salad

PREP: 20 MIN. COOK: 35 MIN. YIELD: 4 SERVINGS

PAT SELLON MONTICELLO, WISCONSIN

A friend served this curry-flavored salad at a luncheon, and I tweaked it to fit our tastes. Since it's a meal in one, it's perfect for weeknights, and the presentation makes it ideal for entertaining.

4-1/2 teaspoons lime juice

1-1/2 teaspoons orange juice

1-1/2 teaspoons Dijon mustard

1/2 teaspoon curry powder

1/4 teaspoon salt

1/8 teaspoon pepper

2 tablespoons olive oil

SPICE RUB:

1/2 teaspoon salt

1/2 teaspoon ground cumin

1/2 teaspoon ground cinnamon

1/2 teaspoon chili powder

1/4 teaspoon pepper

1 pork tenderloin (1 pound)

2 teaspoons olive oil

1/3 cup packed brown sugar

6 garlic cloves, minced

1-1/2 teaspoons hot pepper sauce

1 package (6 ounces) fresh baby spinach

1 In a small bowl, whisk the first six ingredients; gradually whisk in oil. Cover and refrigerate vinaigrette. Combine the salt, cumin, cinnamon, chili powder and pepper; rub over meat.

2 In an ovenproof skillet, brown meat on all sides in oil, about 8 minutes. Combine the brown sugar, garlic and hot pepper sauce; spread over meat.

3 Bake at 350° for 25-35 minutes or until a meat thermometer reads 160°. Let stand for 5 minutes before slicing.

4 Toss spinach with vinaigrette. Arrange spinach on four salad plates; top with sliced pork. Drizzle with pan juices.

 Minced garlic that you can buy, garlic that's been finely chopped by hand and garlic that's been put through a press can all be used interchangeably in recipes. Choose whichever is the easiest and most convenient for you.

ANA COLON
WISCONSIN RAPIDS,
WISCONSIN

I made a large version of this colorful pasta salad for a football party, and all my guests loved it. They wanted to know what I put in it to make it taste so good.

Smoked Turkey Pasta Salad

PREP: 30 MIN. + CHILLING YIELD: 4 CUPS

1 cup uncooked tricolor spiral pasta

1/4 pound cubed deli smoked turkey

1 cup (4 ounces) cubed Monterey Jack cheese

1/2 small cucumber, thinly sliced and halved

1/3 cup chopped sweet red pepper

1 green onion, thinly sliced

3 tablespoons sour cream

2 tablespoons mayonnaise

1-1/2 teaspoons 2% milk

1 teaspoon honey

1 teaspoon Dijon mustard

Dash pepper

1   Cook pasta according to package directions; drain and rinse in cold water. In a serving bowl, combine the pasta, turkey, cheese, cucumber, red pepper and onion.

2   In a small bowl, whisk the sour cream, mayonnaise, milk, honey, mustard and pepper. Pour over salad and toss to coat. Cover and refrigerate for at least 2 hours before serving.

To cook pasta more evenly, prevent it from sticking together and avoid boil-overs, always cook pasta in a large kettle or Dutch oven. It's best if you don't cook more than 2 pounds at a time.

For 8 ounces of pasta, bring 3 quarts water to a full rolling boil. To flavor, add 1 tablespoon salt. Cooking times vary with the size and variety of pasta. Dried pasta can take from 5 to 15 minutes to cook; fresh pasta can cook in as little as 2 to 3 minutes.

Party Carrots

PREP: 15 MIN. BAKE: 20 MIN. YIELD: 8 SERVINGS

BERTHA JOHNSON INDIANAPOLIS, INDIANA

People who don't like carrots often change their minds after tasting this easy-to-fix dish. It's nice for potlucks because you can prepare it ahead of time.

- 2 pounds carrots, sliced
- 2 teaspoons chicken bouillon granules
- 8 ounces process cheese (Velveeta), cubed
- 2 tablespoons butter
- 1 package (8 ounces) cream cheese, cubed
- 4 green onions, sliced
- 1/4 teaspoon salt
- 1/4 teaspoon pepper

1 Place 1 in. of water in a large saucepan; add carrots and bouillon. Bring to a boil. Reduce heat. Cover and simmer for 7-9 minutes or until crisp-tender.

2 Meanwhile, in another large saucepan, combine process cheese and butter. Cook and stir over low heat until melted. Add the cream cheese, onions, salt and pepper. Cook and stir until cream cheese is melted.

3 Drain carrots; stir into cheese sauce. Transfer to a greased shallow 2-qt. baking dish. Cover and bake at 350° for 20-25 minutes or until bubbly.

Tomatoes with Horseradish Sauce

PREP/TOTAL TIME: 15 MIN. YIELD: 4 SERVINGS

PHYLLIS SHAUGHNESSY LIVONIA, NEW YORK

This warm dish of lightly sauteed tomatoes and a tangy sauce is very tasty and quick to make. I occasionally use both red and green tomatoes to add even more color.

Refrigerated butter-flavored spray

- 4 large tomatoes, sliced
- 3 tablespoons mayonnaise
- 2 tablespoons half-and-half cream
- 1 tablespoon prepared horseradish

Minced fresh parsley

1 Coat a large skillet with refrigerated butter-flavored spray. Heat skillet over medium heat. Add tomato slices; cook for 2-3 minutes on each side or until edges begin to brown. In a small bowl, whisk the mayonnaise, cream and horseradish. Spoon over the tomatoes. Sprinkle with parsley.

Brown Rice Salad with Grilled Chicken

PREP/TOTAL TIME: 20 MIN. YIELD: 9 SERVINGS

GLENDA HARPER CABLE, OHIO

This delightful dish is nutritious, simple to fix and brightens up any buffet table. It's a terrific way to use up leftover chicken, and you can add vegetables according to your family's liking.

- 3 cups cooked brown rice
- 2 cups cubed grilled chicken breast
- 2 medium tart apples, diced
- 1 medium sweet red pepper, diced
- 2 celery ribs, finely chopped
- 2/3 cup chopped green onions
- 1/2 cup chopped pecans
- 3 tablespoons minced fresh parsley
- 1/4 cup cider vinegar
- 3 tablespoons canola oil
- 1 tablespoon lemon juice
- 1 teaspoon salt
- 1/4 teaspoon pepper
- Lettuce leaves, optional

1. In a large bowl, combine the first eight ingredients. In a jar with a tight-fitting lid, combine the vinegar, oil, lemon juice, salt and pepper; shake well. Pour over the rice mixture and toss to coat. Serve immediately or refrigerate. Serve in a lettuce-lined bowl if desired.

Almond Chicken Salad

PREP/TOTAL TIME: 15 MIN. YIELD: 6-8 SERVINGS

KATHY KITTELL LENEXA, KANSAS

My mother used to prepare this salad for an evening meal during the hot summer months. It also serves well as a delicious, speedy luncheon or potluck dish. You can't beat the tasty combination of chicken, grapes and almonds.

- 4 cups cubed cooked chicken
- 1-1/2 cups seedless green grapes, halved
- 1 cup chopped celery
- 3/4 cup sliced green onions
- 3 hard-cooked eggs, chopped
- 1/2 cup Miracle Whip
- 1/4 cup sour cream
- 1 tablespoon prepared mustard
- 1 teaspoon salt
- 1/2 teaspoon pepper
- 1/4 teaspoon onion powder
- 1/4 teaspoon celery salt
- 1/8 teaspoon ground mustard
- 1/8 teaspoon paprika
- 1/2 cup slivered almonds, toasted
- 1 kiwifruit, peeled and sliced, optional

1. In a large bowl, combine chicken, grapes, celery, onions and eggs. In another bowl, combine the next nine ingredients; stir until smooth.

2. Pour over the chicken mixture and toss gently. Stir in almonds and serve immediately, or refrigerate and add the almonds just before serving. Garnish with kiwifruit if desired.

Southwestern Spuds

PREP/TOTAL TIME: 30 MIN. YIELD: 4-6 SERVINGS

PENNY DYKSTRA PORTERVILLE, CALIFORNIA

I came up with this attractive side dish when my best friend unexpectedly stayed for dinner. While my husband grilled pork chops, I perked up potatoes with tasty taco fixings. The results received rave reviews. This recipe is even quicker to fix with leftover baked potatoes.

   3 **medium potatoes**

Salt and pepper to taste

   1 **cup (4 ounces) shredded cheddar cheese**

   1 **cup (4 ounces) shredded pepper Jack cheese**

   3 **green onions, chopped**

   1 **can (2-1/4 ounces) sliced ripe olives, drained**

Sour cream and salsa, optional

1 Pierce potatoes; place on a microwave-safe plate. Microwave on high for 6-8 minutes or until almost tender. Cool slightly; peel and cut into 1/8-in. slices.

2 Arrange half of the potatoes in a greased microwave-safe 9-in. pie plate. Season with salt and pepper. Sprinkle with half of the cheeses. Repeat layers. Top with onions and olives.

3 Microwave, uncovered, for 7-8 minutes or until cheese is melted and potatoes are tender. Serve with sour cream and salsa if desired.

Chicken Pear Mixed Greens Salad

PREP/TOTAL TIME: 25 MIN. YIELD: 5 SERVINGS

JANET DURAN DES MOINES, WASHINGTON

I served this fabulous salad at a shower, and received many compliments. The vinaigrette pairs wonderfully with the grilled chicken and Brie, and the nuts offer a fun crunch.

   5 **boneless skinless chicken breasts (4 ounces *each*)**

   7 **cups torn mixed salad greens**

   2 **ounces Brie cheese, cubed**

   2 **medium pears, chopped**

  1/4 **cup chopped pecans, toasted**

  1/4 **cup thawed apple juice concentrate**

   2 **tablespoons canola oil**

4-1/2 **teaspoons cider vinegar**

   2 **teaspoons Dijon mustard**

  1/4 **teaspoon salt**

  1/8 **teaspoon pepper**

1 Coat grill rack with cooking spray before starting the grill. Grill chicken, covered, over medium heat for 6-8 minutes on each side or until juices run clear.

2 Arrange the salad greens, cheese, pears and pecans on individual plates. Slice chicken; arrange over salad. Whisk the apple juice concentrate, oil, vinegar, mustard, salt and pepper. Drizzle over the salad and serve immediately.

3. Drain sweet potatoes; mash with the thyme and remaining milk, cream cheese, butter and salt. Spread over potato mixture. Cut through layers with a knife to swirl. Bake, uncovered, at 350° for 25-30 minutes or until heated through.

Summer Spinach Salad

PREP/TOTAL TIME: 20 MIN. YIELD: 14 SERVINGS

CALLIE BERGER DIAMOND SPRINGS, CALIFORNIA

Guests always request the recipe for this fabulous spinach salad. Tossed with ripe banana chunks, fresh strawberries and toasted almonds, it looks and tastes special enough for company. The tangy poppy seed dressing is a cinch to combine in the blender.

- 1/2 **cup canola oil**
- 1/4 **cup chopped onion**
- 2 **tablespoons plus 2 teaspoons red wine vinegar**
- 2 **tablespoons plus 2 teaspoons sugar**
- 1-1/2 **teaspoons ground mustard**
- 1/2 **teaspoon salt**
- 1-1/2 **teaspoons poppy seeds**
- 8 **cups torn fresh spinach**
- 3 **green onions, sliced**
- 2 **pints fresh strawberries, sliced**
- 3 **large ripe bananas, cut into 1/2-inch slices**
- 1/2 **cup slivered almonds, toasted**

1. In a blender, combine the first six ingredients. Cover and process until the sugar is dissolved. Add the poppy seeds; process just until blended.

2. In a salad bowl, combine the remaining ingredients. Drizzle with dressing; toss to coat.

Swirled Potato Bake

PREP: 35 MIN. BAKE: 25 MIN. YIELD: 7 SERVINGS

MARY ANN DELL PHOENIXVILLE, PENNSYLVANIA

Potato lovers will go crazy for this delicious bake from my mother-in-law. The creamy combination of Yukon Golds and sweet potatoes goes well with poultry or roasts. This recipe tastes great reheated, although leftovers are rare.

- 2-1/2 **pounds sweet potatoes, peeled and cubed**
- 2-1/2 **pounds Yukon Gold potatoes, peeled and cubed**
- 1-1/2 **cups milk,** *divided*
- 1 **package (8 ounces) cream cheese, softened,** *divided*
- 2 **tablespoons butter,** *divided*
- 2 **green onions, finely chopped**
- 1-1/2 **teaspoons salt,** *divided*
- 1/4 **teaspoon pepper**
- 1/2 **teaspoon dried thyme**

1. Place the sweet potatoes in a large saucepan; cover with water. Bring to a boil. Reduce heat; cover and cook for 20-25 minutes or just until tender.

2. Meanwhile, place the Yukon Gold potatoes in another large saucepan; cover with water. Bring to a boil. Reduce heat; cover and cook for 15-20 minutes or until tender. Drain; mash with 3/4 cup milk, half of the cream cheese and 1 tablespoon butter. Add the onions, 3/4 teaspoon salt and pepper; mix well. Spoon into a greased 13-in. x 9-in. baking dish.

LISA HUFF
BIRMINGHAM, ALABAMA

Grilled indoors, this delightful sandwich can be enjoyed any time of year. The honey-mustard dressing gives the chicken plenty of pizzazz, and the apple and pecans lend a lively crunch.

Chicken Salad Panini

PREP/TOTAL TIME: 25 MIN. YIELD: 2 SERVINGS

- 1/4 **cup mayonnaise**
- 1-1/2 **teaspoons honey**
- 3/4 **teaspoon snipped fresh dill**
- 3/4 **teaspoon Dijon mustard**

Dash salt

Dash pepper

- 1 **cup cubed cooked chicken breast**
- 3/4 **cup shredded cheddar cheese**
- 1/2 **cup chopped peeled apple**
- 1/4 **cup chopped pecans, toasted**
- 6 **slices white bread**
- 4 **teaspoons butter, softened**

1. In a small bowl, combine the first six ingredients. In another bowl, combine the chicken, cheese, apple and pecans; add dressing and toss to coat.

2. Spread half of the chicken salad on two slices of bread. Top each with another slice of bread, remaining chicken salad and remaining bread. Spread butter on both sides of sandwiches. Cook on a panini maker or indoor grill until bread is toasted and cheese is melted.

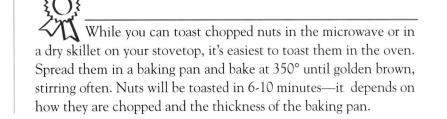

While you can toast chopped nuts in the microwave or in a dry skillet on your stovetop, it's easiest to toast them in the oven. Spread them in a baking pan and bake at 350° until golden brown, stirring often. Nuts will be toasted in 6-10 minutes—it depends on how they are chopped and the thickness of the baking pan.

3 Spoon stuffing into a greased 2-qt. shallow baking dish. Bake, uncovered, at 325° for 40-45 minutes or until stuffing is heated through and the top is lightly browned. Serve warm.

Editor's Note: If using frozen rhubarb, measure rhubarb while still frozen, then thaw completely. Drain in a colander, but do not press liquid out.

Festive Fruit Salad

PREP/TOTAL TIME: 10 MIN. YIELD: 12-16 SERVINGS

FAITH BOWMAN SELAH, WASHINGTON

One year I was asked to bring fruit salad to a family Christmas dinner. I brought this one, and became the "official fruit salad person" for family get-togethers.

     1 can (15 ounces) mandarin oranges, drained
 1-1/2 cups halved red seedless grapes
 1-1/2 cups halved green grapes
     1 jar (10 ounces) red maraschino cherries, halved, rinsed and drained
     1 jar (10 ounces) green maraschino cherries, halved, rinsed and drained
     1 can (8 ounces) unsweetened pineapple chunks, drained
     2 cups miniature marshmallows
     1 cup flaked coconut
     1 cup (8 ounces) sour cream

1 In a large bowl, combine the first eight ingredients. Just before serving, add sour cream and toss to coat.

Rhubarb Corn Bread Stuffing

PREP: 20 MIN. BAKE: 40 MIN. YIELD: 6-8 SERVINGS

KATHY PETRULLO LONG ISLAND CITY, NEW YORK

This distinctive stuffing is awesome alongside ham, chicken or turkey. I've been a fan of rhubarb's unique and tart flavor since I was a girl, so when a friend suggested this recipe, I had to try it. Now when I serve this side dish, my guests are usually curious about my special ingredient… and they love it!

     5 cups chopped fresh *or* frozen rhubarb (1/2-inch pieces), thawed
   1/2 cup sugar
     1 medium onion, chopped
   1/2 cup butter, *divided*
     3 cups crushed corn bread stuffing
   1/2 cup chopped walnuts

1 In a large bowl, toss the chopped rhubarb with the sugar; set aside. In a large skillet, saute the chopped onion in 2 tablespoons butter until tender; add to the rhubarb mixture. Stir in the corn bread stuffing and the walnuts.

2 In a small skillet, melt the remaining butter over medium heat; pour melted butter over the stuffing mixture and toss lightly.

Orange Avocado Salad

PREP/TOTAL TIME: 30 MIN. YIELD: 6-8 SERVINGS

LATRESSA ALLEN FORT WORTH, TEXAS

For a beautiful salad with an unbeatable combination of flavors, you can't miss with this recipe. We love the mellow avocado together with sweet mandarin oranges and crisp cucumber. The tangy dressing makes this dish special. It's a great summertime salad to serve with grilled meat.

DRESSING:
- 1/2 cup orange juice
- 1/4 cup canola oil
- 2 tablespoons red wine vinegar
- 1 tablespoon sugar
- 1 teaspoon grated orange peel
- 1/4 teaspoon salt

SALAD:
- 1 medium head iceberg lettuce, torn
- 2 cups torn red leaf lettuce
- 1 medium ripe avocado, peeled and sliced
- 1/4 cup orange juice
- 1 medium cucumber, sliced
- 1/2 medium red onion, thinly sliced into rings
- 1 can (11 ounces) mandarin oranges, drained

1 In a jar with a tight-fitting lid, combine dressing ingredients; shake well. Chill.

2 Just before serving, toss greens in a large salad bowl. Dip the avocado slices into orange juice. Arrange cucumber, onion and oranges over greens. Add the avocado (discard remaining juice). Serve with dressing.

Warm Mustard Potato Salad

PREP/TOTAL TIME: 30 MIN. YIELD: 8-10 SERVINGS

TIFFANY MITCHELL SUSANVILLE, CALIFORNIA

This tangy mixture is wonderful and so different from traditional potato salads. The Dijon mustard and dill spark the flavor. It's a comforting and tasty side dish that's really simple to assemble.

- 2 pounds small red potatoes
- 1 cup mayonnaise
- 1/4 cup Dijon mustard
- 1/2 to 3/4 cup chopped red onion
- 2 green onions with tops, sliced
- 2 garlic cloves, minced
- 3 tablespoons snipped fresh dill
- 1/2 teaspoon salt
- 1/2 teaspoon pepper
- 1/4 teaspoon lime juice

1 Place the potatoes in a saucepan and cover with water. Cover and bring to a boil; cook until tender, about 25 minutes. Drain thoroughly and cool slightly.

2 Meanwhile, combine the remaining ingredients. Cut potatoes into chunks; place in a bowl. Add the mustard mixture and toss to coat. Serve warm.

sunday chicken stew, p. 60

Discover comforting bowls of goodness that soothe on the chilliest of nights, fill hungry tummies and nourish you, body and soul.

soups & stews

3 Cover and bake at 350° for 1-1/2 hours. Stir in beans; cover and bake 30-40 minutes longer or until beef and vegetables are tender. Discard bay leaves and oregano.

Editor's Note: This recipe was tested with McCormick's Montreal Steak Seasoning. Look for it in the spice aisle.

Curried Pumpkin Soup

PREP/TOTAL TIME: 20 MIN. YIELD: 7 SERVINGS

KIMBERLY KNEPPER EULESS, TEXAS

I whipped up this satisfying soup last Thanksgiving for my family, and everyone was crazy about it! Even my brother, who is one of the pickiest eaters I know, asked for seconds.

- 1/2 **pound fresh mushrooms, sliced**
- 1/2 **cup chopped onion**
-   2 **tablespoons butter**
-   2 **tablespoons all-purpose flour**
- 1/2 to 1 **teaspoon curry powder**
-   3 **cups vegetable broth**
-   1 **can (15 ounces) solid-pack pumpkin**
-   1 **can (12 ounces) evaporated milk**
-   1 **tablespoon honey**
- 1/2 **teaspoon salt**
- 1/4 **teaspoon pepper**
- 1/4 **teaspoon ground nutmeg**

Minced chives

1 In a large saucepan, saute the mushrooms and onion in butter until tender. Stir in the flour and curry powder until blended. Gradually add the broth. Bring to a boil; cook and stir for 2 minutes or until thickened. Add the pumpkin, milk, honey, salt, pepper and nutmeg; heat through. Garnish with chives if desired.

Wintertime Braised Beef Stew

PREP: 40 MIN. BAKE: 2 HOURS YIELD: 8 SERVINGS (2 QUARTS)

MICHAELA ROSENTHAL WOODLAND HILLS, CALIFORNIA

This easy beef stew has a deep, rich taste. It's even better a day or two later, so you may want to make a double batch.

-   2 **tablespoons all-purpose flour**
-   2 **teaspoons steak seasoning**
-   2 **pounds boneless beef sirloin steak, cut into 1-inch cubes**
-   2 **tablespoons olive oil,** *divided*
-   1 **large onion, chopped**
-   2 **celery ribs, chopped**
-   2 **medium parsnips, peeled and cut into 1-1/2-inch pieces**
-   2 **medium carrots, peeled and cut into 1-1/2-inch pieces**
-   2 **garlic cloves, minced**
-   1 **can (14-1/2 ounces) diced tomatoes, undrained**
-   1 **cup dry red wine** *or* **reduced-sodium beef broth**
-   2 **tablespoons red currant jelly**
-   2 **bay leaves**
-   2 **fresh oregano sprigs**
-   1 **can (15 ounces) white kidney** *or* **cannellini beans, rinsed and drained**

1 In a large resealable plastic bag, combine flour and steak seasoning. Add beef, a few pieces at a time, and shake to coat. Heat 1 tablespoon oil in an ovenproof Dutch oven; brown beef in batches on all sides. Remove and keep warm.

2 In the same pan, saute the onion, celery, parsnips and carrots in remaining oil until crisp-tender. Add garlic; cook 1 minute longer. Add the tomatoes, wine, jelly, bay leaves, oregano and beef; bring to a boil.

Hungarian Goulash Soup

PREP: 40 MIN. COOK: 2 HOURS YIELD: 15 SERVINGS

JULIE POLAKOWSKI WEST ALLIS, WISCONSIN

This soup is similar to one my mother made years ago. We loved the flavor and our dad appreciated that it used an inexpensive cut of meat and homegrown vegetables. This soup is brimming with beef, potatoes, rutabagas, carrots and onions—it's a rich, flavorful meal in a bowl!

1-1/4	pounds beef stew meat, cut into 1-inch cubes
2	tablespoons olive oil, *divided*
4	medium onions, chopped
6	garlic cloves, minced
2	teaspoons paprika
1/2	teaspoon caraway seeds, crushed
1/2	teaspoon pepper
1/4	teaspoon cayenne pepper
1	teaspoon salt, optional
2	cans (14-1/2 ounces *each*) beef broth
2	cups cubed peeled potatoes
2	cups sliced carrots
2	cups cubed peeled rutabagas
2	cans (28 ounces *each*) diced tomatoes, undrained
1	large sweet red pepper, chopped

Sour cream, optional

1. In a Dutch oven over medium heat, brown beef in 1 tablespoon oil. Remove beef; drain drippings. Heat remaining oil in the same pan; saute onions and garlic for 8-10 minutes over medium heat or until lightly browned.

2. Add the paprika, caraway, pepper, cayenne and salt if desired; cook and stir 1 minute. Return beef to pan. Add broth, potatoes, carrots and rutabagas; bring to a boil. Reduce heat; cover and simmer for 1-1/2 hours or until vegetables are tender and meat is almost tender.

3. Add tomatoes and red pepper; return to a boil. Reduce heat; cover and simmer 30-40 minutes or until meat and vegetables are tender. Serve with sour cream if desired.

Colorful Chicken 'n' Squash Soup

PREP: 25 MIN. COOK: 1-1/2 HOURS
YIELD: 14 SERVINGS (5-1/2 QUARTS)

TRINA BIGHAM FAIRHAVEN, MASSACHUSETTS

When I turned 40, I decided to live a healthier lifestyle, which included cooking healthier for my family. I make this soup every week, and everyone loves it. Full of delicious winter squash, chunks of chicken and healthy vegetables, it's truly a nutritious meal.

1	broiler/fryer chicken (4 pounds), cut up
13	cups water
5	pounds butternut squash, peeled and cubed (about 10 cups)
1	bunch kale, trimmed and chopped
6	medium carrots, chopped
2	large onions, chopped
3	teaspoons salt

1. Place chicken and water in a stockpot. Bring to a boil. Reduce heat; cover and simmer for 1 hour or until chicken is tender.

2. Remove chicken from broth. Strain broth and skim fat. Return broth to the pan; add the squash, kale, carrots and onions. Bring to a boil. Reduce heat; cover and simmer for 25-30 minutes or until vegetables are tender.

3. When chicken is cool enough to handle, remove meat from bones and cut into bite-size pieces. Discard bones and skin. Add chicken and salt to soup; heat through.

Creamy Carrot Parsnip Soup

PREP: 30 MIN. COOK: 25 MIN. YIELD: 12 SERVINGS (3 QUARTS)

PHYLLIS CLINEHENS MAPLEWOOD, OHIO

Our farm family would eat soup every day as long as it didn't come from a can! This smooth, creamy concoction tastes like it's fresh from the garden. A subtle hint of horseradish and ginger sparks every steaming spoonful.

- 8 cups chopped carrots
- 6 cups chopped peeled parsnips
- 4 cups chicken broth
- 3 cups water
- 2 teaspoons sugar
- 1 teaspoon salt
- 1 medium onion, chopped
- 4 garlic cloves, minced
- 1 teaspoon peeled grated horseradish
- 1 teaspoon minced fresh gingerroot
- 3 tablespoons butter
- 2 cups buttermilk
- 2 tablespoons sour cream

Fresh dill sprigs, optional

1   In a Dutch oven, combine carrots, parsnips, broth, water, sugar and salt; bring to a boil. Reduce heat; cover and cook for 25-30 minutes or until vegetables are tender.

2   In a small skillet, saute onion, garlic, horseradish and ginger in butter until tender. Add to carrot mixture.

3   Transfer soup to a blender in batches; cover and process until smooth. Return to the pan. Stir in buttermilk; heat through (do not boil).

4   Garnish servings with sour cream and dill if desired.

Mexican Shrimp Bisque

PREP/TOTAL TIME: 30 MIN. YIELD: 3 CUPS

KAREN HARRIS CASTLE ROCK, COLORADO

I enjoy Cajun and Mexican cuisine, and this rich, elegant soup combines the best of both. I like to serve it with a crispy, green salad and a glass of white wine for a simple but very special meal.

- 1/2 cup chopped onion
- 2 garlic cloves, minced
- 1 tablespoon olive oil
- 1 tablespoon all-purpose flour
- 1 cup water
- 1/2 cup heavy whipping cream
- 1 tablespoon chili powder
- 2 teaspoons chicken bouillon granules
- 1/2 teaspoon ground cumin
- 1/2 teaspoon ground coriander
- 1/2 pound uncooked medium shrimp, peeled and deveined
- 1/2 cup sour cream

Fresh cilantro and cubed avocado, optional

1   In a large saucepan, saute onion and garlic in oil until tender. Stir in flour until blended. Stir in the water, cream, chili powder, bouillon, cumin and coriander; bring to a boil. Reduce heat; cover and simmer for 5 minutes.

2   Cut shrimp into bite-size pieces; add to soup. Simmer 5 minutes longer or until shrimp turn pink. Gradually stir 1/2 cup hot soup into sour cream; return all to the pan, stirring constantly. Heat through (do not boil). Garnish with cilantro and avocado if desired.

Creamy Swiss Onion Soup

PREP: 40 MIN. BROIL: 5 MIN. YIELD: 4 SERVINGS

MACKAY STARR NORTH SAANICH, BRITISH COLUMBIA

It was a cool spring day when I came up with this sweet and creamy variation of traditional baked French onion soup. I top individual bowls with toasty buttered croutons and a sprinkling of Swiss cheese, then pop them under the broiler. The rich results are delightful!

- 7 tablespoons butter, *divided*
- 1-1/2 cups cubed day-old bread
- 3 large onions, quartered and thinly sliced
- 1-1/2 cups water
- 4-1/2 teaspoons chicken bouillon granules
- 1/4 cup all-purpose flour
- 1-3/4 cups milk, *divided*
- 1-1/2 cups (6 ounces) shredded Swiss cheese, *divided*

Pepper to taste

Fresh minced chives *or* parsley

1. Melt 3 tablespoons of butter; toss with bread cubes. Place on a lightly greased baking sheet. Bake at 350° for 7 minutes; turn and bake 7 minutes longer or until toasted.

2. Meanwhile, in a large saucepan, saute onions in remaining butter until lightly browned, about 12 minutes. Stir in water and bouillon; bring to a boil. Reduce heat; cover and simmer for 15 minutes.

3. Combine flour and 1/2 cup milk until smooth; gradually stir into onion mixture. Stir in remaining milk. Bring to a boil; boil for 2 minutes, stirring until thickened. Reduce heat to low; stir in 3/4 cup Swiss cheese and pepper.

4. Ladle into four ovenproof bowls; sprinkle with reserved croutons and remaining cheese. Broil 4 in. from the heat until cheese is melted and bubbly. Garnish with chives.

Gone-All-Day Stew

PREP: 25 MIN. BAKE: 4 HOURS YIELD: 8 SERVINGS

PATRICIA KILE GREENTOWN, PENNSYLVANIA

This healthy stew is one of my husband's favorite meals. I always use fresh mushrooms and low-sodium bouillon cubes.

- 1/4 cup all-purpose flour
- 1 boneless beef chuck roast (2 pounds), cut into 1-inch cubes
- 2 tablespoons canola oil
- 1 can (10-3/4 ounces) condensed tomato soup, undiluted
- 1 cup water *or* red wine
- 2 teaspoons beef bouillon granules
- 3 teaspoons Italian seasoning
- 1 bay leaf
- 1/2 teaspoon coarsely ground pepper
- 6 medium onions, quartered
- 4 medium potatoes, cut into 1-1/2-inch chunks
- 3 medium carrots, cut into 1-inch slices
- 12 large fresh mushrooms
- 1/2 cup celery, cut into 1-inch slices

Hot noodles

1. Place flour in a large resealable plastic bag. Add beef, a few pieces at a time and shake to coat.

2. In a large skillet, brown meat in oil in batches; drain. Transfer to a 5-qt. slow cooker. Combine the tomato soup, water, bouillon and seasonings; pour over beef. Add the onions, potatoes, carrots, mushrooms and celery. Cover and cook on low for 4-5 hours or until meat is tender. Discard bay leaf before serving. Serve over noodles.

MARGE DRAKE
JUNIATA, NEBRASKA

My chicken stew makes the house smell wonderful as it gently bubbles in the slow cooker. One whiff and my family heads to the kitchen to see if it's ready.

Chicken Stew with Gnocchi

PREP: 25 MIN. COOK: 6-1/2 HOURS YIELD: 8 SERVINGS (ABOUT 3 QUARTS)

3 medium parsnips, peeled and cut into 1/2-inch pieces

2 large carrots, cut into 1/2-inch slices

2 celery ribs, chopped

1 large sweet potato, peeled and cut into 1-inch cubes

4 green onions, chopped

3 pounds bone-in chicken thighs, skin removed

1/2 teaspoon dried sage leaves

1/4 teaspoon salt

1/4 teaspoon pepper

4 cups chicken broth

1 cup water

3 tablespoons cornstarch

1/4 cup cold water

1 package (16 ounces) potato gnocchi

Hot pepper sauce, optional

1 Place the parsnips, carrots, celery, sweet potato and onions in a 5-qt. slow cooker. Top with chicken; sprinkle with the sage, salt and pepper. Add broth and water. Cover and cook on low for 6 hours.

2 Remove the chicken; when cool enough to handle, remove meat from bones and discard bones. Cut the meat into bite-size pieces and return to the slow cooker.

3 Mix cornstarch and cold water until smooth; stir into stew. Add gnocchi. Cover and cook on high for 30 minutes or until gravy is thickened. Season with hot pepper sauce if desired.

Parsnips are a root vegetable that are similar to carrots. Look for small to medium parsnips that are firm and with smooth skin. Store parsnips in a plastic bag for up to 2 weeks. Peel and trim ends just before using. One pound is equivalent to about 4 medium parsnips or 2 cups peeled and chopped.

Red Pepper Soup

PREP: 35 MIN. COOK: 20 MIN. + COOLING
YIELD: 10-12 SERVINGS (ABOUT 3 QUARTS)

BARB NELSON VICTORIA, BRITISH COLUMBIA

While I don't have scientific proof of it, Red Pepper Soup works for me as a head cold remedy! It is a good gift to take when visiting a sick friend, too. For a pretty touch, top the soup with grated cheese and parsley. We enjoy it with jalapeno cheese buns. You can also serve it with warm garlic bread.

> 6 medium sweet red peppers, chopped
>
> 2 medium carrots, chopped
>
> 2 medium onions, chopped
>
> 1 celery rib, chopped
>
> 4 garlic cloves, minced
>
> 1 tablespoon olive oil
>
> 2 cans (one 49-1/2 ounces, one 14-1/2 ounces) chicken broth
>
> 1/2 cup uncooked long grain rice
>
> 2 tablespoons minced fresh thyme *or* 2 teaspoons dried thyme
>
> 1-1/2 teaspoons salt
>
> 1/4 teaspoon pepper
>
> 1/8 to 1/4 teaspoon cayenne pepper
>
> 1/8 to 1/4 teaspoon crushed red pepper flakes

1   In a large Dutch oven or soup kettle, saute red peppers, carrots, onions, celery and garlic in oil until tender.

2   Stir in the broth, rice, thyme, salt, pepper and cayenne; bring to a boil. Reduce heat; cover and simmer for 20-25 minutes or until the vegetables and rice are tender.

3   Cool for 30 minutes. Puree in small batches in a blender; return to pan. Add red pepper flakes; heat through.

Hearty Turkey Vegetable Soup

PREP: 20 MIN. COOK: 45 MIN.
YIELD: 10 SERVINGS (3-3/4 QUARTS)

JULIE ANDERSON BLOOMINGTON, ILLINOIS

I found this recipe on the Internet. After experimenting, I created a more nutritious version. I often double this chili-like soup to freeze or to share with friends.

> 1 pound lean ground turkey
>
> 1 medium onion, chopped
>
> 2 small zucchini, quartered lengthwise and sliced
>
> 1 large carrot, cut into 1-inch julienne strips
>
> 3 cans (14 ounces *each*) reduced-sodium beef broth
>
> 1 jar (26 ounces) garden-style pasta sauce *or* meatless spaghetti sauce
>
> 1 can (16 ounces) kidney beans, rinsed and drained
>
> 1 can (15-1/2 ounces) great northern beans, rinsed and drained
>
> 1 can (14-1/2 ounces) Italian diced tomatoes, undrained
>
> 1 tablespoon dried parsley flakes
>
> 2 teaspoons dried oregano
>
> 1 teaspoon pepper
>
> 1 teaspoon hot pepper sauce
>
> 1 cup uncooked small shell pasta

1   In a Dutch oven coated with cooking spray, cook turkey and onion over medium heat until meat is no longer pink; drain. Add zucchini and carrot; cook and stir 1 minute longer. Stir in the broth, pasta sauce, beans, tomatoes, parsley, oregano, pepper and hot pepper sauce.

2   Bring to a boil. Reduce heat; cover and simmer for 45 minutes. Meanwhile, cook pasta according to package directions; drain. Just before serving, stir in pasta.

Cream of Cauliflower Soup

PREP: 30 MIN. COOK: 40 MIN.
YIELD: 8 SERVINGS (ABOUT 2 QUARTS)

CAROL REAVES SAN ANTONIO, TEXAS

I adapted this creamy concoction from a soup I tasted at a local eatery. It's now a popular item on my menu.

- 2 medium onions, chopped
- 2 medium carrots, grated
- 2 celery ribs, sliced
- 2 garlic cloves, minced
- 1/4 cup plus 6 tablespoons butter, *divided*
- 1 medium head cauliflower, chopped
- 5 cups chicken broth
- 1/4 cup minced fresh parsley
- 1 teaspoon salt
- 1 teaspoon coarsely ground pepper
- 1/2 teaspoon dried basil
- 1/2 teaspoon dried tarragon
- 6 tablespoons all-purpose flour
- 1 cup milk
- 1/2 cup heavy whipping cream
- 1/4 cup sour cream

Fresh tarragon, optional

1 In a Dutch oven, saute onions, carrots, celery and garlic in 1/4 cup butter until tender. Add cauliflower, broth, parsley and seasonings. Cover and simmer for 30 minutes or until the vegetables are tender.

2 Meanwhile, in a saucepan, melt remaining butter. Stir in flour until smooth. Gradually stir in milk and cream. Bring to a boil; cook and stir for 2 minutes or until thickened. Add to cauliflower mixture. Cook for 10 minutes or until thickened, stirring frequently. Remove from heat; stir in sour cream. Garnish with tarragon.

Turkey Pasta Soup

PREP/TOTAL TIME: 30 MIN. YIELD: 10 SERVINGS

MARIE EWERT RICHMOND, MICHIGAN

This quick soup has such a great flavor that everyone I've shared it with has added the recipe to her list of favorites. It also simmers up well in a slow cooker.

- 1 cup uncooked small pasta shells
- 1 pound lean ground turkey
- 2 medium onions, chopped
- 2 garlic cloves, minced
- 3 cans (14-1/2 ounces *each*) reduced-sodium chicken broth
- 2 cans (15 ounces *each*) white kidney *or* cannellini beans, rinsed and drained
- 2 cans (14-1/2 ounces *each*) Italian stewed tomatoes
- 2 teaspoons dried oregano
- 2 teaspoons dried basil
- 1 teaspoon fennel seed, crushed
- 1 teaspoon pepper
- 1/2 teaspoon salt
- 1/4 teaspoon crushed red pepper flakes

1 Cook the pasta according to package directions. Meanwhile, in a large soup kettle or Dutch oven, cook the turkey, onions and garlic over medium heat until meat is no longer pink; drain. Stir in the broth, beans, tomatoes and seasonings. Bring to a boil. Reduce heat; simmer, uncovered, for 10 minutes.

2 Drain pasta and add to the soup. Cook 5 minutes longer or until heated through.

Creamed Cabbage Soup

PREP: 15 MIN. COOK: 25 MIN. YIELD: 8-10 SERVINGS

LAURIE HARMS GRINNELL, IOWA

Although we live in town, we have a big garden. I love planting vegetables, watching them grow, then using the bounty in my favorite recipes.

2 cans (14-1/2 ounces *each*) chicken broth
2 celery ribs, chopped
1 medium head cabbage (3 pounds), shredded
1 medium onion, chopped
1 medium carrot, chopped
1/4 cup butter
3 tablespoons all-purpose flour
1 teaspoon salt
1/4 teaspoon pepper
2 cups half-and-half cream
1 cup milk
2 cups cubed fully cooked ham
1/2 teaspoon dried thyme

Minced fresh parsley

1 In a large soup kettle or Dutch oven, combine broth, celery, cabbage, onion and carrot; bring to a boil. Reduce heat; cover and simmer for 15-20 minutes or until vegetables are tender.

2 Meanwhile, melt butter in a medium saucepan. Add flour, salt and pepper; stir to form a smooth paste. Combine cream and milk; gradually add to flour mixture, stirring constantly. Cook and stir until thickened; continue cooking 1 minute longer. Gradually stir into vegetable mixture. Add ham and thyme and heat through. Garnish with parsley.

Taco Twist Soup

PREP/TOTAL TIME: 20 MIN. YIELD: 6 SERVINGS

COLLEEN ZERTLER MENOMONIE, WISCONSIN

I lightened up this soup recipe by substituting black beans for the ground beef originally called for...and by topping off bowlfuls with reduced-fat sour cream and cheese. Spiral pasta adds a fun twist.

1 medium onion, chopped
2 garlic cloves, minced
2 teaspoons olive oil
3 cups vegetable broth *or* reduced-sodium beef broth
1 can (15 ounces) black beans, rinsed and drained
1 can (14-1/2 ounces) diced tomatoes
1-1/2 cups picante sauce
1 cup uncooked spiral pasta
1 small green pepper, chopped
2 teaspoons chili powder
1 teaspoon ground cumin
1/2 cup shredded reduced-fat cheddar cheese
3 tablespoons reduced-fat sour cream

1 In a large saucepan, saute onion and garlic in oil until tender. Add the broth, beans, tomatoes, picante sauce, pasta, green pepper and seasonings. Bring to a boil, stirring frequently. Reduce heat; cover and simmer for 10-12 minutes or until pasta is tender, stirring occasionally. Serve with cheese and sour cream.

Creamy Sausage Stew

PREP: 15 MIN. BAKE: 1-1/4 HOURS YIELD: 10-12 SERVINGS

ROSEMARY JESSE CABOOL, MISSOURI

Depending on the time of year, I serve my stew with bread or sweet corn muffins and fresh butter, and with salad or fruit. Then, since it tastes even better the next day, we have it for lunch on the rare occasions there are leftovers!

- 8 to 10 medium red potatoes, cut into 1-1/2-inch pieces
- 2 large white onions, quartered
- 1 large green pepper, cut into 1-inch pieces
- 1 large sweet red pepper, cut into 1-inch pieces
- 2 pounds smoked Polish sausage, cut into 1-inch slices
- 1/3 cup canola oil
- 1 tablespoon dried basil
- 2 teaspoons salt
- 1 teaspoon pepper
- 1 pint heavy whipping cream
- 3 tablespoons cornstarch
- 3 tablespoons water

1 Place potatoes in a 5-qt. roasting pan. Add onions, peppers and sausage; toss gently. Combine oil, basil, salt and pepper. Pour over the meat and vegetables; toss well.

2 Cover and bake at 350° for 45 minutes; stir. Add the cream; cover and bake 30-40 minutes longer or until potatoes are tender.

3 Combine cornstarch and water; stir into stew. Place on stovetop and bring to a boil, stirring constantly until thickened.

Ham and Bean Chowder

PREP: 40 MIN. + STANDING COOK: 2 HOURS + CHILLING
YIELD: 12-14 SERVINGS (3-1/4 QUARTS)

JOE ANN HEAVRIN MEMPHIS, TENNESSEE

We also call this 2-Day Bean Chowder, since it can be started, chilled overnight and finished the next day.

- 1 pound dried great northern beans
- 2 cups chopped onion
- 1 cup sliced celery
- 2 garlic cloves, minced
- 3 tablespoons butter
- 1 meaty ham bone
- 2 cups water
- 1 can (14-1/2 ounces) chicken broth
- 1 can (14-1/2 ounces) stewed tomatoes
- 2 bay leaves
- 2 whole cloves
- 1/2 teaspoon pepper
- 2 cups milk
- 2 cups (8 ounces) shredded cheddar cheese

1 Place beans in Dutch oven; add water to cover by 2-in. Bring to a boil; boil for 2 minutes. Remove from the heat; cover and let stand for 1 hour.

2 Drain beans and discard liquid. In the same kettle, saute onion, celery and garlic in butter until tender. Add beans, ham bone, water, broth, tomatoes, bay leaves, cloves and pepper; bring to a boil. Reduce heat; cover and simmer for 2 hours.

3 Remove ham bone, bay leaves and cloves. When cool, remove ham from bone; cut into pieces. Return to soup. Chill for 8 hours or overnight.

4   Skim fat from the soup. Stir in the milk; cook on low until heated through. Just before serving, stir in the cheddar cheese.

Western-Style Beef & Beans

PREP: 15 MIN. BAKE: 1 HOUR YIELD: 12 SERVINGS

JOLENE LOPEZ WICHITA, KANSAS

This hearty, warm dish is a comforting meal on a chilly night with bread and a salad. It also makes a delicious side dish. It has that simmered-all-day flavor.

         3 pounds ground beef
         2 medium onions, chopped
         2 celery ribs, chopped
         2 teaspoons beef bouillon granules
      2/3 cup boiling water
         2 cans (28 ounces *each*) baked beans with molasses
    1-1/2 cups ketchup
      1/4 cup prepared mustard
         3 garlic cloves, minced
    1-1/2 teaspoons salt
      1/2 teaspoon pepper
      1/2 pound sliced bacon, cooked and crumbled

1   In a Dutch oven over medium heat, cook beef, onions and celery until meat is no longer pink and vegetables are tender; drain. Dissolve bouillon in water; stir into beef mixture. Add the beans, ketchup, mustard, garlic, salt and pepper; mix well.

2   Cover and bake at 375° for 60-70 minutes or until bubbly; stir. Top with cooked bacon.

Tomato Dill Soup

PREP/TOTAL TIME: 30 MIN. YIELD: 4 SERVINGS (1 QUART)

PATTY KILE PLYMOUTH MEETING, PENNSYLVANIA

Most often, I make this soup ahead and keep it in the fridge. It's particularly good to take out and heat up with tuna or grilled cheese sandwiches, hard rolls or a salad. It would be fine to serve either hot or cold at a soup supper as well.

        1 medium onion, thinly sliced
        1 garlic clove, minced
        2 tablespoons canola oil
        1 tablespoon butter
        3 large tomatoes, sliced
      1/2 teaspoon salt
  Pinch pepper
        1 can (6 ounces) tomato paste
      1/4 cup all-purpose flour
        2 cups water, *divided*
      3/4 cup heavy whipping cream, whipped
        1 to 2 tablespoons finely minced fresh dill *or*
           1 to 2 teaspoons dill weed

1   In a large saucepan saute onion and garlic in oil and butter until tender. Add tomatoes, salt and pepper; cook over medium-high heat for 3 minutes or until heated through. Remove from heat and stir in tomato paste.

2   In a small bowl, combine the flour and 1/2 cup of water; stir until smooth. Stir into saucepan. Gradually stir in the remaining water until smooth; bring to a boil over medium heat. Cook and stir for 2 minutes or until thickened.

3   Place mixture in a sieve over a large bowl. With back of a spoon, press vegetables through sieve to remove seeds and skin; return puree to pan. Add cream and dill; cook over low heat just until heated through (do not boil).

3. Add carrots and onion. Cover and simmer until vegetables are tender. Stir in green beans.

4. For dumplings, combine biscuit mix and cheese. Stir in enough milk to form a soft dough. Drop by tablespoonfuls into bubbling stew. Cover; simmer 12 minutes (do not lift cover) or until a toothpick inserted into centers of dumplings comes out clean. Serve immediately.

Pepperoni Pizza Chili

PREP: 5 MIN. COOK: 40 MIN. YIELD: 8 SERVINGS

MARILOUISE WYATT COWEN, WEST VIRGINIA

We love this on a chilly day. A big bowl warms you right up, and the leftovers freeze well. I first made this recipe one day when I decided I didn't enjoy making pizza crust so I just put the pizza toppings in a bowl instead.

- 1 pound ground beef
- 1 can (16 ounces) kidney beans, rinsed and drained
- 1 can (15 ounces) pizza sauce
- 1 can (14-1/2 ounces) Italian stewed tomatoes
- 1 can (8 ounces) tomato sauce
- 1-1/2 cups water
- 1 package (3-1/2 ounces) sliced pepperoni
- 1/2 cup chopped green pepper
- 1 teaspoon pizza seasoning *or* Italian seasoning
- 1 teaspoon salt

Shredded part-skim mozzarella cheese, optional

1. In a large saucepan, cook beef over medium heat until no longer pink; drain. Stir in beans, pizza sauce, tomatoes, tomato sauce, water, pepperoni, green pepper, seasoning and salt. Bring to a boil. Reduce heat; simmer, uncovered, for 30 minutes or until chili reaches desired thickness. Sprinkle with cheese if desired.

Beef Stew with Cheddar Dumplings

PREP: 25 MIN. COOK: 1-1/4 HOURS YIELD: 6-8 SERVINGS

JACKIE RILEY GARRETTSVILLE, OHIO

My family asks for this stew just about every week. But it's perfect for company, too–it's easy, and everyone comments on the cheese in the dumplings.

- 1/2 cup all-purpose flour
- 1/2 teaspoon salt
- 1/2 teaspoon pepper
- 2 to 3 pounds beef stew meat, cut into 1-inch pieces
- 2 tablespoons canola oil
- 1/2 teaspoon onion salt
- 1/2 teaspoon garlic salt
- 1 tablespoon browning sauce, optional
- 5 cups water
- 5 teaspoons beef bouillon granules
- 4 medium carrots, sliced
- 1 medium onion, cut into wedges
- 1 can (14-1/2 ounces) cut green beans, drained

DUMPLINGS:
- 2 cups biscuit/baking mix
- 1 cup (4 ounces) shredded cheddar cheese
- 2/3 cup milk

1. Combine flour, salt and pepper. Coat meat with flour mixture. In a Dutch oven, heat oil over medium-high. Brown meat on all sides.

2. Add onion salt and garlic salt, browning sauce, water and bouillon. Bring to a boil; reduce heat and simmer, covered, about 1 hour.

New England Clam Chowder

PREP: 15 MIN. COOK: 30 MIN.
YIELD: 10-12 SERVINGS (3 QUARTS)

RACHEL NYDAM UXBRIDGE, MASSACHUSETTS

I wasn't satisfied with other recipes I came across for clam chowder, so I devised this one. Everyone who's tried it raves about it. The dish is great on a cold day.

- 4 medium potatoes, peeled and cubed
- 2 medium onions, chopped
- 1/2 cup butter
- 3/4 cup all-purpose flour
- 2 quarts milk
- 3 cans (6-1/2 ounces *each*) chopped clams, undrained
- 2 to 3 teaspoons salt
- 1 teaspoon ground sage
- 1 teaspoon ground thyme
- 1/2 teaspoon celery salt
- 1/2 teaspoon pepper

Minced fresh parsley

1 Place potatoes in a large saucepan and cover with water. Bring to a boil. Reduce heat; cover and cook for 10-15 minutes or until tender.

2 Meanwhile, in a Dutch oven, saute onions in butter until tender. Add flour; stir until smooth. Gradually stir in milk. Bring to a boil; cook and stir for 2 minutes or until thickened.

3 Drain potatoes; add to pot. Add clams and remaining ingredients; heat through. Sprinkle with parsley.

Hearty Beef Barley Soup

PREP: 10 MIN. COOK: 30 MIN. YIELD: 4 SERVINGS

BARBARA BEATTIE GLEN ALLEN, VIRGINIA

My entire family just loves this delicious and comforting soup. Loaded with chunks of tender beef, the rich broth also includes plenty of fresh mushrooms, sliced carrots and quick-cooking barley.

- 2 tablespoons all-purpose flour
- 1/2 teaspoon salt
- 1/4 teaspoon pepper, *divided*
- 1 pound lean boneless beef sirloin steak, cut into 1/2-inch cubes
- 1 tablespoon canola oil
- 2 cups sliced fresh mushrooms
- 2 cans (14-1/2 ounces *each*) reduced-sodium beef broth
- 2 medium carrots, sliced
- 1/4 teaspoon garlic powder
- 1/4 teaspoon dried thyme
- 1/2 cup quick-cooking barley

1 In a large resealable plastic bag, combine the flour, salt and 1/8 teaspoon pepper. Add beef and shake to coat. In a Dutch oven, brown beef in oil over medium heat or until the meat is no longer pink. Remove beef and set aside.

2 In the same pan, saute mushrooms until tender. Add the broth, carrots, garlic powder, thyme and remaining pepper; bring to a boil. Add barley and beef. Reduce heat; cover and simmer for 20-25 minutes until the meat, vegetables and barley are tender.

Italian Peasant Soup

PREP/TOTAL TIME: 25 MIN. YIELD: 11 SERVINGS (2-3/4 QUARTS)

KIM KNIGHT HAMBURG, PENNSYLVANIA

My father shared this recipe with me, and I use it when I need a hearty, healthy meal. It's my sons' favorite. Loaded with sausage, chicken, beans and spinach, the quick soup is nice for special occasions, too.

- 1 pound Italian sausage links, casings removed and cut into 1-inch slices
- 2 medium onions, chopped
- 6 garlic cloves, chopped
- 1 pound boneless skinless chicken breasts, cut into 1-inch cubes
- 2 cans (15 ounces *each*) cannellini *or* white kidney beans, rinsed and drained
- 2 cans (14-1/2 ounces *each*) chicken broth
- 2 cans (14-1/2 ounces *each*) diced tomatoes
- 1 teaspoon dried basil
- 1 teaspoon dried oregano
- 6 cups fresh spinach leaves, chopped

Shredded Parmesan cheese, optional

1 In a Dutch oven or soup kettle, cook sausage over medium heat until no longer pink; drain. Add onions and garlic; saute until tender. Add chicken; cook and stir until no longer pink.

2 Stir in the beans, broth, tomatoes, basil and oregano. Cook, uncovered, for 10 minutes. Add the spinach and heat just until wilted. Serve with Parmesan cheese if desired.

Creamy Asparagus Chowder

PREP/TOTAL TIME: 40 MIN. YIELD: 10 SERVINGS (2-1/2 QUARTS)

SHIRLEY BEACHUM SHELBY, MICHIGAN

While this soup's good with fresh asparagus, it can also be prepared with frozen or canned. Since we grow asparagus on our farm—the sandy soil and spring breezes off Lake Michigan are just right for it here—I do my best to promote our wonderful crop.

- 1/4 cup butter
- 2 medium onions, chopped
- 2 cups chopped celery
- 1 garlic clove, minced
- 1/2 cup all-purpose flour
- 1 large potato, peeled and cut into 1/2-inch cubes
- 4 cups milk
- 4 cups chicken broth
- 1/2 teaspoon dried thyme
- 1/2 teaspoon dried marjoram
- 4 cups chopped fresh asparagus, cooked and drained

Salt and pepper to taste

Sliced almonds

Shredded cheddar cheese

Chopped fresh tomato

1 In a Dutch oven, melt butter; saute onions, celery and garlic until tender. Stir in flour. Add potato, milk, broth and herbs; cook over low heat, stirring occasionally until the potato is tender and soup is thickened, about 20-30 minutes.

2 Add asparagus, salt and pepper; heat through. To serve, sprinkle with almonds, cheese and the tomato.

ELAINE SWEET
DALLAS, TEXAS

My son loves the way the kitchen smells when this soup is cooking. He comes into the kitchen and fans the aroma into his face, and I know he is happy.

Corn Soup with Pico de Gallo

PREP: 50 MIN. COOK: 20 MIN. YIELD: 6 SERVINGS

3 corn tortillas (6 inches), cut into 1-inch strips

4 medium ears sweet corn, husks removed

1/2 teaspoon canola oil

1/2 teaspoon *each* salt, pepper and paprika

1 medium red onion, chopped

1 bacon strip, chopped

6 garlic cloves, minced

1/4 cup all-purpose flour

3 cups reduced-sodium chicken broth

1 cup fat-free milk

1 can (4 ounces) chopped green chilies

1 teaspoon ground cumin

1 teaspoon dried oregano

1/2 cup minced fresh cilantro

1/4 cup lime juice

PICO DE GALLO:

2 plum tomatoes, chopped

1 medium ripe avocado, peeled and chopped

1 small serrano pepper, seeded and chopped

1 garlic clove, minced

1/4 teaspoon salt

1/4 teaspoon pepper

1 Place tortilla strips on a baking sheet coated with cooking spray; bake at 350° for 8-10 minutes or until crisp.

2 Coat grill rack with cooking spray before starting the grill. Rub corn with oil; sprinkle with seasonings. Grill, covered, over medium heat for 10-12 minutes or until tender, turning frequently. Cool slightly; cut corn from cobs and set aside.

3 In a large saucepan, saute onion and bacon for 5 minutes; add garlic, cook 1 minute longer. Stir in flour until blended; gradually add broth. Bring to a boil; cook and stir for 2 minutes or until thickened. Add corn, milk, chilies, cumin and oregano; heat through. Remove from heat; stir in cilantro and lime juice.

4 Combine pico de gallo ingredients. Serve with soup and tortilla strips.

Editor's Note: When cutting hot peppers, disposable gloves are recommended. Avoid touching your face.

Shaker Bean Soup

PREP: 10 MIN. + STANDING COOK: 2 HOURS 40 MIN.
YIELD: 5 QUARTS

DEBORAH AMRINE GRAND HAVEN, MICHIGAN

This soup tastes especially good in cold weather–which we have a lot of here on the shore of Lake Michigan! I love cooking and I like to try a new recipe every week. My family loves soup, so I'm always looking for one more.

- 1 pound dried great northern beans
- 1 meaty ham bone *or* 2 smoked ham hocks
- 8 cups water
- 1 large onion, chopped
- 3 celery ribs, diced
- 2 medium carrots, shredded

Salt to taste
- 1/2 teaspoon pepper
- 1/2 teaspoon dried thyme
- 1 can (28 ounces) crushed tomatoes in puree
- 2 tablespoons brown sugar
- 1-1/2 cups finely shredded fresh spinach

1   Sort and rinse beans. Place in a Dutch oven or soup kettle; cover with water and bring to a boil. Boil 2 minutes. Remove from heat; let stand 1 hour. Drain beans and discard liquid.

2   In the same kettle, add ham bone, 8 cups water and beans. Bring to a boil. Reduce heat; cover and simmer for 1-1/2 hours or until meat easily falls from the bone.

3   Remove bone from broth; cool. Trim meat from the bone. Discard bone. Add ham, onion, celery, carrots, salt, pepper and thyme to bean mixture. Cover and simmer for 1 hour or until beans are tender.

4   Add tomatoes and brown sugar. Cook for 10 minutes. Just before serving, add spinach.

Mexican Chicken Corn Chowder

PREP/TOTAL TIME: 30 MIN. YIELD: 6-8 SERVINGS (2 QUARTS)

SUSAN GAROUTTE GEORGETOWN, TEXAS

I like to make this smooth, creamy soup when company comes to visit. Its zippy flavor is full of Southwestern flair. My family enjoys dipping slices of homemade bread in this chowder to soak up every bite!

- 1-1/2 pounds boneless skinless chicken breasts, cut into 1-inch pieces
- 1/2 cup chopped onion
- 1 to 2 garlic cloves, minced
- 3 tablespoons butter
- 1 cup hot water
- 2 teaspoons chicken bouillon granules
- 1/2 to 1 teaspoon ground cumin
- 2 cups half-and-half cream
- 2 cups (8 ounces) shredded Monterey Jack cheese
- 1 can (14-3/4 ounces) cream-style corn
- 1 can (4 ounces) chopped green chilies, undrained
- 1/4 to 1 teaspoon hot pepper sauce
- 1 medium tomato, chopped

Minced fresh cilantro, optional

1   In a Dutch oven, brown chicken, onion and garlic in butter until chicken is no longer pink. Add the water, bouillon and cumin; bring to a boil. Reduce heat; cover and simmer for 5 minutes.

2   Stir in the cream, cheese, corn, chilies and hot pepper sauce. Cook and stir over low heat until the cheese is melted; add tomato. Sprinkle with cilantro if desired.

Savory Cheese Soup

PREP/TOTAL TIME: 25 MIN. YIELD: 4 SERVINGS

DEE FALK STROMSBURG, NEBRASKA

This delicious soup recipe was shared by a friend and instantly became a hit with my husband. Its big cheese taste blends wonderfully with the flavor of the vegetables. I first served this creamy soup as part of a holiday meal, but now we enjoy it throughout the year.

- 1/4 cup chopped onion
- 3 tablespoons butter
- 1/4 cup all-purpose flour
- 1/4 teaspoon salt
- 1/8 teaspoon garlic powder
- 1/8 teaspoon pepper
- 2 cups milk
- 1 can (14-1/2 ounces) chicken *or* vegetable broth
- 1/2 cup shredded carrot
- 1/2 cup finely chopped celery
- 1-1/2 cups (6 ounces) shredded cheddar cheese
- 3/4 cup shredded part-skim mozzarella cheese

Minced chives, optional

1 In a large saucepan, saute onion in butter until tender. Add the flour, salt, garlic powder and pepper; stir until smooth. Gradually add milk; cook and stir over medium heat until thickened and bubbly.

2 Meanwhile, in a small saucepan, bring broth to a boil. Add carrot and celery; simmer for 5 minutes or until vegetables are tender. Add to milk mixture and stir until blended. Add cheeses. Cook and stir until melted (do not boil). Garnish with chives if desired.

Chicken Barley Soup

PREP: 30 MIN. + COOLING COOK: 1 HOUR
YIELD: 5 SERVINGS (ABOUT 1-1/2 QUARTS)

DIANA COSTELLO MARION, KANSAS

No question—this is my favorite soup! It's so filling that I serve it as a hearty main dish, and I have given the recipe to many of our friends and relatives. (Especially with the barley, it simply tastes too good to keep to yourself!)

- 1 broiler/fryer chicken (2 to 3 pounds), cut up
- 2 quarts water
- 1-1/2 cups diced carrots
- 1 cup diced celery
- 1/2 cup medium pearl barley
- 1/2 cup chopped onion
- 1 teaspoon chicken bouillon granules
- 1 teaspoon salt, optional
- 1 bay leaf
- 1/2 teaspoon poultry seasoning
- 1/2 teaspoon pepper
- 1/2 teaspoon rubbed sage

1 In a large kettle, cook chicken in water until tender. Cool broth and skim off fat. Bone the chicken and cut into bite-size pieces; return to kettle along with remaining ingredients. Bring to a boil. Reduce heat; cover and simmer for 1 hour or until vegetables and barley are tender. Discard bay leaf.

1. In a large resealable plastic bag, combine the flour, salt and pepper; add chicken, a few pieces at a time, and shake to coat. In a large skillet, brown chicken in oil; remove and keep warm. Gradually add broth to the skillet; bring to a boil.

2. In a 5-qt. slow cooker, layer the carrots, celery and onion; sprinkle with rosemary. Add the chicken and hot broth. Cover and cook on low for 6-7 hours or until chicken juices run clear, vegetables are tender and stew is bubbling. Stir in peas.

3. For dumplings, in a small bowl, combine the flour, baking powder, salt and rosemary. Combine the egg and milk; stir into dry ingredients. Drop by heaping teaspoonfuls onto simmering chicken mixture. Cover and cook on high for 25-30 minutes or until a toothpick inserted in a dumpling comes out clean (do not lift the cover while simmering).

Sunday Chicken Stew

PREP: 30 MIN. COOK: 6-1/2 HOURS YIELD: 6 SERVINGS

DIANE HALFERTY CORPUS CHRISTI, TEXAS

I love this recipe because I can prepare the veggies the night before. In the morning, I brown the chicken and assemble everything in the slow cooker before church. I can spend time with my family while Sunday dinner cooks.

- 1/2 cup all-purpose flour
- 1 teaspoon salt
- 1/2 teaspoon white pepper
- 1 broiler/fryer chicken (3 pounds), cut up and skin removed
- 2 tablespoons canola oil
- 3 cups chicken broth
- 6 large carrots, cut into 1-inch pieces
- 2 celery ribs, cut into 1/2-inch pieces
- 1 large sweet onion, thinly sliced
- 1 teaspoon dried rosemary, crushed
- 1-1/2 cups frozen peas

DUMPLINGS:

- 1 cup all-purpose flour
- 2 teaspoons baking powder
- 1/2 teaspoon salt
- 1/2 teaspoon dried rosemary, crushed
- 1 egg, lightly beaten
- 1/2 cup 2% milk

Neighborhood Bean Soup

PREP: 30 MIN. + STANDING COOK: 3 HOURS
YIELD: 10 SERVINGS (2-3/4 QUARTS)

CHERYL TROWBRIDGE WINDSOR, ONTARIO

Even though I'm single, I make multiple servings of everything—as reflected in the name of my soup! Actually, that tendency has helped me get to know my neighbors. The local ladies have "adopted" me. They always volunteer to be my guinea pigs whenever I try out a new recipe or two.

- 2 cups dried great northern beans
- 5 cups chicken broth
- 3 cups water
- 1 meaty ham bone *or* 2 smoked ham hocks

2 to 3 tablespoons chicken bouillon granules

1 teaspoon dried thyme

1/2 teaspoon dried marjoram

1/2 teaspoon pepper

1/4 teaspoon rubbed sage

1/4 teaspoon dried savory

2 medium onions, chopped

3 medium carrots, chopped

3 celery ribs, chopped

1 tablespoon canola oil

1 Place the beans in a Dutch oven or soup kettle; add water to cover by 2 in. Bring to a boil; boil for 2 minutes. Remove from the heat; cover and let stand for 1 hour. Drain.

2 Add broth, water, ham bone, bouillon and seasonings; bring to a boil. Reduce heat. Cover; simmer 2 hours.

3 Meanwhile, saute the onions, carrots and celery in oil; add to soup. Cover and simmer 1 hour longer.

4 Debone the ham and cut into chunks; return to the soup. Skim fat before serving.

Meaty Three-Bean Chili

PREP: 25 MIN. COOK: 1 HOUR 40 MIN.
YIELD: 10-12 SERVINGS (3 QUARTS)

SANDRA MILLER LEE'S SUMMIT, MISSOURI

Doubling this recipe is automatic for me—just about every-one wants more than one bowl! If any's left, I freeze it. It's also great the second time around.

3/4 pound Italian sausage links, cut into 1/2-inch chunks

3/4 pound ground beef

1 large onion, chopped

1 medium green pepper, chopped

1 jalapeno pepper, seeded and minced

2 garlic cloves, minced

1 cup beef broth

1/2 cup Worcestershire sauce

1-1/2 teaspoons chili powder

1 teaspoon pepper

1 teaspoon ground mustard

1/2 teaspoon celery seed

1/2 teaspoon salt

6 cups chopped fresh plum tomatoes (about 2 pounds)

6 bacon strips, cooked and crumbled

1 can (16 ounces) kidney beans, rinsed and drained

1 can (15 ounces) pinto beans, rinsed and drained

1 can (15 ounces) garbanzo beans *or* chickpeas, rinsed and drained

Additional chopped onion, optional

1 In a 4-qt. kettle or Dutch oven, cook sausage and beef over medium heat, until meat is no longer pink; drain, reserving 1 tablespoon drippings. Set meat aside.

2 Saute onion, peppers and garlic in the reserved drippings for 3 minutes. Add the broth, Worcestershire sauce and seasonings; bring to a boil over medium heat. Reduce heat; cover and simmer for 10 minutes.

3 Add tomatoes, bacon and browned sausage and beef; return to a boil. Reduce the heat; cover and simmer for 30 minutes.

4 Add all of the beans. Simmer for 1 hour, stirring occasionally. Garnish with chopped onion if desired.

Editor's Note: When cutting hot peppers, disposable gloves are recommended. Avoid touching your face.

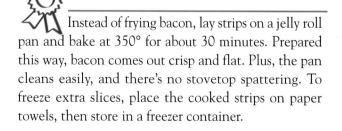

Instead of frying bacon, lay strips on a jelly roll pan and bake at 350° for about 30 minutes. Prepared this way, bacon comes out crisp and flat. Plus, the pan cleans easily, and there's no stovetop spattering. To freeze extra slices, place the cooked strips on paper towels, then store in a freezer container.

savory chicken dinner, p. 81

Inviting, juicy entrees using a variety of cooking techniques and ingredients offer a sensational selection of lip-smacking meals for every occasion.

main dishes

1. In a saucepan, combine the first five ingredients. Bring to a boil. Reduce heat; simmer, uncovered, for 5-7 minutes or until onion is tender and sauce is slightly thickened. Remove from the heat; set aside.

2. In a large bowl, combine the egg, bread crumbs, parsley, Italian seasoning, salt and pepper. Add beef and mix well. Divide into 12 portions. Place a cube of cheese in each mushroom cap; shape each meat portion around a mushroom.

3. On six metal or soaked wooden skewers, alternate meatballs, peppers and onion wedges. Grill, uncovered, over medium heat for 3 minutes on each side.

4. Grill 10-12 minutes longer or until meat juices run clear, turning occasionally. Brush with reserved glaze during the last 2 minutes. Serve with rice if desired.

Surprise Meatball Skewers

PREP: 30 MIN. GRILL: 20 MIN. YIELD: 6 SERVINGS

KRISTEN WONDRA HUDSON, KANSAS

I still remember the first time I served these colorful kabobs. My family was thrilled to find a surprise in the meatballs. Since I make them often, I sometimes substitute different vegetables or cheeses for variety.

- 1/3 cup honey
- 3 tablespoons Dijon mustard
- 2 tablespoons finely chopped onion
- 2 tablespoons apple juice

Dash cayenne pepper

- 1 egg
- 1/4 cup dry bread crumbs
- 1 tablespoon minced fresh parsley
- 1 teaspoon Italian seasoning
- 1/4 teaspoon salt

Pepper to taste

- 1 pound ground beef
- 1 block (1-1/2 ounces) Monterey Jack cheese, cut into 12 cubes
- 12 small mushrooms, stems removed
- 1 medium green pepper, cut into pieces
- 1 medium sweet yellow *or* red pepper, cut into pieces
- 1 medium onion, cut into wedges

Hot rice, optional

Terrific Teriyaki Burgers

PREP: 20 MIN. GRILL: 15 MIN. YIELD: 6 SERVINGS

MARGARET WILSON SUN CITY, CALIFORNIA

Golden flecks of pineapple give these burgers a touch of sweetness, while the gingerroot adds some spice. Ground chicken works well in this recipe, too.

- 1/4 cup ketchup
- 2 tablespoons reduced-sodium soy sauce
- 1 tablespoon brown sugar
- 1 tablespoon unsweetened crushed pineapple
- 1-1/2 teaspoons minced fresh gingerroot
- 1 garlic clove, minced
- 1/2 teaspoon sesame oil

BURGERS:

1 egg white, lightly beaten

1/3 cup dry bread crumbs

3 green onions, chopped

2 tablespoons unsweetened crushed pineapple

3/4 pound lean ground beef

3/4 pound lean ground turkey

6 slices unsweetened pineapple

6 hamburger buns, split and toasted

6 lettuce leaves

6 slices tomato

1 In a small bowl, combine the ketchup, soy sauce, brown sugar, pineapple, ginger, garlic and sesame oil; set aside.

2 For burgers, in a large bowl, combine the egg white, bread crumbs, onions, crushed pineapple and 3 tablespoons reserved ketchup mixture. Crumble beef and turkey over mixture and mix well. Shape into six burgers.

3 Coat grill rack with cooking spray before starting the grill. Grill burgers, covered, over medium heat for 5-7 minutes on each side or until a meat thermometer reads 165° and juices run clear, brushing occasionally with remaining ketchup mixture.

4 Grill pineapple slices for 2-3 minutes on each side or until heated through. Serve burgers and pineapple on buns with lettuce and tomato.

Round Steak with Dumplings

PREP: 30 MIN. BAKE: 1 HOUR 50 MIN. YIELD: 10-12 SERVINGS

SHERRI ODOM PLANT CITY, FLORIDA

My grandma taught me how to make this old-fashioned dish. I like to serve it for special occasions.

3/4 cup all-purpose flour

1 tablespoon paprika

3 pounds boneless beef top round steak, cut into serving-size pieces

2 tablespoons canola oil

1 medium onion, chopped

2-2/3 cups water

2 cans (10-3/4 ounces *each*) condensed cream of chicken soup, undiluted

1/2 teaspoon pepper

DUMPLINGS:

3 cups all-purpose flour

1/4 cup dried minced onion

2 tablespoons baking powder

1 tablespoon poppy seeds

1-1/2 teaspoons celery salt

1-1/2 teaspoons poultry seasoning

3/4 teaspoon salt

1-1/2 cups milk

6 tablespoons canola oil

1 cup dry bread crumbs

1/4 cup butter, melted

1 In a large resealable plastic bag, combine the flour and paprika. Add the beef, a few pieces at a time, and shake to coat.

2 In a Dutch oven over medium-high heat, brown steak in oil on both sides in batches, adding more oil if necessary. Remove and keep warm.

3 In the drippings, saute onion until tender. Stir in the water, soup and pepper. Bring to a boil. Return meat to pan. Cover and bake at 325° for 1-1/2 hours.

4 Meanwhile, for dumplings, combine the flour, minced onion, baking powder, poppy seeds, celery salt, poultry seasoning and salt in a bowl. Combine milk and oil; stir into dry ingredients just until moistened.

5 Increase oven temperature to 425°. In a large bowl, combine bread crumbs and butter. Drop dumpling batter by rounded tablespoonfuls into crumb mixture; roll to form dumplings. Place on top of simmering beef mixture.

6 Cover and bake 20-25 minutes longer or until a toothpick inserted in a dumpling comes out clean (do not lift the cover while baking).

Taco Meat Loaves

PREP: 25 MIN. BAKE: 1 HOUR + STANDING
YIELD: 2 MEAT LOAVES (6 SERVINGS EACH)

SUSAN GAROUTTE GEORGETOWN, TEXAS

We live in Texas and love the Southwest style of cooking.
This recipe spices up plain ol' meat loaf so it tastes like a
filling for tacos.

    3 eggs, lightly beaten
    2 cups picante sauce, *divided*
    1 can (16 ounces) kidney beans, rinsed and drained
    1 can (11 ounces) Mexicorn, drained
    1 medium onion, chopped
    2 cans (2-1/4 ounces *each*) sliced ripe olives,
       drained
  3/4 cup dry bread crumbs
    1 envelope taco seasoning
    1 teaspoon ground cumin
    1 teaspoon chili powder
    2 pounds ground beef
    2 cups (8 ounces) shredded cheddar cheese
Additional picante sauce, optional

1   In a large bowl, combine the eggs, 1/2 cup picante
    sauce, beans, corn, onion, olives, bread crumbs, taco
    seasoning, cumin and chili powder. Crumble beef over
    mixture and mix well.

2   Pat into two ungreased 9-in. x 5-in. loaf pans. Bake,
    uncovered, at 350° for 50-55 minutes or until no pink
    remains and a meat thermometer reads 160°.

3   Spoon remaining picante sauce over each meat loaf;
    sprinkle with cheese. Bake 10-15 minutes longer or
    until cheese is melted. Let stand for 10 minutes before
    slicing. Serve with additional picante sauce if desired.

Onion Beef au Jus

PREP: 20 MIN. BAKE: 2-1/2 HOURS + STANDING YIELD: 12 SERVINGS

MARILYN BROWN WEST UNION, IOWA

Garlic, onions, soy sauce and onion soup mix flavor the
tender beef in these savory hot sandwiches served with a
tasty, rich broth for dipping. The seasoned beef makes
delicious cold sandwiches, too.

    1 beef rump roast *or* bottom round roast
       (4 pounds)
    2 tablespoons canola oil
    2 large sweet onions, cut into 1/4-inch slices
    6 tablespoons butter, softened, *divided*
    5 cups water
  1/2 cup soy sauce
    1 envelope onion soup mix
    1 garlic clove, minced
    1 teaspoon browning sauce, optional
    1 loaf (1 pound) French bread
    1 cup (4 ounces) shredded Swiss cheese

1   In a Dutch oven over medium-high heat, brown roast
    on all sides in oil; drain. In a large skillet, saute onions
    in 2 tablespoons of butter until tender. Add the water,
    soy sauce, soup mix, garlic and browning sauce if
    desired. Pour over roast. Cover and bake at 325° for
    2-1/2 hours or until meat is tender.

2   Let stand for 10 minutes before slicing. Return meat to
    pan juices. Slice bread in half lengthwise; cut into 3-in.
    sections. Spread remaining butter over bread.

3   Place on a baking sheet. Broil 4-6 in. from the heat for 2-3 minutes or until golden brown. Top with beef and onions; sprinkle with cheese. Broil 4-6 in. from the heat for 1-2 minutes or until cheese is melted. Serve with pan juices.

Dressed-Up Meatballs

PREP/TOTAL TIME: 20 MIN.   YIELD: 8 SERVINGS

IVY ERESMAS DADE CITY, FLORIDA

Frozen meatballs and a jar of sweet-and-sour sauce make this microwave meal a last-minute lifesaver when racing against the clock. The flavorful sauce is dressed up with a hint of garlic and nicely coats the colorful combination of meatballs, carrots, green pepper and onion.

- 2 pounds frozen fully cooked meatballs, thawed
- 1 small onion, sliced
- 2 medium carrots, julienned
- 1 small green pepper, julienned
- 1 garlic clove, minced
- 1 jar (10 ounces) sweet-and-sour sauce
- 4-1/2 teaspoons soy sauce

Hot cooked rice

1   Place the meatballs in a 3-qt. microwave-safe dish; top with the onion, carrots, green pepper and garlic. Combine the sauces; pour over meatballs.

2   Cover and microwave on high for 6-8 minutes or until vegetables are tender and meatballs are heated through, stirring twice. Serve with rice.

Pineapple-Stuffed Burgers

PREP/TOTAL TIME: 30 MIN.   YIELD: 2 SERVINGS

ANN COUCH HALIFAX, NORTH CAROLINA

I really enjoy making these special burgers with a sweet surprise inside. The homemade sauce, with brown sugar, mustard and ketchup, makes these tropical-tasting grilled sandwiches even better.

- 1/4 cup packed brown sugar
- 1/4 cup ketchup
- 1 tablespoon prepared mustard
- 1/2 pound lean ground beef
- 2 slices unsweetened pineapple
- 1/8 teaspoon salt
- 1/8 teaspoon pepper
- 2 hamburger buns, split
- 2 lettuce leaves

1   In a small saucepan, combine the brown sugar, ketchup and mustard. Cook over medium heat for 2-3 minutes, stirring occasionally.

2   Meanwhile, shape beef into four patties. Place pineapple slices on two patties; top with remaining patties. Seal edges; sprinkle with salt and pepper.

3   Coat grill rack with cooking spray before starting the grill. Grill burgers, covered, over medium-hot heat for 7-9 minutes on each side or until a meat thermometer reads 160° and juices run clear. Serve on buns with the sauce and lettuce.

Stovetop Pot Roast

PREP: 15 MIN. COOK: 3-1/4 HOURS YIELD: 8-10 SERVINGS

MARY LOU CHERNIK TAOS, NEW MEXICO

I make this stovetop favorite at least twice a month—my husband, Jim, loves it! You can use whatever vegetables are abundant in your garden. I like to cut up the leftovers, add gravy and warm it up like a stew.

- 1 **boneless beef chuck roast (3 to 4 pounds)**
- 2 **to 3 garlic cloves, peeled and halved lengthwise**
- 2 **tablespoons olive oil**
- 1 **large onion, cut into 1/2-inch slices**
- 3 **celery ribs, cut into 1/2-inch slices**
- 2 **medium turnips, peeled and cut into chunks**
- 4 **cups water**
- 2 **teaspoons beef bouillon granules**
- 4 **medium potatoes, peeled and quartered**
- 1 **pound carrots, cut into chunks**
- 1/2 **pound fresh green beans, trimmed**
- 1/2 **pound sliced fresh mushrooms**
- 3 **tablespoons cornstarch**
- 1/4 **cup cold water**

Salt and pepper to taste

1 Cut slits in roast; insert garlic slivers. In a Dutch oven, brown roast in oil on all sides. Remove roast. Add the onion, celery and turnips to skillet. Place roast over vegetables; add water and bouillon. Bring to a boil. Reduce heat; cover and simmer for 2 hours.

2 Add the potatoes, carrots and beans; cover and cook for 45 minutes. Add mushrooms; cover and cook 15 minutes longer or until meat and vegetables are tender. Remove to a serving platter and keep warm.

3 Skim fat from pan juices. Combine cornstarch and cold water until smooth; stir into pan juices. Bring to a boil; cook and stir for 2 minutes. Season with salt and pepper. Serve roast with vegetables and gravy.

Taco Puffs

PREP/TOTAL TIME: 30 MIN. YIELD: 8 SERVINGS

JAN SCHMID HIBBING, MINNESOTA

I got this recipe from a friend years ago and still make these cheesy sandwiches regularly. I serve them for dinner along with a steaming bowl of soup or fresh green salad. Any leftovers taste even better the next day for lunch. A helpful hint: Plain refrigerated biscuits seal together better than buttermilk types.

- 1 **pound ground beef**
- 1/2 **cup chopped onion**
- 1 **envelope taco seasoning**
- 2 **tubes (16.3 ounces *each*) large refrigerated flaky biscuits**
- 2 **cups (8 ounces) shredded cheddar cheese**

1 In a large skillet, cook beef and onion over medium heat until meat is no longer pink; drain. Add the taco seasoning and prepare according to package directions. Cool slightly.

2 Flatten half of the biscuits into 4-in. circles; place in greased 15-in. x 10-in. x 1-in. baking pans. Spoon 1/4 cup meat mixture onto each; sprinkle with 1/4 cup shredded cheese. Flatten the remaining biscuits; place on top and pinch edges to seal tightly. Bake at 400° for 15 minutes or until golden brown.

GINA HATCHELL
MICKLETON, NEW JERSEY
I'm always on the lookout for light meals that will satisfy my family, and these stuffed kabobs fit the bill. Served with a creamy mustard sauce, the colorful bundles are special enough for company.

Asian Steak Skewers

PREP: 25 MIN. + MARINATING GRILL: 5 MIN. YIELD: 4 SERVINGS

1	**pound beef sirloin tip roast**
1/3	**cup reduced-sodium soy sauce**
1/4	**cup sugar**
1/2	**teaspoon ground ginger**
1	**cup water**
4	**medium carrots, julienned**
1/2	**pound fresh green beans, trimmed**
1	**large sweet red pepper, julienned**
1/2	**cup reduced-fat sour cream**
2	**tablespoon Dijon mustard**
1-1/4	**teaspoons prepared horseradish**

1 Cut beef widthwise into 16 slices, 1/4 in. thick. In a large resealable plastic bag, combine the soy sauce, sugar and ginger; add beef. Seal bag and turn to coat; refrigerate for 4 hours.

2 In a large saucepan, bring water and carrots to a boil. Reduce heat; cover and simmer for 3 minutes. Add the beans and red pepper; cover and simmer for 3-5 minutes or until vegetables are crisp-tender. Drain and immediately place vegetables in ice water. Drain and pat dry.

3 Drain and discard marinade from beef. Arrange three beans, one carrot strip and one pepper strip down the center of each beef slice; roll up. For each kabob use metal or soaked wooden skewers and thread two bundles on two parallel skewers.

4 If grilling the kabobs, coat grill rack with cooking spray before starting the grill. Grill kabobs, covered, over medium heat or broil 4-6 in. from the heat for 3-5 minutes on each side or until beef reaches desired doneness.

5 In a small bowl, combine the sour cream, mustard and horseradish. Serve with kabobs.

2 In a large skillet or wok, stir-fry half of the beef in 1 tablespoon oil until no longer pink; remove from the skillet and keep warm. Repeat with remaining beef and 1 tablespoon oil.

3 Stir-fry the asparagus and cauliflower in remaining oil for 4 minutes. Add red pepper and onion; stir-fry for 2 minutes. Return beef to skillet.

4 In a small bowl, combine the bouillon, soy sauce, ketchup, vinegar and remaining water; add to the skillet. Cook and stir for 2 minutes or until heated through. Serve with rice.

Curried Beef with Dumplings

PREP: 30 MIN. COOK: 2-3/4 HOURS YIELD: 8 SERVINGS

JANELL SCHMIDT ATHELSTANE, WISCONSIN

I like making this hearty pot roast in winter and serving leftovers the next day. It's not only easy to prepare, but the aroma is just wonderful while it's cooking.

- 1 beef rump roast *or* bottom round roast (3 pounds)
- 2 tablespoons olive oil
- 6 medium carrots, cut into chunks
- 1 can (14-1/2 ounces) diced tomatoes, undrained
- 1 medium onion, sliced
- 2 teaspoons curry powder
- 1 teaspoon sugar

Beef and Asparagus Stir-Fry

PREP/TOTAL TIME: 30 MIN. YIELD: 6 SERVINGS

JOLYNN HILL ROOSEVELT, UTAH

With tender slices of beef and fresh, colorful vegetables, this mouthwatering stir-fry was designated "a keeper" by my husband the first time I made it. He loves the beef and asparagus, and I appreciate how quick it is to make.

- 1 pound boneless beef top round steak (3/4 inch thick)
- 2 tablespoons cornstarch
- 2 tablespoons plus 1/2 cup water, *divided*
- 1/2 teaspoon salt
- 1/4 teaspoon pepper
- 1/8 teaspoon hot pepper sauce
- 3 tablespoons canola oil, *divided*
- 2 cups fresh asparagus pieces *or* fresh broccoli florets
- 1 cup sliced cauliflower
- 1 small sweet red *or* green pepper, julienned
- 1 small onion, cut into 1/4-inch wedges
- 2 teaspoons beef bouillon granules
- 1 tablespoon soy sauce
- 1 tablespoon ketchup
- 1 teaspoon red wine vinegar

Hot cooked rice

1 Slice beef into thin 3-in. strips. In a large resealable plastic bag, combine the cornstarch, 2 tablespoons water, salt, pepper and hot pepper sauce; add the beef. Seal bag and turn to coat.

2 teaspoons salt, *divided*

1 teaspoon Worcestershire sauce

1 cup hot water

1-2/3 cups all-purpose flour

3 teaspoons baking powder

2 tablespoons cold butter

3/4 cup milk

2 tablespoons minced fresh parsley

2 tablespoons chopped pimientos

1 In a Dutch oven, brown the roast in oil on all sides; drain. Combine the carrots, tomatoes, onion, curry powder, sugar, 1 teaspoon salt and Worcestershire sauce; pour over roast. Bring to a boil. Reduce heat to low; cover and cook for 2-1/2 hours or until meat and carrots are tender.

2 Remove roast and carrots; keep warm. Add hot water to pan; bring to a boil. For dumplings, combine the flour, baking powder and remaining salt in a large bowl. Cut in butter until mixture resembles fine crumbs. Stir in the milk, parsley and pimientos just until moistened.

3 Drop by tablespoonfuls onto simmering liquid. Cover and cook for 15 minutes or until a toothpick inserted in a dumpling comes out clean (do not lift cover while simmering). Remove dumplings. Strain cooking juices; serve with roast, dumplings and carrots.

Teriyaki Shish Kabobs

PREP: 20 MIN. + MARINATING GRILL: 15 MIN.
YIELD: 6-8 SERVINGS

SUZANNE PELEGRIN OCALA, FLORIDA

My father worked for an airline in the 1960s, when I was a teenager, and my family lived on the island of Guam in the South Pacific. A friend of Mother's there gave her this wonderful recipe. We ate this delicious warm-weather dish often, and now I serve it to my family.

1 cup ketchup

1 cup sugar

1 cup soy sauce

2 teaspoons garlic powder

2 teaspoons ground ginger

1 beef top sirloin steak (1-1/2 inches thick and 2 pounds), cut into 1-1/2-inch cubes

1/2 fresh pineapple, trimmed and cut into 1-inch chunks

2 to 3 small zucchini, cut into 1-inch chunks

1/2 pound medium fresh mushrooms

1/2 pound pearl onions

1 large green *or* sweet red pepper, cut into 1-inch pieces

1 Combine first five ingredients in a large resealable plastic bag; reserving half the marinade. Add beef. Seal bag and turn to coat; refrigerate overnight. Cover and refrigerate reserved marinade.

2 Drain and discard marinade from beef. Thread the meat, pineapple and vegetables alternately on metal or soaked wooden skewers.

3 Grill over hot heat for 15-20 minutes, turning often, or until meat reaches desired doneness and vegetables are tender.

4 In a saucepan, bring reserved marinade to a boil; boil for 1 minute. Remove the meat and vegetables from skewers; serve with marinade.

 To easily peel pearl onions, in a Dutch oven, bring 6 cups of water to a boil. Add the pearl onions and boil for about 2 minutes. Drain the onions and rinse with cold water. After trimming off the stem ends, the skins should slip right off.

Tangy Beef Brisket

PREP: 50 MIN. BAKE: 4 HOURS
YIELD: 12-14 SERVINGS (6 CUPS SAUCE)

JACQUE WATKINS GREEN RIVER, WYOMING

We like the sauce for my tasty brisket over elk, moose and venison salami as well. And we also use it to spice up hamburgers and hot dogs that we sizzle on the grill.

- 1 large onion, diced
- 1/2 cup butter
- 1 bottle (28 ounces) ketchup
- 1-1/2 cups packed brown sugar
- 1/2 cup Worcestershire sauce
- 1/3 cup lemon juice
- 2 tablespoons chili powder
- 1-1/2 teaspoons hot pepper sauce
- 1 teaspoon salt
- 1 teaspoon prepared horseradish
- 1/2 teaspoon garlic powder
- 1 boneless beef brisket (6 pounds)

1   In a large saucepan, saute onion in butter until tender. Add the next nine ingredients; bring to a boil. Reduce heat; simmer, uncovered, for 30-40 minutes.

2   Place brisket in a roasting pan. Add 3 cups of sauce. Cover and bake at 350° for 4 hours or until tender, basting occasionally. Skim fat. To serve, thinly slice across the grain. Top with remaining sauce if desired.

Editor's Note: This is a fresh beef brisket, not corned beef.

Perfect Pot Roast

PREP: 20 MIN. BAKE: 2 HOURS 40 MIN. YIELD: 8-10 SERVINGS

MELODY SROUFE WICHITA, KANSAS

Cooking meats, I have to confess, isn't my specialty. But everyone who tastes this main-course dish wants more! I'm a mostly at-home mom. I like to sew and read. I also enjoy gardening—we grow a good-sized patch, and it's so nice to have fresh-picked tomatoes and spinach when I make salads.

- 1 teaspoon seasoned salt
- 1/2 teaspoon onion powder
- 1/4 teaspoon pepper
- 1/8 teaspoon garlic powder
- 1 beef chuck pot roast (3 to 4 pounds)
- 1 tablespoon olive oil
- 3/4 cup water
- 1 large onion, chopped
- 1/4 cup chopped green pepper
- 2 garlic cloves, minced
- 2 bay leaves
- 2 teaspoons dried parsley flakes
- 1/4 teaspoon dried thyme

All-purpose flour

1   Combine first four ingredients; rub onto roast. In skillet, brown roast in oil. Place in a roasting pan. Add water, onion, green pepper and seasonings. Cover and bake at 325° for 2-1/2 to 3 hours or until roast is tender.

2   Remove and keep warm. Discard bay leaves. Skim fat from pan juices. Measure juices and transfer to a saucepan.

3   For each cup of juices, combine 1 tablespoon flour with 2 tablespoons water; mix well. Stir flour mixture into pan. Bring to a boil; cook and stir for 2 minutes or until thickened. Serve gravy with roast.

SHAWN SOLLEY
MORGANTOWN,
WEST VIRGINIA

This recipe is a variation of the marinated ginger-sake flank steak my mother used to make. It was so good. The wonderful flavor and aroma of this tender, lighter version is one you'll want to try!

Grilled Asian Flank Steak

PREP: 15 MIN. + MARINATING   GRILL: 15 MIN.   YIELD: 6 SERVINGS

1/4 **cup Worcestershire sauce**

1/4 **cup reduced-sodium soy sauce**

3 **tablespoons honey**

1 **tablespoon sesame oil**

1 **teaspoon Chinese five-spice powder**

1 **teaspoon minced garlic**

1/2 **teaspoon minced fresh gingerroot**

1 **beef flank steak (1-1/2 pounds)**

2 **tablespoons hoisin sauce, warmed**

3 **green onions, thinly sliced**

1 **tablespoon sesame seeds, toasted, optional**

1   In a large resealable plastic bag, combine the first seven ingredients; add steak. Seal bag and turn to coat; refrigerate overnight.

2   Drain and discard marinade. Grill steak, covered, over medium heat for 6-7 minutes on each side or until meat reaches desired doneness (for medium-rare, a meat thermometer should read 145°; medium, 160°; well-done, 170°). Let stand for 5 minutes.

3   Thinly slice steak across the grain. Drizzle with hoisin sauce; garnish with onions. Sprinkle with sesame seeds if desired.

Fresh gingerroot is available in your grocer's produce section. It should have a smooth skin. If wrinkled and cracked, the root is dry and past its prime. When stored in a heavy-duty resealable plastic bag, unpeeled gingerroot can be frozen for up to 1 year. When needed, simply peel and grate.

Pasta with Chicken And Squash

PREP/TOTAL TIME: 25 MIN. YIELD: 8 SERVINGS

PAM HALL ELIZABETH CITY, NORTH CAROLINA

This is a special dish that we enjoy often. A bed of noodles is covered with a creamy cheese sauce, tender squash and strips of chicken that've been stir-fried with tasty herbs. It's delicious and pretty too!

- 1 package (16 ounces) spiral pasta
- 2 cups heavy whipping cream
- 1 tablespoon butter
- 2 cups (8 ounces) shredded Mexican cheese blend
- 1 small onion, chopped
- 1 garlic clove, minced
- 5 tablespoons olive oil, *divided*
- 2 medium zucchini, julienned
- 2 medium yellow summer squash, julienned
- 1-1/4 teaspoons salt, *divided*
- 1/8 teaspoon pepper
- 1 pound boneless skinless chicken breasts, sliced
- 1/4 teaspoon *each* dried basil, marjoram and savory
- 1/4 teaspoon dried rosemary, crushed
- 1/8 teaspoon rubbed sage

1   Cook pasta according to package directions. Meanwhile, in a large saucepan, add cream and butter; cook until butter is melted. Stir until smooth. Add cheese; cook and stir until cheese is melted. Rinse and drain pasta; add to cheese mixture. Cover and keep warm.

2   In a large skillet, saute onion and garlic in 3 tablespoons olive oil until onion is tender. Add squash; cook until tender. Add 1 teaspoon of salt and pepper; remove and keep warm.

3   Add remaining oil to skillet; cook chicken with herbs and remaining salt until juices run clear. Place pasta on a serving platter; top with chicken and squash.

Sweet 'n' Spicy Chicken

PREP/TOTAL TIME: 20 MIN. YIELD: 4 SERVINGS

SHERI WHITE HIGLEY, ARIZONA

My husband and three children love this tender chicken that has a spicy sauce. Peach preserves add just a touch of sweetness, while taco seasoning and salsa give this dish some kick. This entree can be made zippier by adding more taco seasoning and using spicier salsa.

- 3 tablespoons taco seasoning
- 1 pound boneless skinless chicken breasts, cut into 1/2-inch cubes
- 1 to 2 tablespoons canola oil
- 1 jar (11 ounces) chunky salsa
- 1/2 cup peach preserves

Hot cooked rice

1   Place taco seasoning in a large resealable plastic bag; add chicken and toss to coat.

2   In a large skillet, brown chicken in oil until no longer pink. Combine salsa and preserves; stir into skillet. Bring to a boil. Reduce heat; cover and simmer for 2-3 minutes or until heated through. Serve with rice.

Herb-Roasted Turkey

PREP: 10 MIN. BAKE: 4 HOURS YIELD: 12-14 SERVINGS

BECKY GOLDSMITH EDEN PRAIRIE, MINNESOTA

Our guests always comment on how flavorful this elegant entree is. Rubbed with garden-fresh herbs, this turkey has such a wonderful aroma when it's roasting that it lures everyone into the kitchen!

> 1 turkey (14 pounds)
> 1 tablespoon salt
> 1 teaspoon pepper
> 18 sprigs fresh thyme, *divided*
> 4 medium onions, sliced
> 4 celery ribs, sliced
> 2 medium carrots, sliced
> 3 bay leaves
> 1 tablespoon peppercorns
> 1/2 cup butter, melted
> 1 teaspoon minced fresh sage *or* 1/2 teaspoon rubbed sage
> 1 teaspoon minced fresh thyme *or* 1/2 teaspoon dried thyme
> 1 teaspoon minced chives

1 Rub the surface of the turkey and sprinkle cavity with salt and pepper. Place 12 sprigs of thyme in cavity. In a large heavy roasting pan, place onions, celery, carrots, bay leaves, peppercorns and remaining thyme sprigs. Place the turkey, breast side up, over vegetables. Drizzle butter over turkey and sprinkle with minced herbs.

2 Cover loosely with foil. Bake at 325° for 2-1/2 hours. Remove foil; bake 1-1/2 to 2 hours longer or until a meat thermometer reads 180°, basting every 20 minutes.

3 Cover and let stand for 20 minutes before carving. Discard bay leaves and peppercorns; thicken pan drippings for gravy if desired.

Honey Rosemary Chicken

PREP: 5 MIN. + MARINATING BAKE: 55 MIN. YIELD: 6 SERVINGS

ELSIE BARTON HOOVER, ALABAMA

I never get tired of finding new ways to cook with herbs! A rosemary marinade sweetened with honey gives this moist chicken wonderful flavor and a pretty golden sheen.

> 1/4 cup honey
> 1/4 cup balsamic vinegar
> 1/4 cup minced fresh rosemary
> 2 tablespoons olive oil
> 6 bone-in skinless chicken breast halves (7 ounces *each*)
> 1 teaspoon salt
> 1/4 teaspoon pepper

1 In a small bowl, combine the honey, vinegar, rosemary and oil. Pour half of the marinade into a large resealable plastic bag; add the chicken. Seal bag and turn to coat; refrigerate for 2 hours. Cover and refrigerate for 2 hours. Cover and refrigerate remaining marinade.

2 Drain and discard marinade from chicken. Place chicken bone side down in a 13-in. x 9-in. baking pan. Sprinkle with salt and pepper. Bake, uncovered, at 350° for 55-65 minutes or until a meat thermometer reaches 170°, basting occasionally with reserved marinade.

Herbed Turkey and Dressing

PREP: 55 MIN. + CHILLING BAKE: 5 HOURS
YIELD: 14-16 SERVINGS (18 CUPS DRESSING)

MARILYN CLAY PALATINE, ILLINOIS

When I serve this succulent golden turkey and tasty dressing, guests fill their plates and I'm buried in compliments. This recipe always makes a holiday dinner one to remember.

BASTING SAUCE:
- 2-1/4 cups chicken broth
- 1/2 cup butter, cubed
- 1/2 teaspoon salt
- 1 teaspoon dried thyme
- 1/4 teaspoon *each* dried marjoram, rubbed sage and dried crushed rosemary
- 1/4 cup minced fresh parsley
- 2 tablespoons minced chives

DRESSING:
- 1 loaf (1 pound) sliced bread
- 1 pound bulk pork sausage
- 1/2 cup butter, cubed
- 4 cups thinly sliced celery
- 3 cups thinly sliced carrots
- 1/2 pound fresh mushrooms, chopped
- 1/2 pound cubed fully cooked ham
- 2 cups green onions
- 2 cups chopped pecans
- 1 large tart apple, chopped
- 1 cup chopped dried apricots
- 1 tablespoon rubbed sage
- 2 teaspoons dried marjoram
- 1 teaspoon dried crushed rosemary
- 1 teaspoon salt
- 1/8 teaspoon ground nutmeg
- 1 cup egg substitute
- 1 turkey (16 to 18 pounds)
- 1 cup chicken broth

1. In a pan, bring broth, butter and salt to a boil. Add the herbs; set aside.

2. For dressing, toast bread; cut into 1/2-in. cubes. Place in a bowl. In a skillet, cook sausage over medium heat until no longer pink; remove with slotted spoon and add to bread. Add butter to drippings. Stir in celery, carrots, mushrooms, ham and onions; cook over medium heat for 15 minutes.

3. Add to bread mixture; stir in the nuts, fruit and seasonings. Add egg substitute and 3/4 cup basting sauce; mix lightly.

4. Stuff the turkey with about 8 cups dressing. Skewer the openings; tie the drumsticks together. Place on a rack in roasting pan. Baste with some of the remaining basting sauce.

5. Bake, uncovered, at 325° for 5 to 5-1/2 hours or until a meat thermometer reads 180° for the turkey and 165° for the stuffing, basting every 30 minutes. When turkey begins to brown, cover lightly with foil.

6. Add broth to remaining dressing; mix lightly. Place in a greased 2-1/2-qt. baking dish; refrigerate. Remove from the refrigerator 30 minutes before baking. Cover and bake at 325° for 1 hour; uncover and bake 10 minutes.

Chicken and Asparagus Kabobs

PREP: 25 MIN. + MARINATING GRILL: 10 MIN. YIELD: 6 SERVINGS

KELLY TOWNSEND SYRACUSE, NEBRASKA

These Asian-flavored kabobs, served with a delicious dipping sauce, are special enough to make for guests at your next backyard get-together. Sometimes I substitute salmon for the chicken.

DIPPING SAUCE:
- 2 cups mayonnaise
- 1/4 cup sugar
- 1/4 cup soy sauce
- 2 tablespoons sesame seeds, toasted
- 1 tablespoon sesame oil
- 1/2 teaspoon white pepper

Garden Turkey Burgers

PREP/TOTAL TIME: 30 MIN. YIELD: 6 SERVINGS

SANDY KITZMILLER UNITYVILLE, PENNSYLVANIA

These moist burgers get plenty of color and flavor from onion, zucchini and red pepper. I often make the mixture ahead of time and put it in the refrigerator. Later, after helping my husband with farm chores, I can put the burgers on the grill while whipping up a salad or side dish.

> 1 cup old-fashioned oats
> 3/4 cup chopped onion
> 3/4 cup finely chopped sweet red *or* green pepper
> 1/2 cup shredded zucchini
> 1/4 cup ketchup
> 2 garlic cloves, minced
> 1/4 teaspoon salt, optional
> 1 pound ground turkey
> 6 whole wheat hamburger buns, split and toasted

1 Coat grill rack with cooking spray before starting the grill. In a bowl, combine the first seven ingredients. Crumble turkey over mixture and mix well. Shape into six 1/2-in.-thick patties.

2 Grill, covered, over indirect medium heat for 6 minutes on each side or until a meat thermometer reads 165° and juices run clear. Serve on buns.

KABOBS:

> 1/4 cup soy sauce
> 2 tablespoons brown sugar
> 2 tablespoons water
> 1 tablespoon sesame oil
> 1 teaspoon crushed red pepper flakes
> 1 teaspoon minced fresh gingerroot
> 1-1/2 pounds boneless skinless chicken breasts, cut into 1-1/2-inch pieces
> 1 pound fresh asparagus, trimmed and cut into 2-inch pieces
> 2 tablespoons olive oil
> 1/2 teaspoon salt

1 In a small bowl, combine the sauce ingredients. Cover and refrigerate for 2-4 hours.

2 For kabobs, in a large resealable plastic bag, combine the soy sauce, brown sugar, water, sesame oil, pepper flakes and ginger. Add the chicken; seal bag and turn to coat. Refrigerate for 2 hours, turning occasionally.

3 Drain and discard marinade. In a large bowl, toss the asparagus with olive oil and salt. On six metal or soaked wooden skewers, alternately thread one chicken piece and two asparagus pieces.

4 Grill, covered, over medium heat for 4-5 minutes on each side or until chicken is no longer pink and asparagus is crisp-tender. Serve with dipping sauce.

HEATHER THOMPSON
WOODLAND HILLS, CALIFORNIA

This is the only pizza I make. We love it! Keeping the spices simple helps the flavor of the chicken and vegetables to come through. The entree is great for casual get-togethers.

Chicken Pesto Pizza

PREP: 35 MIN. + RISING BAKE: 20 MIN. YIELD: 8 SLICES

2 teaspoons active dry yeast

1 cup warm water (110° to 115°)

2-3/4 cups bread flour, *divided*

1 tablespoon plus 2 teaspoons olive oil, *divided*

1 tablespoon sugar

1-1/2 teaspoons salt, *divided*

1/2 pound boneless skinless chicken breasts, cut into 1/2-inch pieces

1 small onion, halved and thinly sliced

1/2 *each* small green, sweet red and yellow peppers, julienned

1/2 cup sliced fresh mushrooms

3 tablespoons prepared pesto

1-1/2 cups (6 ounces) shredded part-skim mozzarella cheese

1/4 teaspoon pepper

1 In a large bowl, dissolve the yeast in warm water. Beat in 1 cup flour, 1 tablespoon oil, sugar and 1 teaspoon salt. Add the remaining flour; beat until combined.

2 Turn onto a lightly floured surface; knead until smooth and elastic, about 6-8 minutes. Place in a bowl coated with cooking spray, turning once to coat top. Cover and let rise in a warm place until doubled, about 1 hour.

3 In a large nonstick skillet over medium heat, cook the chicken, onion, peppers and mushrooms in remaining oil until chicken is no longer pink and vegetables are tender. Remove from the heat; set aside.

4 Punch dough down; roll into a 15-in. circle. Transfer to a 14-in. pizza pan. Build up edges slightly. Spread with pesto. Top with chicken mixture and cheese. Sprinkle with pepper and remaining salt.

5 Bake at 400° for 18-20 minutes or until crust and cheese are lightly browned.

Bombay Chicken

PREP: 10 MIN. + MARINATING GRILL: 25 MIN. YIELD: 8 SERVINGS

JUNE THOMAS CHESTERTON, INDIANA

This grilled dinner always turns out moist and tender. The marinade has a Middle Eastern flair, giving the dish a zesty flavor. It makes a beautiful presentation as well.

- 1-1/2 cups (12 ounces) plain yogurt
- 1/4 cup lemon juice
- 2 tablespoons chili powder
- 2 tablespoons paprika
- 2 tablespoons olive oil
- 1-1/2 teaspoons salt
- 1/2 to 1 teaspoon cayenne pepper
- 1/2 teaspoon garlic powder
- 1/4 teaspoon ground ginger
- 1/4 teaspoon ground cardamom
- 1/8 teaspoon ground cinnamon
- 4 to 5 pounds bone-in chicken thighs and legs, skin removed

1 In a large resealable plastic bag, combine the first 11 ingredients. Add the chicken; seal bag and turn to coat. Refrigerate overnight.

2 Rub grill rack with oil or coat with cooking spray before starting the grill. Drain and discard marinade.

3 Grill the chicken, covered, over medium-hot heat for 10-15 minutes on each side or until a meat thermometer reads 180°.

Smothered Chicken Breasts

PREP/TOTAL TIME: 30 MIN. YIELD: 4 SERVINGS

BRENDA CARPENTER WARRENSBURG, MISSOURI

After trying this delicious dish in a restaurant, I decided to re-create it at home. Topped with bacon, caramelized onions and zippy shredded cheese, it comes together in no time with ingredients I usually have on hand. Plus, it cooks in only one skillet, so it's a cinch to clean up!

- 4 boneless skinless chicken breast halves (6 ounces *each*)
- 1/4 teaspoon salt
- 1/4 teaspoon lemon-pepper seasoning
- 1 tablespoon canola oil
- 8 bacon strips
- 1 medium onion, sliced
- 1/4 cup packed brown sugar
- 1/2 cup shredded Colby-Monterey Jack cheese

1 Sprinkle chicken with salt and lemon-pepper. In a large skillet, cook chicken in oil for 6-7 minutes on each side or until a meat thermometer reads 170°; remove and keep warm.

2 In the same skillet, cook bacon over medium heat until crisp. Using a slotted spoon, remove to paper towels; drain, reserving 2 tablespoons drippings.

3 In the drippings, saute onion and brown sugar until onion is tender and golden brown. Place two bacon strips on each chicken breast half; top with caramelized onions and cheese.

Baked Chicken And Acorn Squash

PREP: 20 MIN. BAKE: 1 HOUR YIELD: 4 SERVINGS

CONNIE SVOBODA ELKO, MINNESOTA

This eye-pleasing main dish is ideal for harvesttime with its colorful acorn squash and sweet peaches. The fragrance of rosemary-seasoned chicken baking is heavenly. My family says it's every bit as delicious as it smells.

- 2 small acorn squash (1-1/4 pounds)
- 2 to 4 garlic cloves, minced
- 2 tablespoons canola oil, *divided*
- 4 chicken drumsticks (4 ounces *each*)
- 4 bone-in chicken thighs (about 1-1/2 pounds), skin removed
- 1/4 cup packed brown sugar
- 1 tablespoon minced fresh rosemary *or* 1 teaspoon dried rosemary, crushed
- 1 teaspoon salt
- 1 can (15-1/4 ounces) sliced peaches, undrained

1 Cut squash in half lengthwise; discard seeds. Cut each half widthwise into 1/2-in. slices; discard ends. Place slices in an ungreased 13-in. x 9-in. baking dish. Sprinkle with garlic and drizzle with 1 tablespoon oil.

2 In a large skillet, brown chicken in remaining oil. Arrange chicken over squash. Combine the brown sugar, rosemary and salt; sprinkle over chicken. Bake, uncovered, at 350° for 45 minutes, basting with pan juices twice.

3 Pour peaches over chicken and squash. Bake, uncovered, 15 minutes longer or until a meat thermometer reads 180°.

Chicken in Basil Cream

PREP/TOTAL TIME: 25 MIN. YIELD: 4 SERVINGS

JUDY BAKER CRAIG, COLORADO

When I first read this recipe, I thought it looked difficult. But because I had all the ingredients readily at hand, I gave it a try. Am I glad I did! It's simple to make and tastes great.

- 1/4 cup milk
- 1/4 cup dry bread crumbs
- 4 boneless skinless chicken breast halves (4 ounces *each*)
- 3 tablespoons butter
- 1/2 cup chicken broth
- 1 cup heavy whipping cream
- 1 jar (4 ounces) sliced pimientos, drained
- 1/2 cup grated Parmesan cheese
- 1/4 cup minced fresh basil
- 1/8 teaspoon pepper

1 Place milk and bread crumbs in separate shallow bowls. Dip chicken in milk, then coat with crumbs. In a skillet over medium-high heat, cook chicken in butter for about 5 minutes on each side or until a meat thermometer reads 170°. Remove and keep warm.

2 Add broth to the skillet. Bring to a boil over medium heat; stir to loosen browned bits. Stir in the cream and pimientos; boil and stir for 1 minute. Reduce heat. Add Parmesan cheese, basil and pepper; cook and stir until heated through. Serve with chicken.

Southern Barbecued Chicken

PREP: 25 MIN. + MARINATING GRILL: 40 MIN. YIELD: 4 SERVINGS

REVONDA STROUD FORT WORTH, TEXAS

Nothing says Texas like outdoor grilling. And summer is a prime time for patio picnics featuring my barbecued chicken. Guests are surprised to find the basis for my "mystery marinade" is simply vinegar and oil.

- 2 cups cider vinegar
- 1 cup canola oil
- 1 egg, lightly beaten
- 2 tablespoons hot pepper sauce
- 1 tablespoon garlic powder
- 1 tablespoon poultry seasoning
- 2 teaspoons salt
- 1 teaspoon pepper
- 1 broiler/fryer chicken (3 to 4 pounds), cut up

1 In a large saucepan, combine the first eight ingredients. Bring to a boil, stirring constantly. Reduce the heat; simmer, uncovered, for 10 minutes, stirring often. Cool.

2 Pour 1-2/3 cups marinade into a large resealable plastic bag; add the chicken.

3 Seal bag and turn to coat; refrigerate overnight, turning occasionally. Cover and refrigerate remaining marinade for basting.

4 Prepare grill for indirect heat, using a drip pan. Drain and discard marinade from chicken. Place skin side down over pan. Grill, covered, over indirect medium heat for 20-25 minutes on each side or until juices run clear, basting occasionally with reserved marinade.

Savory Chicken Dinner

PREP: 10 MIN. BAKE: 45 MIN. YIELD: 4 SERVINGS

LESLIE ADAMS SPRINGFIELD, MISSOURI

No one would guess that these moist chicken breasts and tender potatoes are seasoned with herb- and garlic-flavored soup mix. The meal-in-one is simple to assemble, and it all bakes in one dish so there's little cleanup.

- 2 envelopes savory herb with garlic soup mix
- 6 tablespoons water
- 4 boneless skinless chicken breast halves (6 to 8 ounces *each*)
- 2 large red potatoes, cubed
- 1 large onion, halved and cut into small wedges

1 In a small bowl, combine soup mix and water; pour half into a large resealable plastic bag. Add chicken. Seal bag and toss to coat. Pour the remaining soup mix in another large resealable plastic bag. Add potatoes and onion. Seal bag and toss to coat.

2 Drain and discard marinade from chicken. Transfer to a greased 13-in. x 9-in. baking dish. Pour potato mixture with marinade over chicken.

3 Bake, uncovered, at 350° for 40-45 minutes or until vegetables are tender and a meat thermometer reads 170°, stirring vegetables occasionally.

Buying skinned and boned chicken breasts can cut up to 15 minutes off your cooking time. Save money by buying larger size packages, then rewrap individually or in family-size portions and freeze.

Chicken with Spicy Fruit

PREP/TOTAL TIME: 30 MIN. YIELD: 4 SERVINGS

KATHY RAIRIGH MILFORD, INDIANA

This speedy stovetop entree is special enough for company, yet easy enough for everyday meals. The succulent chicken gets wonderful flavor from a sweet sauce made with strawberry jam, dried cranberries and pineapple juice. I like to serve it with rice pilaf, peas, a garden salad and cloverleaf rolls.

1-1/4 cups unsweetened pineapple juice
1/4 cup dried cranberries
2 garlic cloves, minced
1/8 to 1/4 teaspoon crushed red pepper flakes
4 boneless skinless chicken breast halves (4 ounces *each*)
1/4 cup strawberry spreadable fruit
1 teaspoon cornstarch
2 green onions, thinly sliced

1 In a large skillet, combine the pineapple juice, cranberries, garlic and red pepper flakes; bring to a boil. Add chicken. Reduce heat; cover and simmer for 10 minutes or until a meat thermometer reaches 170°. Remove chicken to a platter and keep warm.

2 Bring cooking liquid to a boil; cook for 5-7 minutes or until liquid is reduced to 3/4 cup. Combine spreadable fruit and cornstarch until blended; add to the skillet. Boil and stir for 1 minute or until thickened. Spoon over chicken. Sprinkle with onions.

Squash-Stuffed Chicken

PREP: 20 MIN. BAKE: 50 MIN. YIELD: 4 SERVINGS

BERNADETTE ROMANO SHAFTSBURY, VERMONT

Even people who don't like zucchini comment on how flavorful this is! If you want, you can also bake the stuffing by itself and serve it as a side dish.

3 tablespoons butter
1/2 small onion, chopped
1 tablespoon chopped fresh parsley
1/2 teaspoon dried basil
2 medium zucchini, shredded (about 2-1/2 cups)
3 slices white bread, torn into coarse crumbs
1 egg, beaten
3/4 cup shredded Swiss cheese
1/2 teaspoon salt
1/8 teaspoon pepper
4 bone-in chicken breast halves

1 In a skillet, melt butter over medium-high heat. Saute onion, parsley and basil until the onion is tender. Add zucchini and continue to cook for 2 minutes. Remove from the heat; stir in bread crumbs, egg, cheese, salt and pepper.

2 Carefully loosen the skin of the chicken on one side to form a pocket. Stuff each breast with the zucchini mixture. Bake at 375° for 50-60 minutes or until chicken is done.

3 Remove chicken and keep warm. Pour cooking juices into a small saucepan; skim fat. Combine cornstarch and water until smooth; gradually stir into cooking juices. Bring to a boil; cook and stir for 2 minutes or until smooth. Pour over chicken. Sprinkle with basil, pimientos and parsley.

Editor's Note: Look for herbes de Provence in the spice aisle. It is also available from Penzeys Spices. Call 1-800-741-7787 or visit www.penzeys.com.

Nutty Oven-Fried Chicken

PREP: 10 MIN. BAKE: 1 HOUR YIELD: 6-8 SERVINGS

DIANE HIXON NICEVILLE, FLORIDA

I love to make and serve this easy dish because the chicken comes out delectable, tasty and crispy.

- 1/2 cup evaporated milk
-   1 cup biscuit/baking mix
- 1/3 cup finely chopped pecans
-   2 teaspoons paprika
- 1/2 teaspoon salt
- 1/2 teaspoon poultry seasoning
- 1/2 teaspoon rubbed sage
-   1 broiler/fryer chicken (3 to 4 pounds), cut up
- 1/3 cup butter, melted

1 Place milk in a shallow bowl. In another shallow bowl, combine baking mix, pecans and seasonings. Dip chicken pieces in milk, then coat generously with pecan mixture.

2 Place in a lightly greased 13-in. x 9-in. baking dish. Drizzle with butter. Bake, uncovered, at 350° for 1 hour or until chicken is golden brown, crispy and the juices run clear.

Corsican Chicken

PREP: 20 MIN. COOK: 4-1/2 HOURS YIELD: 6-8 SERVINGS

MARY BERGFELD EUGENE, OREGON

Moist and tender chicken thighs make a delicious hot entree for winter months. Just add a salad and a lemon dessert. I set the table with warm, sunny Mediterranean shades and patterns that look gorgeous with this colorful meal.

-   3 tablespoons butter, softened
-   2 tablespoons herbes de Provence
-   1 teaspoon salt
-   2 garlic cloves, minced
- 1/2 teaspoon coarsely ground pepper
-   2 pounds boneless skinless chicken thighs
-   1 large onion, chopped
- 1/2 cup oil-packed sun-dried tomatoes, julienned
-   1 can (10-1/2 ounces) condensed beef consomme, undiluted
- 1/2 cup dry vermouth *or* orange juice
- 1/2 cup pitted Greek olives, quartered
-   1 teaspoon grated orange peel
-   2 teaspoons cornstarch
-   1 tablespoon cold water
-   2 tablespoons minced fresh basil
-   2 tablespoons diced pimientos
-   2 tablespoons minced fresh parsley

1 In a small bowl, combine the butter, herbes de Provence, salt, garlic and pepper; rub over chicken. Place in a 5-qt. slow cooker. Add the onion, tomatoes, consomme and vermouth or orange juice.

2 Cover and cook on low for 4-5 hours or until chicken is no longer pink. Add olives and orange peel. Cover and cook on high for 30 minutes.

Sesame Chicken with Mustard Sauce

PREP: 10 MIN. + MARINATING BAKE: 35 MIN. YIELD: 6 SERVINGS

WANDA WHITE ANTIOCH, TENNESSEE

For variety, you can make a cracker-crumb coating for my chicken…substitute turkey for chicken…or grill it instead of baking it. I've even served the chicken in strips with a sauce so it becomes a fun finger food for dipping.

1-1/2 cups buttermilk
2 tablespoons lemon juice
2 teaspoons Worcestershire sauce
1 teaspoon salt
1 teaspoon pepper
1 teaspoon paprika
1 teaspoon soy sauce
1/2 teaspoon dried oregano
2 garlic cloves, minced
6 boneless skinless chicken breast halves (about 1-1/2 pounds)
2 cups dry bread crumbs
1/2 cup sesame seeds
1/4 cup butter, melted
1/4 cup shortening, melted

SAUCE:
1-1/2 cups prepared mustard
1-1/2 cups plum jam
4-1/2 teaspoons prepared horseradish
1-1/2 teaspoons lemon juice

1 In a large resealable plastic bag or shallow glass container, combine the first nine ingredients; mix well. Add chicken and turn to coat. Seal or cover and refrigerate for 8 hours or overnight, turning occasionally. Drain and discard marinade.

2 In a shallow dish, combine bread crumbs and sesame seeds. Dredge the chicken in the crumb mixture. Place in a greased 13-in. x 9-in. baking dish. Combine butter and shortening; drizzle over chicken. Bake, uncovered, at 350° for 35-40 minutes or until juices run clear.

3 Meanwhile, combine sauce ingredients in a saucepan; heat through. Serve with the chicken.

Orange Walnut Chicken

PREP: 10 MIN. + MARINATING COOK: 30 MIN. YIELD: 4 SERVINGS

TERRYANN MOORE OAKLYN, NEW JERSEY

For an impressive main dish that's not tricky to prepare, try this mouthwatering chicken. With orange juice concentrate, orange juice, lemon juice and marmalade, the pretty sauce has a zesty taste.

1/3 cup thawed orange juice concentrate
5 tablespoons canola oil, *divided*
2 tablespoons soy sauce
2 garlic cloves, minced
4 boneless skinless chicken breast halves (4 ounces *each*)
1/2 cup coarsely chopped walnuts
1 tablespoon butter
4 green onions, thinly sliced, *divided*
1/2 cup orange marmalade
1/2 cup orange juice
1/4 cup lemon juice
2 tablespoons honey
1 to 2 tablespoons grated orange peel
2 to 3 teaspoons grated lemon peel
1/2 teaspoon salt
1/8 teaspoon pepper

Hot cooked rice

1 In a small bowl, combine the orange juice concentrate, 4 tablespoons oil, soy sauce and garlic. Pour half of marinade into a large resealable plastic bag; add the chicken. Seal bag and turn to coat; refrigerate for 2-3 hours. Cover and refrigerate remaining marinade.

2 Discard marinade from chicken. In a large skillet, cook chicken in remaining oil until a meat thermometer reads 170°.

2 tablespoons steak sauce

2 tablespoons cornstarch

2 tablespoons brown sugar

1 cup water

1 tablespoon lemon juice

1 Sprinkle inside of hens with 1/4 teaspoon salt; set aside. Drain pineapple, reserving juice. In a bowl, combine the pineapple, bread cubes, celery and coconut. Add 6 tablespoons butter; toss to coat.

2 Loosely stuff hens; tie legs together with kitchen string. Place on a rack in a greased shallow roasting pan. Place remaining stuffing in a greased 1-1/2-cup baking dish; cover and set aside. Add poultry seasoning and remaining salt to remaining butter. Spoon some butter mixture over hens. Bake, uncovered, at 350° for 40 minutes, basting twice with butter mixture.

3 Stir steak sauce and reserved pineapple juice into remaining butter mixture; baste hens. Bake reserved stuffing with hens for 30 minutes; baste hens twice.

4 Uncover stuffing; baste hens with remaining butter mixture. Bake 15-20 minutes longer or until a meat thermometer reads 185° for hens and 165° for stuffing in hens. Remove hens from pan; keep warm.

5 Pour drippings into a saucepan, skim fat. Combine cornstarch, brown sugar, water and lemon juice until smooth; add to the drippings. Bring to a boil; cook and stir for 1-2 minutes or until thickened. Serve with hens and stuffing.

3 Meanwhile, in a small saucepan, saute walnuts in butter until lightly browned; remove and set aside. Set aside 1/4 cup green onions for garnish.

4 Add remaining onions to saucepan; saute until tender. Add the next eight ingredients and reserved marinade. Bring to a boil. Reduce heat; simmer, uncovered, for 5-10 minutes or until sauce reaches desired consistency. Serve chicken with rice; top with sauce and garnish with reserved walnuts and onions.

Pineapple-Stuffed Cornish Hens

PREP: 20 MIN. BAKE: 55 MIN. YIELD: 2 SERVINGS

VICKI CORNERS ROCK ISLAND, ILLINOIS

My mother brought this recipe back with her from Hawaii about 25 years ago. The tender meat, pineapple-coconut stuffing and sweet-sour sauce made it a favorite of my family and friends. I keep the recipe on hand to share.

2 Cornish game hens (20 ounces *each*)

1/2 teaspoon salt, *divided*

1 can (8 ounces) crushed pineapple

3 cups cubed day-old bread (1/2-inch cubes), crusts removed

1 celery rib, chopped

1/2 cup flaked coconut

2/3 cup butter melted, *divided*

1/4 teaspoon poultry seasoning

Next Day Turkey Primavera

PREP/TOTAL TIME: 30 MIN. YIELD: 4 SERVINGS

ROBYN HARDISTY LAKEWOOD, CALIFORNIA

I make this recipe around the holidays. It's a wonderful way to use leftover turkey without feeling like it's a "repeat" meal. I love pasta, and the creamy sauce in this primavera is so easy to make.

- 1 cup uncooked penne pasta
- 8 fresh asparagus spears, trimmed and cut into 1-inch pieces
- 2/3 cup julienned carrot
- 3 tablespoons butter
- 4 large fresh mushrooms, sliced
- 1/2 cup chopped yellow summer squash
- 1/2 cup chopped zucchini
- 1-1/2 cups shredded cooked turkey
- 1 medium tomato, chopped
- 1 envelope Italian salad dressing mix
- 1 cup heavy whipping cream
- 1/4 cup grated Parmesan cheese

1 Cook pasta according to package directions. Meanwhile, in a large skillet, saute asparagus and carrot in butter for 3 minutes. Add the mushrooms, yellow squash and zucchini; saute until crisp-tender.

2 Stir in the turkey, tomato, dressing mix and cream. Bring to a boil; cook and stir for 2 minutes.

3 Drain pasta; add to vegetable mixture and toss to combine. Sprinkle with cheese and toss again.

Apricot Chicken

PREP/TOTAL TIME: 15 MIN. YIELD: 4 SERVINGS

VICKI RUIZ TWIN FALLS, IDAHO

This is one of my favorite ways to fix chicken in a hurry. Everybody just loves it, and leftovers are always just as good the next day. For variation, I've used pork instead of chicken and added additional ingredients like pineapple, mandarin oranges, snow peas and broccoli.

- 1/2 cup apricot preserves
- 2 tablespoons soy sauce
- 1 tablespoon chicken broth *or* sherry
- 1 tablespoon canola oil
- 1 tablespoon cornstarch
- 1 teaspoon minced garlic
- 1/4 teaspoon ground ginger
- 1 pound boneless skinless chicken breasts, cut into strips
- 1 medium green pepper, chopped
- 1/2 cup salted cashews

Hot cooked rice

1 In a large bowl, combine the first seven ingredients. Add chicken and toss to coat. Transfer to a shallow microwave-safe dish. Cover and microwave on high for 3 minutes, stirring once.

2 Add green pepper and cashews. Cover and microwave on high for 2-4 minutes or until chicken is no longer pink, stirring once. Let stand for 3 minutes. Serve with rice.

SHERI SIDWELL
ALTON, ILLINOIS

This garlic-kissed chicken is delicious, plain or fancy. It's an elegant entree for guests—and my husband and I love its leftovers in rice casseroles and hot, open-face sandwiches.

Roasted Chicken with Garlic-Sherry Sauce

PREP: 30 MIN. + MARINATING BAKE: 20 MIN. YIELD: 4 SERVINGS

- 2 **quarts water**
- 1/2 **cup salt**
- 4 **bone-in chicken breast halves (12 ounces *each*)**
- 3/4 **teaspoon pepper, *divided***
- 2 **teaspoons canola oil**
- 8 **garlic cloves, peeled and thinly sliced**
- 1 **cup reduced-sodium chicken broth**
- 1/2 **cup sherry *or* additional reduced-sodium chicken broth**
- 3 **fresh thyme sprigs**
- 1/4 **cup butter, cubed**
- 1 **teaspoon lemon juice**

1. For brine, in a large saucepan, bring water and salt to a boil. Cook and stir until salt is dissolved. Remove from the heat; cool to room temperature.

2. Place a large heavy-duty resealable plastic bag inside a second large resealable plastic bag; add chicken. Carefully pour cooled brine into bag. Squeeze out as much air as possible; seal bags and turn to coat. Refrigerate for 1-2 hours, turning several times.

3. Drain and discard brine. Rinse chicken with cold water; pat dry. Sprinkle with 1/2 teaspoon pepper. In a large ovenproof skillet, brown chicken in oil over medium heat.

4. Bake, uncovered, at 400° for 20-25 minutes or until juices run clear. Remove chicken and keep warm. Drain drippings, reserving 1 tablespoon.

5. In the drippings, saute garlic until tender. Add the broth, sherry or additional broth and thyme. Bring to a boil; cook until liquid is reduced to 1 cup. Discard thyme. Stir in the butter, lemon juice and remaining pepper. Serve with chicken.

Orange-Glazed Cornish Hens

PREP: 10 MIN. BAKE: 1-1/4 HOURS YIELD: 4 SERVINGS

LAURIE BARTLEY LAKE HIAWATHA, NEW JERSEY

This is a wonderfully elegant entree to serve at a cozy dinner party for four. Your guests will think you spent hours in the kitchen preparing the tender, golden-brown hens and perfecting the full-flavored basting sauce.

    4 Cornish game hens (22 ounces *each*)
  1/4 cup butter, melted
    1 teaspoon salt
  1/2 teaspoon pepper
  3/4 cup orange juice
  1/2 cup packed brown sugar
  1/2 cup Madeira wine, sherry *or* chicken broth
    2 tablespoons lemon juice
    1 teaspoon ground mustard
  1/4 teaspoon ground allspice

1 Tie legs of each hen together; turn wing tips under backs. Place on a greased rack in a roasting pan. Brush with butter; sprinkle with salt and pepper. Bake, uncovered, at 350° for 1 hour.

2 In a saucepan, combine the remaining ingredients; bring to a boil. Reduce heat; simmer, uncovered, for 15 minutes. Spoon over hens. Bake 15 minutes longer or until a meat thermometer reads 180°.

Parmesan Chicken

PREP: 15 MIN. BAKE: 50 MIN. YIELD: 4 SERVINGS

SHARON CRIDER ST. ROBERT, MISSOURI

This oven-fried chicken is the perfect dish to prepare in advance and take on a picnic because it tastes just as good cold as it does warm. It's been a family favorite for years.

    1 cup all-purpose flour
    2 teaspoons salt
    2 teaspoons paprika
  1/4 teaspoon pepper
    2 eggs
    3 tablespoons milk
  2/3 cup grated Parmesan cheese
  1/3 cup dry bread crumbs
    1 broiler/fryer chicken (3 to 4 pounds), cut up

1 In a shallow bowl, combine the flour, salt, paprika and pepper. In another shallow bowl, beat the eggs and milk. In a third bowl, combine the Parmesan cheese and bread crumbs. Coat chicken pieces with flour mixture, dip in egg mixture, then roll in crumb mixture.

2 Place in a well-greased 15-in. x 10-in. x 1-in. baking pan. Bake at 400° for 50-55 minutes or until chicken juices run clear.

Peppery Grilled Turkey Breast

PREP: 15 MIN. GRILL: 1-1/2 HOURS + STANDING YIELD: 15 SERVINGS

MARY RELYEA CANASTOTA, NEW YORK

This is a combination of several traditional recipes. People who try it for the first time are amazed to find that it's not only flavorful but healthy as well.

2 tablespoons light brown sugar

1 tablespoon salt

2 teaspoons ground cinnamon

1 teaspoon cayenne pepper

1/2 teaspoon ground mustard

1 bone-in turkey breast (5 pounds)

1 cup reduced-sodium chicken broth

1/4 cup white vinegar

1/4 cup jalapeno pepper jelly

2 tablespoons olive oil

1   In a small bowl, combine the brown sugar, salt, cinnamon, cayenne and mustard. With fingers, carefully loosen the skin from both sides of turkey breast. Spread half of spice mixture under turkey skin; secure skin to underside of breast with wooden toothpicks. Spread remaining spice mixture over the skin.

2   Coat grill rack with cooking spray before starting the grill. Prepare grill for indirect heat, using a drip pan. Place turkey over drip pan. Grill, covered, over indirect medium heat for 30 minutes.

3   In a small saucepan, combine broth, vinegar, jelly and oil. Cook and stir over medium heat for 2 minutes or until jelly is melted. Set aside 1/2 cup. Baste turkey with some of the remaining jelly mixture. Grill 1 to 1-1/2 hours longer or until a meat thermometer reads 170° and juices run clear, basting every 15 minutes.

4   Cover and let stand for 10 minutes. Remove and discard turkey skin if desired. Brush with reserved jelly mixture before slicing.

Chicken Pizza Packets

PREP: 15 MIN. GRILL: 20 MIN. YIELD: 4 SERVINGS

AMBER ZURBRUGG ALLIANCE, OHIO

Basil, garlic, pepperoni and mozzarella cheese give plenty of pizza taste to chicken, green pepper, zucchini and cherry tomatoes in these individual foil dinners. This speedy grilled supper is a tasty way to get kids to eat their veggies.

1 pound boneless skinless chicken breasts, cut into 1-inch pieces

2 tablespoons olive oil

1 small zucchini, thinly sliced

16 pepperoni slices

1 small green pepper, julienned

1 small onion, sliced

1/2 teaspoon dried oregano

1/2 teaspoon dried basil

1/4 teaspoon salt

1/4 teaspoon garlic powder

1/4 teaspoon pepper

1 cup halved cherry tomatoes

1/2 cup shredded part-skim mozzarella cheese

1/2 cup shredded Parmesan cheese

1   In a large bowl, combine the first 11 ingredients. Coat four pieces of heavy-duty foil (about 12 in. square) with cooking spray. Place a quarter of the chicken mixture in the center of each piece. Fold foil round mixture and seal tightly.

2   Grill, covered, over medium-hot heat for 15-18 minutes or until chicken is no longer pink.

3   Carefully open each packet. Sprinkle with tomatoes and cheeses. Seal loosely; grill 2 minutes longer or until cheese is melted.

Turkey with Country Ham Stuffing

PREP: 45 MIN. BAKE: 4-1/2 HOURS YIELD: 10-12 SERVINGS

BOBBIE LOVE KAPAA, HAWAII

As delicious as this is right out of the oven, the bird and stuffing both taste great as leftovers, too. I am careful, though, not to overcook the turkey.

- 3 cups cubed day-old white bread, crust removed
- 3 cups cubed day-old whole wheat bread, crust removed
- 1-1/2 cups cubed fully cooked ham
- 1/2 cup butter, cubed
- 3 cups chopped onion
- 2 cups chopped celery
- 1-1/2 teaspoons rubbed sage
- 1-1/2 teaspoons dried thyme
- 1/2 teaspoon pepper
- 1 to 1-1/2 cups chicken broth
- 1 turkey (12 to 14 pounds)

1 Place bread cubes in a single layer in a 13-in. x 9-in. baking pan. Bake at 325° for 20-25 minutes or until golden brown, stirring occasionally. Place in a large bowl; set aside.

2 In a large skillet, cook ham in butter for 5-10 minutes or until edges are crisp. Remove with a slotted spoon and place over bread cubes.

3 In the same skillet, saute the onion, celery, sage, thyme and pepper until vegetables are tender; toss with bread and ham. Stir in enough broth to moisten.

4 Just before baking, stuff the turkey. Skewer openings; tie drumsticks together. Place on a rack in a roasting pan. Bake at 325° for 4-1/2 to 5 hours or until the thermometer reads 185°.

5 When the turkey begins to brown, cover lightly with a tent of aluminum foil and baste if needed. Cover turkey and let stand for 20 minutes before removing stuffing and carving turkey.

Zesty Turkey Burgers

PREP/TOTAL TIME: 25 MIN. YIELD: 4 SERVINGS

LOUISE GILBERT QUESNEL, BRITISH COLUMBIA

My husband and I were watching our weight last summer, and we found that this recipe was an easy addition to our diets. Best of all, it's delicious!

- 1/2 cup ketchup
- 1 tablespoon cider vinegar
- 1 tablespoon Worcestershire sauce
- 2 garlic cloves, minced
- 1/4 teaspoon pepper
- 1/4 teaspoon crushed red pepper flakes
- 1/4 teaspoon hot pepper sauce
- 1/3 cup quick-cooking oats
- 1 pound lean ground turkey
- 4 lettuce leaves
- 4 hamburger buns, split

1 In a small bowl, combine the first seven ingredients. Transfer half of the mixture to a large bowl; stir in oats. Set remaining ketchup mixture aside for basting. Crumble turkey over oat mixture and mix well. Shape into four patties.

2 Coat grill rack with cooking spray before starting the grill. Grill patties, covered, over medium heat for 5-7 minutes on each side or until a meat thermometer reads 165° and meat juices run clear, basting occasionally with ketchup mixture. Serve on lettuce-lined buns.

1/2 cup sauce. Spoon 1/4 cup down the center of each chicken breast half. Roll up; secure with toothpicks. Place seam side down in a greased 13-in. x 9-in. baking dish. Top with remaining sauce.

3 Cover and bake at 375° for 35-45 minutes or until chicken is no longer pink. Sprinkle with cheese. Broil 4-6 in. from the heat for 5 minutes or until lightly browned. Discard toothpicks. Serve with rice.

Chicken in Lime Butter
PREP/TOTAL TIME: 20 MIN. YIELD: 4 SERVINGS

DENISE SEGURA DRAPER, UTAH

A few ordinary, on-hand ingredients make this moist and tender chicken something really extraordinary! The flavor added by the rich, buttery sauce with a splash of lime juice is unmatched. It's been a hands-down winner at our house for 20 some years.

- 4 boneless skinless chicken breast halves (4 ounces *each*)
- 1/8 teaspoon salt
- 1/8 teaspoon pepper
- 2 tablespoons canola oil
- 1/4 cup butter
- 1 tablespoon lime juice
- 1/2 teaspoon dill weed
- 1/4 teaspoon minced chives

1 Sprinkle chicken with salt and pepper. In a large skillet, cook chicken in oil over medium heat for 5-7 minutes on each side or until a meat thermometer reaches 170°; drain. Remove and keep warm.

2 Add butter and lime juice to the skillet; cook and stir until butter is melted. Stir in dill and chives. Drizzle over chicken.

Spinach Crab Chicken
PREP: 45 MIN. COOK: 40 MIN. YIELD: 4 SERVINGS

VICKI MELIES ELKHORN, NEBRASKA

I altered a friend's recipe for crab-stuffed chicken to include one of my favorite vegetables–spinach. Now my husband requests this elegant entree all the time. Served over rice, it's special enough for company.

- 1/2 cup finely chopped onion
- 1/4 cup chopped fresh mushrooms
- 1/4 cup finely chopped celery
- 3 tablespoons butter
- 3 tablespoons all-purpose flour
- 1/2 teaspoon salt, *divided*
- 1 cup chicken broth
- 1/2 cup milk
- 4 boneless skinless chicken breast halves (6 ounces *each*)
- 1/8 teaspoon white pepper
- 1/2 cup dry bread crumbs
- 1 can (6 ounces) crabmeat, drained, flaked and cartilage removed
- 12 fresh spinach leaves, chopped
- 1 tablespoon minced fresh parsley
- 1 cup (4 ounces) shredded Swiss cheese

Hot cooked rice

1 For sauce, in a large skillet, saute the onion, mushrooms and celery in butter until tender. Stir in flour and 1/4 teaspoon salt until blended. Gradually add broth and milk. Bring to a boil; cook and stir for 1-2 minutes or until thickened. Remove from the heat.

2 Flatten chicken to 1/4-in. thickness; sprinkle with pepper and remaining salt. In a large bowl, combine the bread crumbs, crab, spinach and parsley; stir in

Sweet 'n' Sour Ribs

PREP: 10 MIN. COOK: 8 HOURS YIELD: 8 SERVINGS

DOROTHY VOELZ CHAMPAIGN, ILLINOIS

If you're looking for a change from typical barbecued ribs, you'll enjoy these. Mom prepared them on birthdays and special occasions. The tender ribs have a slight sweet-and-sour taste that my family loves. I usually serve them with garlic mashed potatoes and a salad or coleslaw.

- 3 to 4 pounds boneless country-style pork ribs
- 1 can (20 ounces) pineapple tidbits, undrained
- 2 cans (8 ounces *each*) tomato sauce
- 1/2 cup thinly sliced onion
- 1/2 cup thinly sliced green pepper
- 1/2 cup packed brown sugar
- 1/4 cup cider vinegar
- 1/4 cup tomato paste
- 2 tablespoons Worcestershire sauce
- 1 garlic clove, minced

Salt and pepper to taste

1. Place ribs in an ungreased 5-qt. slow cooker. In a large bowl, combine the remaining ingredients; pour over the ribs.

2. Cover and cook on low for 8-10 hours or until meat is tender. Thicken the sauce if desired.

Teriyaki Pork Roast

PREP: 10 MIN. COOK: 6 HOURS + STANDING YIELD: 6-8 SERVINGS

DEBBIE DUNAWAY KETTERING, OHIO

How tasty is this dish? Well, it's the only kind of meat my two kids will eat and enjoy—other than hot dogs! It's also incredibly easy to make and simply delicious!

- 1 boneless pork shoulder roast (3 to 4 pounds), trimmed
- 1 cup packed brown sugar
- 1/3 cup unsweetened apple juice
- 1/3 cup soy sauce
- 1/2 teaspoon salt
- 1/4 teaspoon pepper
- 2 tablespoons cornstarch
- 3 tablespoons cold water

1. Cut roast in half; rub with brown sugar. Place in a 5-qt. slow cooker. Pour apple juice and soy sauce over roast. Sprinkle with salt and pepper. Cover and cook on low for 6 to 6-1/2 hours or until meat is tender.

2. Remove roast; cover and let stand for 15 minutes. Meanwhile, strain cooking juices and return to slow cooker. Combine cornstarch and cold water until smooth; gradually stir into juices.

3. Cover and cook on high for 15 minutes or until thickened. Slice pork; serve with gravy.

To soften brown sugar, microwave on high for 20-30 seconds. Repeat if necessary, but watch carefully, because the sugar will begin to melt. Always store brown sugar in an airtight container.

Chicago-Style Pan Pizza

PREP: 20 MIN. BAKE: 30 MIN. YIELD: 4 SLICES

NIKKI MACDONALD SHEBOYGAN, WISCONSIN

I developed a love for Chicago's deep-dish pizzas while attending college in the Windy City. This simple recipe relies on frozen bread dough, so I can indulge in the mouthwatering sensation without leaving home.

- 1 loaf (1 pound) frozen bread dough, thawed
- 1 pound bulk Italian sausage
- 2 cups (8 ounces) shredded part-skim mozzarella cheese
- 1/2 pound sliced fresh mushrooms
- 1 small onion, chopped
- 2 teaspoons olive oil
- 1 can (28 ounces) diced tomatoes, drained
- 3/4 teaspoon dried oregano
- 1/2 teaspoon salt
- 1/2 teaspoon fennel seed, crushed
- 1/4 teaspoon garlic powder
- 1/2 cup grated Parmesan cheese

1 Press dough onto the bottom and up the sides of a greased 13-in. x 9-in. baking dish. In a large skillet, cook sausage over medium heat until no longer pink; drain. Sprinkle over dough. Top with mozzarella cheese.

2 In a large skillet, saute mushrooms and onion in oil until onion is tender. Stir in the tomatoes, oregano, salt, fennel seed and garlic powder.

3 Spoon over mozzarella cheese. Sprinkle with Parmesan cheese. Bake at 350° for 25-35 minutes or until crust is golden brown.

Country-Style Pork Medallions

PREP: 20 MIN. COOK: 20 MIN. YIELD: 6 SERVINGS

PAMELA JESSEN CALGARY, ALBERTA

Be prepared to hand out recipes after you pass around this impressive pork entree. Dinner guests can't believe how good it is. I think leftovers would make great sandwiches… but I've never had any to sample!

- 2 pork tenderloins (1 pound *each*)
- 6 tablespoons butter, *divided*
- 2 small onions, sliced and separated into rings
- 3/4 pound small fresh mushrooms
- 2 small apples, cored and cut into rings

APPLE CREAM SAUCE:

- 1 cup apple cider *or* juice
- 1 package (8 ounces) cream cheese, cubed
- 1/4 cup apple brandy *or* additional apple cider
- 1 teaspoon dried basil

1 Cut pork into 1/2-in. slices; flatten to 1/4-in. thickness. In a large skillet over medium-high heat, cook pork in batches in 3 tablespoons butter until juices run clear. Remove to a serving platter and keep warm.

2 In the same skillet, saute onions and mushrooms in remaining butter for 4 minutes or until crisp-tender. Add apples; saute for 3-4 minutes or until vegetables and apples are tender. Arrange over pork.

3 For sauce, add cider and cream cheese to the skillet; cook and stir over medium heat for 3 minutes or until cheese is melted and sauce is smooth. Stir in brandy and basil; heat through. Serve with pork and vegetables.

3 Remove chops from skillet and keep warm. Increase heat to medium. Stir cornstarch mixture into skillet, cook and stir until thickened. Add chopped apple and heat through. On a platter, arrange chops over rice. Spoon sauce over chops and top with green onions.

Italian Sausage and Zucchini Stir-Fry

PREP/TOTAL TIME: 25 MIN. YIELD: 4 SERVINGS

MARY BALLARD LA CRESCENT, MINNESOTA

I'm always looking for new recipes to put variety into our meals. I like this one especially because it doesn't call for too many ingredients and makes an attractive, natural dish. We recently moved into a log home in the country with plenty of room outdoors for a garden, and I plan to grow lots of vegetables to use in similar stir-fry dishes.

- 1 pound Italian sausage links, cut into 1/4-inch slices
- 1/2 cup chopped onion
- 4 cups julienned *or* coarsely shredded zucchini
- 2 cups seeded chopped tomatoes
- 1 teaspoon lemon juice
- 1/4 teaspoon salt
- 1/4 teaspoon dried oregano
- 1/4 teaspoon hot pepper sauce

Grated Parmesan cheese

1 In a large skillet, cook sausage and onion until meat is no longer pink; drain.

2 Stir in the zucchini, tomatoes, lemon juice, salt, oregano and pepper sauce. Cook, uncovered, for 5 minutes, stirring frequently. Garnish with cheese.

Fruited Chops

PREP: 20 MIN. COOK: 20 MIN. YIELD: 4 SERVINGS

TERESA LILLYCROP PUSLINCH, ONTARIO

This one-skillet supper is served often in our farmhouse! We cash-crop plus run a 400-head cow-calf operation...I have a large garden to tend during growing season...and, if that isn't enough to keep me busy, I also work full-time in my husband's tractor dealership. So I appreciate quick and easy recipes like this.

- 1 tablespoon canola oil
- 4 pork chops, about 1 inch thick
- 1 can (10-3/4 ounces) condensed chicken broth, undiluted
- 2 tablespoons soy sauce
- 1 tablespoon vinegar
- 1/2 cup apple juice
- 2 tablespoons brown sugar
- 2 tablespoons cornstarch
- 1 teaspoon ground ginger
- 1 large apple, coarsely chopped

Cooked rice

Sliced green onions

1 In a 10-in. skillet, heat oil over medium-high. Brown chops on both sides. Stir in chicken broth, soy sauce and vinegar; bring to a boil. Reduce heat, cover and simmer 20 minutes or until chops are tender.

2 Meanwhile, in a small bowl, combine apple juice, brown sugar, cornstarch and ginger; stir until smooth.

JUANITA MOORE
DANA POINT, CALIFORNIA

My physical therapist shared this recipe with me and said it was completely fool-proof. She was right. It's a real winner. I serve it with sauteed green beans.

Spicy Pork with Ginger-Maple Sauce

PREP: 25 MIN. BAKE: 20 MIN. YIELD: 2 SERVINGS

2 teaspoons chili powder

1 teaspoon ground cinnamon

1 teaspoon pepper

1/2 teaspoon salt

1/4 teaspoon ground allspice

1 pork tenderloin (3/4 pound)

1/2 teaspoon olive oil

SAUCE:

1/2 cup chopped onion

1 tablespoon butter

1 teaspoon minced fresh gingerroot

1/2 cup chicken broth

1/4 cup maple syrup

1 tablespoon diced candied ginger

1 In a small bowl, combine the chili powder, cinnamon, pepper, salt and allspice. Rub over the pork tenderloin. In a large skillet, brown the pork in olive oil on all sides.

2 Transfer to an 11-in. x 7-in. baking dish coated with cooking spray. Bake, uncovered, at 375° for 15 minutes.

3 Meanwhile, for sauce, in a small skillet, saute onion in butter until tender. Add fresh ginger; saute 1-2 minutes longer. Stir in the broth, syrup and candied ginger. Bring to a boil; cook until sauce is reduced to about 1/2 cup. Pour over the pork.

4 Bake 5-10 minutes longer or until a meat thermometer reads 160°. Let stand for 5 minutes before slicing.

To quickly chop an onion, peel and cut in half from the root to the top. Leaving root attached, place flat side down on work surface. Cut vertically through the onion, leaving the root end uncut. Cut across the onion, discarding root end. The closer the cuts, the finer the onion will be chopped.

Melt-in-Your-Mouth Sausages

PREP: 10 MIN. COOK: 5 HOURS YIELD: 8 SERVINGS

ILEAN SCHULTHEISS COHOCTON, NEW YORK

My family loves this recipe. It's such a good all-around dish. For a heartier meal, eat the sausage with spaghetti.

    8 Italian sausage links (2 pounds)

    1 jar (26 ounces) meatless spaghetti sauce

1/2 cup water

    1 can (6 ounces) tomato paste

    1 large green pepper, thinly sliced

    1 large onion, thinly sliced

    1 tablespoon grated Parmesan cheese

    1 teaspoon dried parsley flakes

    8 brat buns, split

Additional Parmesan cheese, optional

1   Place sausages in a large skillet; cover with water. Bring to a boil. Reduce heat; cover and simmer for 10 minutes; drain well.

2   Meanwhile, in a 3-qt. slow cooker, combine the spaghetti sauce, water, tomato paste, green pepper, onion, Parmesan and parsley. Add sausages. Cover and cook on low for 4 hours. Increase temperature to high; cook 1 hour longer.

3   Serve in buns. Sprinkle with additional Parmesan if desired.

Tangy Pork Chops

PREP: 15 MIN. COOK: 5-1/2 HOURS YIELD: 4 SERVINGS

KAROL HINES KITTY HAWK, NORTH CAROLINA

Fancy enough for company, these mouthwatering pork chops also make a great family meal. I usually have all the ingredients on hand. Since my husband and I just had our first child, this recipe is so convenient—I start it during naptime for a no-fuss supper later.

    4 bone-in pork loin chops (1/2 inch thick)

1/2 teaspoon salt, optional

1/8 teaspoon pepper

    2 medium onions, chopped

    2 celery ribs, chopped

    1 large green pepper, sliced

    1 can (14-1/2 ounces) stewed tomatoes

1/2 cup ketchup

    2 tablespoons cider vinegar

    2 tablespoons brown sugar

    2 tablespoons Worcestershire sauce

    1 tablespoon lemon juice

    1 teaspoon beef bouillon granules

    2 tablespoons cornstarch

    2 tablespoons water

Hot cooked rice, optional

1   Place chops in a 3-qt. slow cooker; sprinkle with salt, if desired, and pepper. Add the onions, celery, green pepper and tomatoes. Combine the ketchup, vinegar, brown sugar, Worcestershire sauce, lemon juice and bouillon; pour over vegetables. Cover and cook on low for 5-6 hours.

2   Mix cornstarch and water until smooth; stir into liquid in slow cooker. Cover and cook on high for 30 minutes or until thickened. Serve with rice if desired.

Onion Italian Sausage

PREP/TOTAL TIME: 30 MIN. YIELD: 6 SERVINGS

RUTH VAN DER LEEST LYNON, ILLINOIS

When my five children were still all at home, this was one of their most-requested meals. I've long had this recipe among my standbys, and, like all cooks who improvise and experiment, I've changed it as our tastes have changed.

> 2 **tablespoons butter**
> 6 **medium onions, peeled and sliced 1/4 inch thick**
> 6 **sweet Italian sausages**
> 1 **small green pepper, chopped**
> 1-1/2 **tablespoons Italian seasoning**

Dash reduced-sodium soy sauce

Buns

1   Melt butter in large skillet; add onions and cook until lightly browned. Remove; set aside. Brown sausages lightly in skillet, turning frequently. Remove; set aside with onions.

2   Add more butter to skillet if necessary and lightly brown pepper. Add onions, sausages, Italian seasoning and soy sauce to skillet. Add water to 1-in. depth and simmer until sausages are done and water is cooked away. Serve with buns.

Sliced Ham with Roasted Vegetables

PREP: 10 MIN. BAKE: 35 MIN. YIELD: 6 SERVINGS

MARGARET PACHE MESA, ARIZONA

To prepare this colorful, zesty oven meal, I "shop" in my backyard for the fresh garden vegetables and oranges (we have our own tree!) that spark the ham's hearty flavor. It's my family's favorite main dish.

> 6 **medium potatoes, peeled and cubed**
> 5 **medium carrots, julienned**
> 1 **medium turnip, peeled and cubed**
> 1 **large onion, cut into thin wedges**
> 6 **slices (4 to 6 ounces *each*) fully cooked ham, halved**
> 1/4 **cup thawed orange juice concentrate**
> 2 **tablespoons brown sugar**
> 1 **teaspoon prepared horseradish**
> 1 **teaspoon grated orange peel**

1   Line two 15-in. x 10-in. x 1-in. baking pans with foil and coat with cooking spray. Add potatoes, carrots, turnip and onion; generously coat with cooking spray. Bake, uncovered, at 425° for 25-30 minutes or until tender.

2   Arrange ham slices over the vegetables. In a bowl, combine remaining ingredients. Spoon over ham and vegetables. Cover and bake 10 minutes longer or until the ham is heated through.

To preserve the fresh taste of a just-opened bottle of horseradish, place tablespoonfuls on a parchment paper-lined baking sheet and freeze. Place the mounds in a resealable plastic bag and store in the freezer.

Indonesian-Style Pork Roast

PREP: 20 MIN. + STANDING BAKE: 1-1/4 HOURS + STANDING
YIELD: 6 SERVINGS

ALICE VIDOVICH WALNUT CREEK, CALIFORNIA

Your family and friends won't believe you when you reveal that the "secret ingredient" for this flavorful pork roast is peanut butter! I've served this roast to guests for years, and I can't tell you how many times I've sent copies of the recipe home with guests. For a change of taste, you can substitute toasted walnuts for peanuts.

    2 pounds boneless pork loin roast

COATING:

    1/4 cup creamy peanut butter

    3 tablespoons soy sauce

    2 tablespoons ground coriander

1-1/2 teaspoons ground cumin

    1/2 teaspoon chili powder

    1 large clove garlic, crushed

    1 tablespoon lemon juice

PEANUT SAUCE:

    1 cup soy sauce

    2 tablespoons pineapple juice

    1 clove garlic, crushed

    1/4 cup dry sherry, optional

    1/2 teaspoon minced fresh gingerroot

    1/2 cup chopped unsalted peanuts

1 Combine the coating ingredients in a bowl; mix until smooth. Rub the coating over all exposed surfaces of the pork roast; let stand for 30 minutes.

2 Place roast in greased baking dish; cook at 325° until meat thermometer inserted in center registers 160° (about 75 minutes).

3 To make sauce, combine all ingredients except peanuts in saucepan; bring to a boil. Let cool; add peanuts. Set aside. Remove roast from oven; let stand for 15 minutes. Slice into serving portions and serve with sauce.

Fruit-Pecan Pork Roast

PREP: 20 MIN. BAKE: 1-3/4 HOURS + STANDING
YIELD: 10-12 SERVINGS

GAY FLYNN BELLEVUE, NEBRASKA

This spectacular roast was a huge hit with members of the cooking club I belong to. It's a family favorite.

    1 boneless rolled pork loin roast (3-1/2 pounds)

    1/2 cup chopped green onions

    4 tablespoons butter, *divided*

    1/4 cup orange juice

    1 bay leaf

    1 can (14 ounces) whole-berry cranberry sauce

    1/2 cup chicken broth

    1/2 cup chopped pecans

    1 tablespoon red wine vinegar

    1/4 teaspoon salt

1/8 teaspoon pepper

1/8 teaspoon sugar

1/4 cup apricot preserves

1   Place roast on a rack in a shallow roasting pan. Bake, uncovered, at 350° for 1 hour.

2   Meanwhile, in a skillet, saute onions in 1 tablespoon of butter for 1 minute. Add orange juice and bay leaf; cook and stir over medium-high until thickened, about 4 minutes. Add cranberry sauce, broth, pecans and vinegar. Cook; stir until slightly thickened, 5 minutes. Reduce heat; stir in salt, pepper, sugar and remaining butter until butter is melted. Discard bay leaf.

3   Remove 1/4 cup sauce and stir in preserves; spoon over roast. Set remaining sauce aside. Bake roast 45 minutes longer or until a meat thermometer reads 160°-170°. Let stand 10-15 minutes before slicing. Serve with reserved sauce.

Stuffed Ham With Raisin Sauce

PREP: 30 MIN. BAKE: 1-3/4 HOURS YIELD: 12-14 SERVINGS

JEANNE MILLER BIG SKY, MONTANA

This impressive ham, stuffed with a simple mixture, makes a great centerpiece for a holiday dinner. I often serve it for brunch, because it's perfect for a unique and special entree. It always draws raves. Be sure to make the sauce, because it adds a deliciously sweet and sour flavor to the meat.

> 1   boneless fully cooked ham (6 to 7 pounds)
> 1   large onion, chopped
> 1/4 cup butter, cubed
> 2   cups corn bread stuffing mix
> 1-1/2 cups chopped pecans, toasted
> 1/2 cup minced fresh parsley
> 1/4 cup egg substitute
> 2   tablespoons prepared mustard
> 1/2 cup honey
> 2   tablespoons orange juice concentrate

RAISIN SAUCE:
> 1/2 cup packed brown sugar
> 2   tablespoons all-purpose flour
> 1/2 teaspoon ground mustard
> 1/2 cup raisins
> 1-1/2 cups water
> 1/4 cup cider vinegar

1   Using a sharp thin-bladed knife and beginning at one end of the ham, carefully cut a 2-1/2-in. circle about 6 in. deep; remove cutout. Cut a 1-1/2-in. slice from the end of removed piece; set aside.

2   Continue cutting a 2-1/2-in. tunnel halfway through ham, using a spoon to remove pieces of ham (save for another use). Repeat from opposite end of ham, cutting and removing ham until a tunnel has been cut through entire length of ham.

3   In a small skillet, saute onion in butter until tender. In a large bowl, combine the stuffing mix, pecans, parsley, egg substitute and mustard. Stir in onion. Stuff ham; cover end openings with reserved ham slices. Place in a shallow roasting pan.

4   Bake, uncovered, at 325° for 1-1/4 hours. In a small saucepan, combine honey and orange juice concentrate; cook and stir for 1-2 minutes or until blended. Brush over ham. Bake 30 minutes longer or until a meat thermometer reads 140°.

5   For sauce, combine the brown sugar, flour, mustard and raisins in a saucepan. Gradually add water and vinegar. Bring to a boil; cook and stir for 1-2 minutes or until thickened. Serve with ham.

Editor's Note: Two fully cooked boneless ham halves can be substituted for the whole ham. Simply hollow out each ham; loosely spoon stuffing into each half, then bake as directed.

Spiced Ham With Apple Relish

PREP: 45 MIN. BAKE: 1 HOUR
YIELD: 8-10 SERVINGS (4 CUPS RELISH)

VICKI TASKER OAKLAND, MARYLAND

If you think Thanksgiving turkey tastes good as a leftover, try this. The ham's wonderful served cold on a bun with hot or cold relish spooned on the top. The meat can be sliced and cooked up in a soup as well or added to a green bean casserole. The only problem I've had is having any leftovers to begin with!

> 1 teaspoon ground cloves
>
> 1 teaspoon ground allspice
>
> 1 boneless fully cooked ham (3 to 4 pounds)

APPLE RELISH:

> 4 medium tart apples, peeled and chopped
>
> 2 cups sugar
>
> 1 cup chopped dried apricots
>
> 1 cup golden raisins
>
> 1/4 cup vinegar
>
> 2 tablespoons grated orange peel
>
> 1/2 cup slivered almonds, toasted

1 Combine cloves and allspice; rub over ham. Wrap tightly in foil and place in a shallow baking pan. Bake at 325° for 1 to 1-1/2 hours or until a meat thermometer reads 140° and the ham is heated through.

2 In a large saucepan, combine the first six relish ingredients. Bring to a boil, stirring constantly. Reduce heat; simmer for 25-30 minutes or until thickened. Stir in almonds. Slice ham; serve with the relish.

Pork with Tangy Mustard Sauce

PREP: 10 MIN. + MARINATING GRILL: 1-1/4 HOURS + STANDING
YIELD: 10-12 SERVINGS

GINGER JOHNSON POTTSTOWN, PENNSYLVANIA

About any side dish would accompany this entree well. In summer, we like to have our homegrown sweet corn and cheesy potatoes hot off the grill, a cold salad and green vegetables alongside it. If you ever have extras—it's rare that we do—the pork would be good in a breakfast casserole or even an omelet.

> 1 boneless pork loin roast (2-1/2 to 3 pounds)
>
> 2 teaspoons olive oil
>
> 1-1/4 teaspoons ground mustard
>
> 3/4 teaspoon garlic powder
>
> 1/4 teaspoon ground ginger
>
> 1/2 cup horseradish mustard *or* spicy brown mustard
>
> 1/2 cup apricot *or* pineapple preserves

1 Rub roast with oil. Combine mustard, garlic powder and ginger; rub over roast. Place in a large resealable plastic bag or shallow glass container; seal bag or cover container. Refrigerate overnight.

2 Grill roast, covered, over indirect heat for 60 minutes. Combine the horseradish mustard and preserves. Continue grilling for 15-30 minutes, basting twice with sauce, or until a meat thermometer reads 160°-170°. Let stand for 10 minutes before slicing. Heat remaining sauce to serve with roast.

Pork Chop Potato Dinner

PREP: 10 MIN. COOK: 2-1/2 HOURS YIELD: 6 SERVINGS

DAWN HUIZINGA OWATONNA, MINNESOTA

Tender chops are slow cooked over a bed of creamy potatoes in this all-in-one meal. It's a snap to assemble, thanks to frozen hash browns, canned cream soup, shredded cheddar cheese and french-fried onions.

- 6 **bone-in pork loin chops (1/2 inch thick and 8 ounces** *each***)**
- 1 **tablespoon canola oil**
- 1 **package (30 ounces) frozen shredded hash brown potatoes, thawed**
- 1-1/2 **cups (6 ounces) shredded cheddar cheese,** *divided*
- 1 **can (10-3/4 ounces) condensed cream of celery soup, undiluted**
- 1/2 **cup milk**
- 1/2 **cup sour cream**
- 1/2 **teaspoon seasoned salt**
- 1/8 **teaspoon pepper**
- 1 **can (2.8 ounces) french-fried onions,** *divided*

1 In a large skillet, brown chops in oil on both sides; set aside and keep warm. In a large bowl, combine the potatoes, 1 cup cheese, soup, milk, sour cream, seasoned salt and pepper. Stir in half of the onions.

2 Transfer to a greased 5-qt. slow cooker; top with pork chops. Cover and cook on high for 2-1/2 to 3 hours or until meat is tender. Sprinkle with remaining cheese and onions. Cover and cook 10 minutes longer or until cheese is melted.

Pork with Pineapple Salsa

PREP: 10 MIN. BAKE: 30 MIN. YIELD: 4 SERVINGS

NICOLE PICKETT ORO VALLEY, ARIZONA

Not only does this easy entree taste awesome, but it's good for you, too. A little brown sugar, ground ginger and Dijon mustard help give the moist tenderloin its incredible flavor, and the tangy salsa can be made in no time.

- 1 **can (20 ounces) unsweetened pineapple tidbits**
- 1 **pork tenderloin (1-1/4 pounds)**
- 3 **tablespoons brown sugar,** *divided*
- 2 **tablespoons Dijon mustard**
- 1 **teaspoon paprika**
- 1/2 **teaspoon ground ginger**
- 1/3 **cup finely chopped sweet red** *or* **green pepper**
- 1/4 **cup chopped green onions**
- 1/8 **teaspoon crushed red pepper flakes, optional**

1 Drain pineapple, reserving 1/4 cup juice. Set aside 1 cup of pineapple (save remaining pineapple for another use). Place pork on a rack in a shallow roasting pan. Combine 2 tablespoons brown sugar, mustard, paprika and ginger. Spread half over the pork.

2 Bake, uncovered at 450° for 15 minutes. Spread with remaining brown sugar mixture. Bake 15-20 minutes longer or until a meat thermometer reads 160°.

3 Meanwhile, for salsa, in a small bowl, combine the red pepper, onions, pepper flakes if desired, remaining brown sugar, reserved pineapple and juice. Let pork stand for 5 minutes before slicing. Serve with salsa.

3 Pour ham drippings into a saucepan; blend in flour. Gradually add water and stir until smooth. Bring to a boil; cook and stir for 2 minutes or until thickened. Reduce heat to low. Add sour cream and remaining dill and pepper; heat through, but do not boil. Pour over the ham balls. Serve over noodles.

Pork Chops with Apples and Stuffing
PREP: 15 MIN. BAKE: 45 MIN. YIELD: 6 SERVINGS

JOAN HAMILTON WORCESTER, MASSACHUSETTS

The heartwarming taste of cinnamon and apples is the perfect accompaniment to these tender pork chops. This dish is always a winner with my family. Because it calls for only four ingredients, it's a main course I can serve with little preparation.

> 6 boneless pork loin chops (1 inch thick and 4 ounces *each*)
>
> 1 tablespoon canola oil
>
> 1 package (6 ounces) crushed stuffing mix
>
> 1 can (21 ounces) apple pie filling with cinnamon

1 In a large skillet, brown pork chops in oil over medium-high heat. Meanwhile, prepare stuffing according to package directions. Spread pie filling into a greased 13-in. x 9-in. baking dish. Place the pork chops on top; spoon stuffing over chops.

2 Cover; bake at 350° for 35 minutes. Uncover; bake pork chops 10 minutes longer or until a meat thermometer reads 160°.

Dilly Ham Balls
PREP: 20 MIN. COOK: 20 MIN. YIELD: 6 SERVINGS

DIXIE TERRY GOREVILLE, ILLINOIS

I'm pretty sure these ham balls would taste good reheated. I can't guarantee it–I've never had any of them left over to find out!

> 1 pound ground fully cooked ham
>
> 1/2 cup dry bread crumbs
>
> 1/4 cup finely chopped green onions
>
> 3 tablespoons finely chopped fresh dill *or* 3 teaspoons dried dill, *divided*
>
> 1/4 cup milk
>
> 1 egg, lightly beaten
>
> 1 teaspoon Dijon mustard
>
> 1/2 teaspoon pepper, *divided*
>
> 1 to 2 tablespoons butter
>
> 1 to 2 tablespoons canola oil
>
> 2 tablespoons all-purpose flour
>
> 1 cup water
>
> 1 cup (8 ounces) sour cream
>
> Hot cooked noodles

1 In a bowl, combine ham, bread crumbs, onions, 1 tablespoon fresh dill (or 1 teaspoon dried), milk, egg, mustard and 1/4 teaspoon pepper. Shape into 1-in. balls.

2 In a large skillet, heat 1 tablespoon butter and 1 tablespoon oil. Brown ham balls, adding remaining butter and oil as needed. Remove ham balls to a serving dish; cover and keep warm.

Glazed Holiday Pork Roast

PREP: 10 MIN. BAKE: 3 HOURS + STANDING YIELD: 6-8 SERVINGS

SHERRY KREIGER YORK, PENNSYLVANIA

With the sweet and tangy fruit glaze, this pretty pork roast is wonderful for a holiday meal. But don't save it just for special occasions! My husband and son love this warm and satisfying supper whenever I serve it.

- 1 pork rib roast (4 to 4-1/2 pounds)
- 1 cup dried fruit bits, *divided*
- 2/3 cup water
- 2/3 cup honey
- 1 envelope onion soup mix
- 1/4 cup ketchup
- 2 tablespoons lemon juice
- 2 teaspoons grated lemon peel

1 Make 15-20 slits, about 1 to 1-1/2 in. deep, in the roast; place some fruit in each slit. In a small bowl, combine the water, honey, soup mix, ketchup, lemon juice, peel and remaining fruit.

2 Place roast fat side up in a roasting pan. Pour fruit mixture over the top. Cover and bake at 325° for 3 to 3-1/2 hours or until a meat thermometer reads 160°. Let stand for 10-15 minutes before carving.

When measuring honey for baking, coat inside of the measuring cup with a thin layer of cooking spray or oil first. The honey comes out easily, and you'll get the full measure without needing to scrape the cup.

Pork Loin with Currant Sauce

PREP: 5 MIN. BAKE: 2-1/2 HOURS + STANDING YIELD: 10 SERVINGS

EDIE URSO SPOKANE, WASHINGTON

I serve this roast often to family and friends…and someone at the table always asks for the recipe. To complete the meal, I make stir-fried green beans and a lightened-up version of twice-baked potatoes.

- 3/4 cup sherry *or* apple juice
- 3/4 cup reduced-sodium soy sauce
- 6 garlic cloves, minced
- 4 teaspoons ground mustard
- 1-1/2 teaspoons ground ginger
- 1-1/2 teaspoons dried thyme
- 1 bone-in pork loin roast (5 pounds)

SAUCE:
- 2/3 cup currant jelly
- 1 tablespoon sherry *or* apple juice
- 1-1/2 teaspoons reduced-sodium soy sauce

1 In a bowl, combine the first six ingredients; mix well. Pour 1-1/4 cups marinade into a 2-gal. resealable plastic bag; add the pork roast. Seal bag and turn to coat; refrigerate overnight. Cover and refrigerate remaining marinade.

2 Drain and discard marinade from roast. Place on a rack in a shallow roasting pan. Bake, uncovered, at 325° for 2-1/2 to 3 hours or until a meat thermometer reads 160°, basting every 30 minutes with reserved marinade. Let stand for 10 minutes before slicing. In a small saucepan, combine sauce ingredients; bring to a boil over medium heat. Serve with the pork.

Broccoli Shrimp Alfredo

PREP/TOTAL TIME: 30 MIN. YIELD: 4 SERVINGS

RAE NATOLI KINGSTON, NEW YORK

After tasting fettuccine Alfredo at a restaurant, I tried to duplicate the recipe at home. You can't imagine how pleased I was when I came up with this delicious version. Not only does my family love the creamy dish, but my husband prefers it to the one at the restaurant.

- 1 package (16 ounces) fettuccine
- 1 pound uncooked medium shrimp, peeled and deveined
- 3 garlic cloves, minced
- 1/2 cup butter, cubed
- 1 package (8 ounces) cream cheese, cubed
- 1 cup milk
- 1/2 cup shredded Parmesan cheese
- 6 cups frozen broccoli florets
- 1/2 teaspoon salt

Dash pepper

1   Cook fettuccine according to package directions. Meanwhile, in a large skillet, saute shrimp and garlic in butter until shrimp turn pink. Remove and keep warm. In the same skillet, combine the cream cheese, milk and Parmesan cheese; cook and stir until cheeses are melted and mixture is smooth.

2   Place 1 in. of water in a saucepan; add broccoli. Bring to a boil. Reduce heat; cover and simmer for 6-8 minutes or until tender. Drain. Stir the broccoli, shrimp, salt and pepper into cheese sauce; cook until heated through. Drain the fettuccine; top with the shrimp mixture.

Lemony Vegetables And Pasta

PREP: 25 MIN. COOK: 15 MIN. YIELD: 7 SERVINGS

ERIN RENOUF MYLROIE SANTA CLARA, UTAH

My refreshing pasta dish comes together in 30 minutes. Its simplicity and flavor combinations are typical of authentic Italian cuisine. Buon appetito!

- 1 pound fresh asparagus, trimmed and cut into 1-inch pieces
- 1 medium sweet red pepper, cut into 1-inch pieces
- 1 medium red onion, sliced
- 1 tablespoon olive oil
- 1/2 teaspoon salt
- 1/4 teaspoon pepper
- 4-1/2 cups uncooked bow tie pasta
- 1 tablespoon butter
- 1 tablespoon all-purpose flour
- 3 garlic cloves, minced
- 1/4 teaspoon crushed red pepper flakes
- 1 cup vegetable broth
- 1 cup shredded Parmesan cheese
- 1/2 cup sour cream
- 2 tablespoons lemon juice
- 1 tablespoon grated lemon peel
- 1/2 cup chopped pistachios
- 1/4 cup fresh basil leaves, thinly sliced

Additional shredded Parmesan cheese

1   In a large bowl, combine the asparagus, red pepper, onion, olive oil, salt and pepper. Transfer to a greased 15-in. x 10-in. x 1-in. baking pan. Bake at 450° for 10-15 minutes or until golden brown, stirring once.

2. Meanwhile, cook pasta according to package directions. In a large saucepan, melt butter over medium heat. Stir in the flour, garlic and pepper flakes until blended. Whisk in broth until blended. Bring to a boil over medium-high heat; cook and stir for 2 minutes or until thickened and bubbly.

3. Reduce heat. Stir in the Parmesan cheese, sour cream, lemon juice and peel; heat through. Drain pasta and place in a large bowl. Add cheese sauce and asparagus mixture; toss to coat. Sprinkle with pistachios, basil and additional Parmesan cheese.

Greek Pizzas

PREP/TOTAL TIME: 30 MIN. YIELD: 4 SERVINGS

DORIS ALLERS PORTAGE, MICHIGAN

Pita breads make crispy crusts for these individual pizzas. Topped with feta and ricotta cheese as well as spinach, tomatoes and basil, the fast pizzas are a hit with everyone who tries them.

- 4 pita breads (6 inches)
- 1 cup reduced-fat ricotta cheese
- 1/2 teaspoon garlic powder
- 1 package (10 ounces) frozen chopped spinach, thawed and squeezed dry
- 3 medium tomatoes, sliced
- 3/4 cup crumbled feta cheese
- 3/4 teaspoon dried basil

1. Place pita breads on a baking sheet. Combine the ricotta cheese and garlic powder; spread over pitas. Top with spinach, tomatoes, feta cheese and basil.

2. Bake at 400° for 12-15 minutes or until bread is lightly browned.

Southwestern Scallops

PREP/TOTAL TIME: 20 MIN. YIELD: 4 SERVINGS

MAGGIE FONTENOT THE WOODLANDS, TEXAS

My saucy sea scallops are popular at dinner parties, but they're also in my repertoire of easy weekday meals.

- 2 teaspoons chili powder
- 1/2 teaspoon ground cumin
- 1/4 teaspoon salt
- 1/8 teaspoon pepper
- 1 pound sea scallops (about 12)
- 2 tablespoons butter, *divided*
- 1/2 cup white wine *or* chicken broth

1. In a small bowl, combine the chili powder, cumin, salt and pepper. Pat scallops dry with paper towels. Rub seasoning mixture over scallops.

2. In a large heavy skillet over medium heat, melt 1 tablespoon butter. Cook scallops for 2 minutes on each side or until golden and opaque. Remove from the skillet; keep warm.

3. Add wine or broth to skillet, stirring to loosen any browned bits from pan. Bring to a boil; cook until liquid is reduced by half. Stir in remaining butter until melted. Serve with scallops.

Be sure you buy the right scallops for the above recipe! Sea scallops are from 1-1/2 to 2 inches wide, and are much bigger than their smaller cousin, bay scallops. Bay scallops are 1/2 to 1 inch in diameter, and are not well-suited for sauteing.

KATHRYN PEHL
PRESCOTT, ARIZONA

This fabulous, meat-less main dish is a great way to get the kids to eat lots of vegetables…and a great way for you to use some of the fresh harvest from your garden.

Spaghetti Squash with Red Sauce

PREP: 25 MIN. COOK: 15 MIN. YIELD: 6 SERVINGS

1 medium spaghetti squash (about 4 pounds)
2 cups chopped fresh tomatoes
1 cup sliced fresh mushrooms
1 cup diced green pepper
1/2 cup shredded carrot
1/4 cup diced red onion
2 garlic cloves, minced
2 teaspoons Italian seasoning
1/8 teaspoon pepper
1 tablespoon olive oil
1 can (15 ounces) tomato sauce
Grated Parmesan cheese, optional

1 Cut squash in half lengthwise; discard seeds. Place squash, cut side down, on a microwave-safe plate. Microwave, uncovered, on high for 14-16 minutes or until tender.

2 Meanwhile, in a large skillet, saute the tomatoes, mushrooms, green pepper, carrot, onion, garlic, Italian seasoning and pepper in oil for 6-8 minutes or until tender. Add tomato sauce; heat through.

3 When squash is cool enough to handle, use a fork to separate strands. Place squash on a serving platter; top with sauce. Sprinkle with cheese if desired.

 The most common varieties of winter squash are but-ternut, acorn, hubbard, spaghetti and turban. Look for squash which feel heavy for their size and have hard, deep-colored rinds that are free of blemishes. Unwashed winter squash can be stored in a dry, cool, well-ventilated place for up to 1 month.

Pleasing Potato Pizza

PREP: 30 MIN. BAKE: 20 MIN. YIELD: 8 SLICES

BARBARA ZIMMER WANLESS, MANITOBA

I first heard of this delicious and distinctive pizza when a friend tried it at a restaurant. It sounded great so I experimented to come up with my own recipe. The way the slices disappear, there's no doubt about their popularity. Guests are always excited when my potato pizza is on the menu.

- 3 large potatoes, peeled and cubed
- 1 tube (13.8 ounces) refrigerated pizza crust
- 1/4 cup milk
- 1/2 teaspoon salt
- 1 pound sliced bacon, diced
- 1 large onion, chopped
- 1/2 cup chopped sweet red pepper
- 1-1/2 cups (6 ounces) shredded cheddar cheese
- 1-1/2 cups (6 ounces) shredded part-skim mozzarella cheese

Sour cream, optional

1. Place potatoes in a saucepan and cover with water. Bring to a boil; cook for 20-25 minutes or until very tender.

2. Meanwhile, unroll the pizza crust onto an ungreased 14-in. pizza pan; flatten dough and build up edges slightly. Prick dough several times with a fork. Bake at 350° for 15 minutes or until lightly browned. Cool on a wire rack.

3. Drain potatoes and transfer to a bowl. Mash with milk and salt until smooth. Spread over crust. In a skillet, partially cook the bacon. Add onion and red pepper; cook until bacon is crisp and vegetables are tender. Drain well; sprinkle over potatoes. Top with cheeses.

4. Bake at 375° for 20 minutes or until cheese is melted. Serve with sour cream if desired.

The Ultimate Grilled Cheese

PREP/TOTAL TIME: 15 MIN. YIELD: 5 SERVINGS

KATHY NORRIS STREATOR, ILLINOIS

These gooey grilled cheese sandwiches, subtly seasoned with garlic, taste great for lunch with sliced apples. And they're really fast to whip up, too. To save seconds, I soften the cream cheese in the microwave, then blend it with the rest of the ingredients in the same bowl. That makes cleanup a breeze.

- 1 package (3 ounces) cream cheese, softened
- 3/4 cup mayonnaise
- 1 cup (4 ounces) shredded part-skim mozzarella cheese
- 1 cup (4 ounces) shredded cheddar cheese
- 1/2 teaspoon garlic powder
- 1/8 teaspoon seasoned salt
- 10 slices Italian bread (1/2 inch thick)
- 2 tablespoons butter, softened

1. In a large bowl, beat cream cheese and mayonnaise until smooth. Stir in the cheeses, garlic powder and seasoned salt. Spread five slices of bread with the cheese mixture, about 1/3 cup on each. Top with remaining bread.

2. Butter the outsides of sandwiches. In a skillet over medium heat, toast sandwiches for 4-5 minutes on each side or until bread is lightly browned and cheese is melted.

3 In a large bowl, combine the tomato, onions, olives, basil, olive oil, vinegar and garlic; sprinkle over the spinach mixture.

4 Top with the feta cheese and remaining mozzarella cheese. Bake at 400° for 12-14 minutes or until cheese softens and is lightly browned.

Shrimp 'n' Noodle Bowls

PREP/TOTAL TIME: 25 MIN. YIELD: 6 SERVINGS

MARY BERGFELD EUGENE, OREGON

This is a great quick meal that can be made with pick-up ingredients from the grocery store. Cooked shrimp and bagged slaw reduce the time and work required to get it on the table.

     8 ounces uncooked angel hair pasta
     1 pound cooked small shrimp
     2 cups broccoli coleslaw mix
     6 green onions, thinly sliced
  1/2 cup minced fresh cilantro
  2/3 cup reduced-fat sesame ginger salad dressing

1 Cook pasta according to package directions; drain and rinse in cold water. Transfer to a large bowl. Add shrimp, coleslaw mix, onions and cilantro. Drizzle with dressing; toss to coat. Cover and refrigerate until serving.

Four-Cheese Spinach Pizza

PREP/TOTAL TIME: 30 MIN. YIELD: 6 SERVINGS

BARBRA ROBINSON HAMBURG, PENNSYLVANIA

I adapted this recipe from one given to me by my Aunt Rosemary. I especially like to make this pizza in summer when fresh spinach and basil are plentiful–they are key to the wonderful taste.

     2 packages (10 ounces *each*) fresh spinach
  3/4 cup shredded part-skim mozzarella cheese, *divided*
  1/2 cup fat-free cottage cheese
  1/3 cup grated Parmesan cheese
  1/4 teaspoon salt
  1/8 teaspoon pepper
     1 prebaked Italian bread shell crust (10 ounces)
     1 medium tomato, chopped
  1/4 cup chopped green onions
  1/4 cup sliced ripe olives
     1 teaspoon minced fresh basil
     1 teaspoon olive oil
     1 teaspoon balsamic vinegar
     1 garlic clove, minced
  1/2 cup crumbled feta cheese

1 In a large nonstick skillet coated with cooking spray, saute spinach for 2-3 minutes or until wilted; remove from the skillet. Cool slightly; chop.

2 In a large bowl, combine 1/4 cup mozzarella cheese, cottage cheese and Parmesan cheese. Stir in the spinach, salt and pepper. Spread over crust to within 1/2 in. of edge.

Sweet Pepper Sandwiches

PREP/TOTAL TIME: 25 MIN. YIELD: 4 SERVINGS

CARA NETH FORT COLLINS, COLORADO

We love this recipe because it's easy and meatless. Family members assemble their own sandwiches to their liking.

- 1 *each* small green, sweet red and yellow pepper, thinly sliced
- 1 small onion, thinly sliced
- 1 garlic clove, minced
- 1 tablespoon olive oil
- 1 tablespoon balsamic vinegar
- 2 ounces fresh mozzarella cheese
- 1/4 cup fat-free mayonnaise
- 1/2 teaspoon prepared horseradish
- 4 hard rolls, split and toasted
- 8 fresh basil leaves
- 1 plum tomato, thinly sliced

1 In a large nonstick skillet, saute peppers, onion and garlic in oil until crisp-tender. Drizzle with vinegar; toss to coat.

2 Cut mozzarella cheese into four slices. Combine the mayonnaise and horseradish; spread over cut sides of rolls. Spoon vegetable mixture onto bottom halves; top with cheese. Broil 4-6 in. from the heat for 2-4 minutes or until cheese is melted. Top with basil leaves and tomato. Replace roll tops.

Mediterranean Vegetable Pasta

PREP/TOTAL TIME: 25 MIN. YIELD: 2 SERVINGS

JAN CLARK NEW FLORENCE, MISSOURI

I created this fast-to-fix recipe to use up excess zucchini from our garden, and at the same time, serve a pasta dish that was lower in calories.

- 3 ounces uncooked angel hair pasta
- 1 cup chopped zucchini
- 1/2 cup chopped fresh mushrooms
- 1/3 cup chopped green pepper
- 1/4 cup chopped onion
- 1 garlic clove, minced
- 2 teaspoons olive oil
- 1 cup canned Italian diced tomatoes
- 6 pitted ripe olives, halved
- 1/8 teaspoon pepper
- 1/4 cup crumbled reduced-fat feta cheese
- 1 tablespoon shredded Parmesan cheese

1 Cook pasta according to package directions. Meanwhile, in a large skillet, saute the zucchini, mushrooms, green pepper, onion and garlic in oil until vegetables are crisp-tender. Stir in the tomatoes, olives and pepper; heat through.

2 Drain pasta; divide between two plates. Top with vegetable mixture and cheeses.

marvelous chicken enchiladas, p. 120

Satisfying, convenient hot dishes are America's favorite comfort food because they are easy to prepare, filling, versatile and economical.

casseroles

3 Drain manicotti and rinse in cold water; stuff each with about 1/4 cupful chicken mixture. Arrange over sauce in baking dish. Pour remaining sauce over shells.

4 Cover and bake at 350° for 30 minutes. Uncover; sprinkle with remaining Monterey Jack cheese. Bake 10 minutes longer or until cheese is melted.

Green Bean Mushroom Pie

PREP: 45 MIN. BAKE: 25 MIN. YIELD: 8-10 SERVINGS

TARA WALWORTH MAPLE PARK, ILLINOIS

Fresh green bean flavor stands out in this pretty lattice-topped pie. A flaky golden crust holds the savory bean, mushroom and cream cheese filling. It tastes wonderfully different every time I make it depending on the variety of mushroom I use.

    3 cups sliced fresh mushrooms
    4 tablespoons butter, *divided*
2-1/2 cups chopped onions
    6 cups cut fresh green beans (1-inch pieces)
    2 teaspoons minced fresh thyme *or* 3/4 teaspoon dried thyme
  1/2 teaspoon salt
  1/4 teaspoon pepper
    1 package (8 ounces) cream cheese, cubed
  1/2 cup milk

Mexican Chicken Manicotti

PREP: 25 MIN. BAKE: 40 MIN. YIELD: 7 SERVINGS

KEELY JANKUNAS CORVALLIS, MONTANA

Our family of five enjoys trying different ethnic cuisines. This Italian specialty has a little Mexican zip. Be careful not to overcook the manicotti. If the filled shells happen to break, just place them in the pan seam-side down.

    1 package (8 ounces) manicotti shells
    2 cups cubed cooked chicken
    2 cups (8 ounces) shredded Monterey Jack cheese, *divided*
1-1/2 cups (6 ounces) shredded cheddar cheese
    1 cup (8 ounces) sour cream
    1 small onion, diced, *divided*
    1 can (4 ounces) chopped green chilies, *divided*
    1 can (10-3/4 ounces) condensed cream of chicken soup, undiluted
    1 cup salsa
  2/3 cup milk

1 Cook manicotti according to package directions. Meanwhile, in a large bowl, combine chicken, 1-1/2 cups Monterey Jack cheese, cheddar cheese, sour cream, half of the onion and 6 tablespoons chilies.

2 In another bowl, combine the soup, salsa, milk and remaining onion and chilies. Spread 1/2 cup in a greased 13-in. x 9-in. baking dish.

CRUST:

- 2-1/2 cups all-purpose flour
- 2 teaspoons baking powder
- 1 teaspoon dill weed
- 1/4 teaspoon salt
- 1 cup cold butter
- 1 cup (8 ounces) sour cream
- 1 egg
- 1 tablespoon heavy whipping cream

1. In a large skillet, saute mushrooms in 1 tablespoon butter until tender; drain and set aside. In the same skillet, saute onions and beans in remaining butter for 18-20 minutes or until beans are crisp-tender. Add the thyme, salt, pepper, cream cheese, milk and mushrooms. Cook and stir until the cheese is melted. Remove from the heat; set aside.

2. For crust, in a large bowl, combine the flour, baking powder, dill and salt. Cut in butter until mixture resembles coarse crumbs. Stir in sour cream to form a soft dough.

3. Divide dough in half. On a well-floured surface, roll out one portion to fit a deep-dish 9-in. pie plate; trim pastry even with edge.

4. Pour green bean mixture into crust. Roll out remaining pastry; make a lattice crust. Trim, seal and flute edge.

5. In a small bowl, beat the egg and cream; brush over lattice top. Bake at 400° for 25-35 minutes or until golden brown.

Creamy Chicken Lasagna

PREP: 40 MIN. BAKE: 45 MIN. + STANDING YIELD: 9-12 SERVINGS

JANICE CHRISTOFFERSON EAGLE RIVER, WISCONSIN

As a girl, I spent summers on my grandparents' farm and helped harvest bushels of fresh vegetables. To this day, I enjoy making recipes like this lasagna, laden with juicy tomatoes and herbs straight from my own garden.

- 12 uncooked lasagna noodles
- 2 tablespoons cornstarch
- 1 can (12 ounces) evaporated milk
- 2 cups chicken broth
- 1 can (8 ounces) tomato sauce
- 1/2 cup grated Parmesan cheese
- 2 garlic cloves, minced
- 2 teaspoons Dijon mustard
- 1/2 teaspoon dried basil

- 1/4 teaspoon ground nutmeg
- 1/8 teaspoon cayenne pepper
- 2 cups cooked chicken strips (12 ounces)
- 24 cherry tomatoes, thinly sliced
- 1 cup (4 ounces) shredded cheddar cheese

Paprika and minced fresh parsley

1. Cook noodles according to package directions. Meanwhile, in a large saucepan, combine the cornstarch and milk until smooth. Whisk in the broth, tomato sauce, Parmesan cheese, garlic, mustard, basil, nutmeg and cayenne. Bring to a boil over medium heat; cook and stir for 2 minutes or until thickened. Remove from the heat.

2. Drain noodles. Spread 1/4 cup sauce into a greased 13-in. x 9-in. baking dish. Set aside 1 cup sauce. Stir chicken and tomatoes into the remaining sauce. Layer four noodles and half of the chicken mixture in baking dish. Repeat layers. Top with remaining noodles; spread with reserved sauce. Sprinkle with cheddar cheese and paprika.

3. Cover and bake at 350° for 45-50 minutes or until bubbly. Let stand for 15 minutes before cutting. Sprinkle with parsley.

To keep lasagna from becoming watery when baking, it's important to drain the noodles well. Here's a good way to do that: Drain and rinse the cooked noodles in a colander. Take each noodle, shake off excess water and lay flat on pieces of waxed paper until most of the water has evaporated.

Spicy Bean and Beef Pie

PREP: 20 MIN. BAKE: 30 MIN. YIELD: 8 SERVINGS

DEBRA DOHY MASSILLON, OHIO

My daughter helped me come up with this recipe when we wanted a one-dish meal that was different than a casserole. This pie slices nicely, is a fun and filling dish and goes over great at potluck suppers.

- 1 pound ground beef
- 2 to 3 garlic cloves, minced
- 1 can (11-1/2 ounces) condensed bean with bacon soup, undiluted
- 1 jar (16 ounces) thick and chunky picante sauce, *divided*
- 1/4 cup cornstarch
- 1 tablespoon chopped fresh parsley
- 1 teaspoon paprika
- 1 teaspoon salt
- 1/4 teaspoon pepper
- 1 can (16 ounces) kidney beans, rinsed and drained
- 1 can (15 ounces) black beans, rinsed and drained
- 2 cups (8 ounces) shredded cheddar cheese, *divided*
- 3/4 cup sliced green onions, *divided*

Pastry for double-crust pie (10 inches)

- 1 cup (8 ounces) sour cream
- 1 can (2-1/4 ounces) sliced ripe olives, drained

1 In a skillet, cook beef and garlic over medium heat until beef is no longer pink; drain.

2 In a large bowl, combine soup, 1 cup of picante sauce, cornstarch, parsley, paprika, salt and pepper; mix well. Fold in beans, 1-1/2 cups of cheese, 1/2 cup onions and the beef mixture.

3 Line pie plate with bottom pastry; fill with bean mixture. Top with remaining pastry; seal and flute edges. Cut slits in the top crust.

4 Bake at 425° for 30-35 minutes or until lightly browned. Let stand for 5 minutes before cutting. Garnish with sour cream, olives, remaining picante sauce, cheese and onions.

Seafood Lasagna

PREP: 35 MIN. BAKE: 35 MIN. + STANDING YIELD: 12 SERVINGS

ELENA HANSEN RUIDOSO, NEW MEXICO

This rich satisfying dish, adapted from a recipe given to me by a friend, is my husband's favorite. It's loaded with scallops, shrimp and crab in a creamy sauce. I consider this the "crown jewel" in my repertoire of recipes.

- 1 green onion, finely chopped
- 2 tablespoons canola oil
- 2 tablespoons plus 1/2 cup butter, *divided*
- 1/2 cup chicken broth
- 1 bottle (8 ounces) clam juice
- 1 pound bay scallops
- 1 pound uncooked small shrimp, peeled and deveined
- 1 package (8 ounces) imitation crabmeat, chopped
- 1/4 teaspoon white pepper, *divided*
- 1/2 cup all-purpose flour
- 1-1/2 cups milk
- 1/2 teaspoon salt
- 1 cup heavy whipping cream
- 1/2 cup shredded Parmesan cheese, *divided*
- 9 lasagna noodles, cooked and drained

1 In a large skillet, saute onion in oil and 2 tablespoons butter until tender. Stir in broth and clam juice; bring to a boil. Add the scallops, shrimp, crab and 1/8 teaspoon pepper; return to a boil. Reduce heat; simmer, uncovered, for 4-5 minutes or until shrimp turn pink and scallops are firm and opaque, stirring gently. Drain, reserving cooking liquid; set seafood mixture aside.

2 In a large saucepan, melt the remaining butter; stir in flour until smooth. Combine milk and reserved cooking liquid; gradually add to the saucepan. Add

1/2 pound sliced fresh mushrooms

1 teaspoon *each* dried basil, oregano and dill weed

Dash hot pepper sauce

1-1/2 cups (6 ounces) shredded part-skim mozzarella cheese

1/4 cup grated Parmesan cheese

1 For polenta, in a small bowl, whisk cornmeal, salt and 1 cup water until smooth. In a large saucepan, bring remaining water to a boil. Add cornmeal mixture, stirring constantly. Bring to a boil; cook and stir for 3 minutes or until thickened.

2 Reduce heat to low; cover and cook for 15 minutes. Divide mixture between two greased 8-in. square baking dishes. Cover and refrigerate until firm, about 1-1/2 hours.

3 In a large skillet, cook the beef, onion, green pepper and garlic over medium heat until meat is no longer pink; drain. Stir in the tomatoes, tomato sauce, mushrooms, herbs and hot pepper sauce; bring to a boil. Reduce heat; simmer, uncovered, for 20 minutes or until thickened.

4 Loosen one polenta from sides and bottom of dish; invert onto a waxed paper-lined baking sheet and set aside. Spoon half of the meat mixture over the remaining polenta. Sprinkle with half the mozzarella and half the Parmesan cheese. Top with reserved polenta and remaining meat mixture.

5 Cover and bake at 350° for 40 minutes or until heated through. Uncover; sprinkle with remaining cheese. Bake 5 minutes longer or until cheese is melted. Let stand for 10 minutes before cutting.

salt and remaining pepper. Bring to a boil; cook and stir for 2 minutes or until thickened. Remove from the heat; stir in cream and 1/4 cup Parmesan cheese. Stir 3/4 cup white sauce into the seafood mixture.

3 Spread 1/2 cup white sauce in a greased 13-in. x 9-in. baking dish. Top with three noodles; spread with half of the seafood mixture and 1-1/4 cups sauce. Repeat layers. Top with remaining noodles, sauce and Parmesan.

4 Bake, uncovered, at 350° for 35-40 minutes or until golden brown. Let stand for 15 minutes before cutting.

Ole Polenta Casserole

PREP: 1 HOUR + CHILLING BAKE: 40 MIN. + STANDING
YIELD: 6 SERVINGS

ANGELA BIGGIN LYONS, ILLINOIS

This casserole has been a family favorite for over 25 years! Servings are great dolloped with sour cream.

1 cup yellow cornmeal

1 teaspoon salt

4 cups water, *divided*

1 pound ground beef

1 cup chopped onion

1/2 cup chopped green pepper

2 garlic cloves, minced

1 can (14-1/2 ounces) diced tomatoes, undrained

1 can (8 ounces) tomato sauce

Rich 'n' Cheesy Macaroni

PREP: 30 MIN. BAKE: 30 MIN. YIELD: 6-8 SERVINGS

GWEN MILLER ROLLING HILLS, ALBERTA

This delicious dish puts a new twist on traditional macaroni and cheese. I make it often when my husband and I travel.

2-1/2 cups uncooked elbow macaroni
   6 tablespoons butter, *divided*
  1/4 cup all-purpose flour
   1 teaspoon salt
   1 teaspoon sugar
   2 cups milk
   8 ounces process American cheese (Velveeta), cubed
1-1/3 cups 4% cottage cheese
  2/3 cup sour cream
   2 cups (8 ounces) shredded sharp cheddar cheese
1-1/2 cups soft bread crumbs

1   Cook macaroni according to package directions; drain. Place in a greased 2-1/2-qt. baking dish. In a saucepan, melt 4 tablespoons butter. Stir in the flour, salt and sugar until smooth. Gradually stir in milk. Bring to a boil; cook and stir for 2 minutes or until thickened.

2   Reduce heat; stir in American cheese until melted. Stir in cottage cheese and sour cream. Pour over macaroni. Sprinkle with cheddar cheese. Melt remaining butter and toss with bread crumbs; sprinkle over top.

3   Bake, uncovered, at 350° for 30 minutes or until golden brown.

To make soft bread crumbs, tear a few slices of bread into 1-1/2-in. pieces and place in a food processor or blender. Cover and pulse (short on/off actions) until the bread turns to crumbs.

Swiss Potato Squares

PREP: 45 MIN. BAKE: 45 MIN. YIELD: 8-9 SERVINGS

NANCY FOUST STONEBORO, PENNSYLVANIA

To vary these squares, you can substitute cheddar cheese for Swiss or try Canadian bacon in place of ham. However you make them, they taste wonderful reheated in the microwave. So you can serve the squares warm as leftovers, pack them in a thermal lunch carrier or put them on a potluck table.

   8 medium russet potatoes (about 3 pounds), peeled and cubed
  1/3 cup butter, melted
   1 tablespoon minced fresh parsley
1-1/2 teaspoons salt
  1/4 teaspoon pepper
1-1/2 cups cubed Swiss cheese
   1 cup cubed fully cooked ham
   1 small onion, grated
   1 teaspoon garlic powder
   3 eggs
  1/2 cup milk
Paprika

1   Place potatoes in a saucepan and cover with water. Cover and bring to a boil; cook for 20-25 minutes or until very tender. Drain well. Mash with butter, parsley, salt and pepper.

2   Spread about 4 cups of the potato mixture onto the bottom and up the sides of a greased 8-in. square baking dish. Combine cheese, ham, onion and garlic powder; spoon into potato shell. Combine eggs and milk; pour over all. Top with remaining potato mixture. Sprinkle with paprika.

3   Bake, uncovered, at 400° for 45-50 minutes or until golden. Let stand 5 minutes before cutting.

Chicken and Stuffing Pie

PREP: 20 MIN. BAKE: 25 MIN. YIELD: 6-8 SERVINGS

INA SCHMILLEN ELKHORN, NEBRASKA

This is an exceptional recipe to have on hand when turkey and chicken leftovers begin to crowd your refrigerator, during the holiday season or at any other time. Thanks to the stuffing crust, this pie's easy to make, and it's pretty to serve with its colorful meat and vegetable filling.

CRUST:

- 1 package (8 ounces) herb seasoning stuffing mix
- 3/4 cup chicken broth
- 1/2 cup butter, melted
- 1 egg, beaten

FILLING:

- 2 tablespoons all-purpose flour
- 1 can (4 ounces) mushroom stems and pieces, drained and liquid reserved
- 1/2 cup chopped onion
- 1 tablespoon butter
- 1 jar (12 ounces) chicken gravy
- 1 teaspoon Worcestershire sauce
- 1/2 teaspoon thyme
- 3 cups cubed cooked chicken
- 1 cup fresh *or* frozen peas
- 2 tablespoons diced pimientos
- 1 tablespoon dried parsley flakes
- 4 ounces sliced Colby *or* American cheese

1 In a small bowl, combine crust ingredients; press into a greased 10-in. pie plate and set aside.

2 For filling, in a small bowl, combine flour and mushroom liquid until smooth; set aside.

3 In a large saucepan, saute mushrooms and onion in butter. Stir in all remaining ingredients except cheese. Heat through; pour into stuffing crust.

4 Bake, uncovered, at 375° for 20 minutes. Cut cheese slices into strips; arrange in a lattice design on pie. Bake 5 minutes longer or until cheese is melted.

Taco Lasagna

PREP: 20 MIN. BAKE: 25 MIN. YIELD: 9 SERVINGS

TERRI KEENAN TUSCALOOSA, ALABAMA

If you like foods with Southwestern flair, this just might become a new favorite. Loaded with cheese, meat and beans, the casserole comes together in a snap. There are never any leftovers when I take this dish to potlucks.

- 1 pound ground beef
- 1/2 cup chopped green pepper
- 1/2 cup chopped onion
- 2/3 cup water
- 1 envelope taco seasoning
- 1 can (15 ounces) black beans, rinsed and drained
- 1 can (14-1/2 ounces) Mexican diced tomatoes, undrained
- 6 flour tortillas (8 inches)
- 1 can (16 ounces) refried beans
- 3 cups (12 ounces) shredded Mexican cheese blend

1 In a large skillet, cook beef, green pepper and onion over medium heat until meat is no longer pink; drain. Add water and taco seasoning; bring to a boil. Reduce heat; simmer, uncovered, for 2 minutes. Stir in the black beans and tomatoes. Simmer, uncovered, for 10 minutes.

2 Place two tortillas in a greased 13-in. x 9-in. baking dish. Spread with half of the refried beans and beef mixture; sprinkle with 1 cup cheese. Repeat layers. Top with remaining tortillas and cheese.

3 Cover and bake at 350° for 25-30 minutes or until heated through and cheese is melted.

Meatball Pie

PREP: 30 MIN. BAKE: 45 MIN. + STANDING YIELD: 6 SERVINGS

SUSAN KEITH FORT PLAIN, NEW YORK

Growing up on a farm, I took part in 4-H cooking club activities. I still love to prepare classic, wholesome recipes, such as this meal-in-one pie. I like serving them, too!

 1 pound ground beef
3/4 cup soft bread crumbs
1/4 cup chopped onion
 2 tablespoons minced fresh parsley
 1 teaspoon salt
1/2 teaspoon dried marjoram
1/8 teaspoon pepper
1/4 cup milk
 1 egg, lightly beaten
 1 can (14-1/2 ounces) stewed tomatoes
 1 tablespoon cornstarch
 2 teaspoons beef bouillon granules
 1 cup frozen peas
 1 cup sliced carrots, cooked

CRUST:
2-2/3 cups all-purpose flour
 1/2 teaspoon salt
 1 cup shortening
 7 to 8 tablespoons ice water

Half-and-half cream

1 In a large bowl, combine the first nine ingredients (mixture will be soft). Divide into fourths; shape each portion into 12 small meatballs. Brown meatballs, a few at a time, in a large skillet; drain and set aside.

2 Drain tomatoes, reserving liquid. Combine the liquid with cornstarch; pour into the skillet. Add tomatoes and bouillon; bring to a boil over medium heat, stirring constantly. Stir in peas and carrots. Remove from the heat and set aside.

3 For crust, in a large bowl, combine flour and salt. Cut in shortening until the mixture resembles coarse crumbs. Add water, 1 tablespoon at a time, tossing lightly with a fork until dough forms a ball. On a lightly floured surface, roll half of dough to fit a 10-in. pie plate.

4 Place in ungreased plate; add meatballs. Spoon tomato mixture over top. Roll remaining pastry to fit top of pie. Place over filling; seal and flute edges. Cut vents in top crust. Brush with cream.

5 Bake at 400° for 45-50 minutes or until golden brown. If needed, cover edges with foil for the last 10 minutes to prevent overbrowning. Let stand for 10 minutes before cutting.

Meatball Sub Casserole

PREP: 15 MIN. BAKE: 45 MIN. YIELD: 6-8 SERVINGS

GINA HARRIS SENECA, SOUTH CAROLINA

If you like meatball subs, you'll love this tangy casserole. It has all the rich flavor of the popular sandwiches with none of the mess. Italian bread is spread with a cream cheese mixture, then topped with meatballs, spaghetti sauce and cheese. Served with a green salad, it's a hearty meal the whole family enjoys.

1/3 cup chopped green onions
1/4 cup seasoned bread crumbs
 3 tablespoons grated Parmesan cheese
 1 pound ground beef
 1 loaf (1 pound) Italian bread, cut into 1-inch slices
 1 package (8 ounces) cream cheese, softened
1/2 cup mayonnaise
 1 teaspoon Italian seasoning
1/4 teaspoon pepper
 2 cups (8 ounces) shredded part-skim mozzarella cheese, *divided*
 1 jar (28 ounces) spaghetti sauce
 1 cup water
 2 garlic cloves, minced

1 In a bowl, combine the onions, crumbs and Parmesan cheese. Add beef and mix well. Shape into 1-in. balls; place on a greased rack in a shallow baking pan. Bake at 400° for 15-20 minutes or until no longer pink.

2. Meanwhile, arrange bread in a single layer in an ungreased 13-in. x 9-in. baking dish (all of the bread might not be used). Combine the cream cheese, mayonnaise, Italian seasoning and pepper; spread over the bread. Sprinkle with 1/2 cup mozzarella.

3. Combine the sauce, water and garlic; add meatballs. Pour over cheese mixture; sprinkle with remaining mozzarella. Bake, uncovered, at 350° for 30 minutes or until heated through.

Editor's Note: Reduced-fat or fat-free mayonnaise is not recommended for this recipe.

Worth It Lasagna

PREP: 1 HOUR BAKE: 55 MIN. + STANDING
YIELD: 2 CASSEROLES (12 SERVINGS EACH)

JOAN BROXHOLME BOULDER CITY, NEVADA

I break out this lasagna recipe whenever I need to feed a crowd. It has such an abundance of tasty ingredients. Often, I'll serve one pan to guests and freeze the other for a family meal later.

- 2 jars (26 ounces *each*) meatless spaghetti sauce
- 1 can (14-1/2 ounces) diced tomatoes, drained
- 1/2 cup Burgundy wine
- 2 tablespoons brown sugar
- 3 garlic cloves, minced
- 2 pounds Italian turkey sausage links, casings removed
- 3/4 cup raisins
- 2 teaspoons Italian seasoning
- 1-1/2 pounds sliced fresh mushrooms
- 1 medium onion, chopped
- 2 eggs, lightly beaten
- 2 containers (15 ounces *each*) ricotta cheese
- 1 package (10 ounces) frozen chopped spinach, thawed and squeezed dry
- 1 cup grated Parmesan cheese
- 2 packages (24 ounces *each*) frozen cheese ravioli, thawed
- 1 cup shredded Parmesan cheese
- 18 slices provolone cheese, cut in half
- 6 cups (24 ounces) shredded Monterey Jack cheese
- 5 large tomatoes, sliced

1. In a Dutch oven, bring first five ingredients to a boil. Reduce heat; simmer, uncovered, for 20 minutes, stirring often.

2. In a large skillet, cook sausage over medium heat until no longer pink; drain. Stir in raisins and Italian seasoning; add to sauce. In the same skillet, saute mushrooms and onion until moisture has evaporated. Stir into sauce. In a large bowl, combine the eggs, ricotta, spinach and grated Parmesan; set aside.

3. In each of two greased 13-in. x 9-in. baking dishes, layer 1-1/3 cups sauce, half of a package of ravioli, 1-1/3 cups sauce, 1/4 cup shredded Parmesan, six half slices of provolone, 1 cup Monterey Jack and 2-1/2 cups spinach mixture.

4. Top each with six half slices of provolone, 1 cup Monterey Jack, 1-1/3 cups sauce, remaining ravioli and sauce, 1/4 cup shredded Parmesan, six half slices of provolone, sliced tomatoes and remaining Monterey Jack (dishes will be full).

5. Cover and bake at 375° for 45 minutes. Uncover; bake 10-15 minutes longer or until bubbly. Let stand 15 minutes before serving.

Marvelous Chicken Enchiladas

PREP: 30 MIN. BAKE: 25 MIN. YIELD: 6 ENCHILADAS

REBEKAH SABO ROCHESTER, NEW YORK

I love Mexican food, and this is one of my favorites. Try using Monterey Jack instead of cheddar for a milder taste.

- 1 pound boneless skinless chicken breasts, cut into thin strips
- 4 teaspoons chili powder
- 2 teaspoons olive oil
- 2 tablespoons all-purpose flour
- 1-1/2 teaspoons ground coriander
- 1 teaspoon baking cocoa
- 1 cup fat-free milk
- 1 cup frozen corn, thawed
- 4 green onions, chopped
- 1 can (4 ounces) chopped green chilies, drained
- 1/2 teaspoon salt
- 1/2 cup minced fresh cilantro, *divided*
- 6 whole wheat tortillas (8 inches)
- 1/2 cup salsa
- 1/2 cup tomato sauce
- 1/2 cup shredded reduced-fat cheddar cheese

1. Sprinkle chicken with chili powder. In a large nonstick skillet coated with cooking spray, cook chicken in oil over medium heat until no longer pink. Sprinkle with flour, coriander and cocoa; stir until blended.

2. Gradually stir in milk. Bring to a boil; cook and stir for 2 minutes or until thickened. Add the corn, onions, chilies and salt; cook and stir 2 minutes longer or until heated through. Remove from the heat. Stir in 1/4 cup cilantro.

3. Spread 2/3 cup filling down the center of each tortilla. Roll up and place seam side down in a 13-in. x 9-in. baking dish coated with cooking spray.

4. Combine salsa, tomato sauce and remaining cilantro; pour over enchiladas. Sprinkle with cheese.

5. Cover and bake at 375° for 25 minutes or until heated through.

Easy Chicken Potpie

PREP/TOTAL TIME: 30 MIN. YIELD: 6 SERVINGS

AMY BRIGGS GOVE, KANSAS

Why look for potpie in the frozen food aisle when this easy, homemade version tastes so much better?

- 1 medium onion, chopped
- 2 tablespoons canola oil
- 1/2 cup all-purpose flour
- 1 teaspoon poultry seasoning
- 1 can (14-1/2 ounces) chicken broth
- 3/4 cup milk
- 3 cups cubed cooked chicken
- 2 cups frozen mixed vegetables, thawed
- 1 sheet refrigerated pie pastry

1. In a large saucepan, saute onion in oil until tender. Stir in flour and seasoning until blended; gradually add broth and milk. Bring to a boil; cook and stir for 2 minutes or until thickened. Add chicken and vegetables.

2. Transfer to a greased 9-in. deep-dish pie plate. Top with pastry. Trim, seal and flute edges. Cut slits in pastry. Bake at 450° for 15-20 minutes or until crust is golden brown and filling is bubbly.

MARGE HODEL
ROANOKE, ILLINOIS

I've been stuffing pasta shells with different fillings for years, but my family enjoys this version with taco-seasoned meat the most. The frozen shells are so convenient, because you can take out only the number you need for a single-serving lunch or family dinner. Just add zippy taco sauce and bake.

Taco-Filled Pasta Shells

PREP: 20 MIN. + CHILLING BAKE: 45 MIN. YIELD: 2 CASSEROLES (6 SERVINGS EACH)

- 2 **pounds ground beef**
- 2 **envelopes taco seasoning**
- 1 **package (8 ounces) cream cheese, cubed**
- 24 **uncooked jumbo pasta shells**
- 1/4 **cup butter, melted**

ADDITIONAL INGREDIENTS
(for each casserole):

- 1 **cup salsa**
- 1 **cup taco sauce**
- 1 **cup (4 ounces) shredded cheddar cheese**
- 1 **cup (4 ounces) shredded Monterey Jack cheese**
- 1-1/2 **cups crushed tortilla chips**
- 1 **cup (8 ounces) sour cream**
- 3 **green onions, chopped**

1 In a Dutch oven, cook beef over medium heat until no longer pink; drain. Add taco seasoning; prepare according to package directions. Add cream cheese; cook and stir for 5-10 minutes or until melted. Transfer to a bowl; chill for 1 hour.

2 Cook pasta according to package directions; drain. Gently toss with butter. Fill each shell with about 3 tablespoons of meat mixture. Place 12 shells in a freezer container. Cover and freeze for up to 3 months.

3 To prepare remaining shells, spoon salsa into a greased 9-in. square baking dish. Top with stuffed shells and taco sauce. Cover and bake at 350° for 30 minutes. Uncover; sprinkle with cheeses and chips. Bake 15 minutes longer or until heated through. Serve with sour cream and onions.

4 To use frozen shells: Thaw in the refrigerator for 24 hours (shells will be partially frozen). Spoon salsa into a greased 9-in. square baking dish; top with shells and taco sauce. Cover and bake at 350° for 40 minutes. Uncover and continue as above.

Ham and Asparagus Casserole

PREP: 15 MIN. BAKE: 25 MIN. YIELD: 6 SERVINGS

DONETTA BRUNNER SAVANNA, ILLINOIS

This family-favorite casserole is perfect for all occasions. But it's especially nice for an Easter brunch, because the ham, hard-cooked eggs and asparagus in it are so much a part of that special day. Cinnamon-flavored yeast bread makes a tasty accompaniment for this easy casserole, as do rolls.

- 1 package (10 ounces) frozen cut asparagus *or* 1 pound fresh asparagus, 1/2-inch cuts
- 4 hard-cooked eggs, peeled and chopped
- 1 cup cubed fully cooked ham
- 2 tablespoons quick-cooking tapioca
- 1/4 cup shredded process cheese (Velveeta)
- 2 tablespoons chopped green pepper
- 2 tablespoons chopped onion
- 1 tablespoon minced fresh parsley
- 1 tablespoon lemon juice
- 1/2 cup half-and-half cream *or* evaporated milk
- 1 cup condensed cream of mushroom soup, undiluted

TOPPING:
- 1 cup soft bread crumbs
- 2 tablespoons butter, melted

1 In a large saucepan, bring 1/2 in. of water to a boil. Add asparagus; cover and boil for 3 minutes. Drain and immediately place asparagus in ice water. Drain and pat dry.

2 In a 2-1/2-qt. baking dish, combine the asparagus, eggs and ham; sprinkle tapioca evenly over all. Stir in the cheese, green pepper, onion and parsley.

3 In a small bowl, combine the lemon juice, cream and soup; add to casserole and mix thoroughly. Combine topping ingredients; sprinkle over top.

4 Bake, uncovered, at 375° for 25-30 minutes or until heated through. Let stand a few minutes before serving.

Sloppy Joe Under a Bun

PREP/TOTAL TIME: 30 MIN. YIELD: 8 SERVINGS

TRISH BLOOM RAY, MICHIGAN

I usually keep a can of sloppy joe sauce in the pantry, because our kids love sloppy joes. But sometimes I don't have buns on hand. With this fun casserole, we can still enjoy the flavor that they love in a flash. The bun-like top crust is made with biscuit mix, sprinkled with sesame seeds and baked until golden.

- 1-1/2 pounds ground beef
- 1 can (15-1/2 ounces) sloppy joe sauce
- 2 cups (8 ounces) shredded cheddar cheese
- 2 cups biscuit/baking mix
- 2 eggs, lightly beaten
- 1 cup milk
- 1 tablespoon sesame seeds

1 In a large skillet, cook the beef over medium heat until no longer pink; drain. Stir in the sloppy joe sauce. Transfer to a lightly greased 13-in. x 9-in. baking dish; sprinkle with cheese.

2 In a large bowl, combine the biscuit mix, eggs and milk just until blended. Pour over cheese; sprinkle with sesame seeds. Bake, uncovered, at 400° for 25 minutes or until golden brown.

Florentine Spaghetti Bake

PREP: 30 MIN. BAKE: 1 HOUR + STANDING YIELD: 9 SERVINGS

LORRAINE MARTIN LINCOLN, CALIFORNIA

This plate-filling sausage dish appeals to basic meat-and-potatoes fans to gourmets.

- 8 ounces uncooked spaghetti
- 1 pound bulk Italian sausage
- 1 cup chopped onion
- 1 garlic clove, minced
- 1 jar (26 ounces) spaghetti sauce
- 1 can (4 ounces) mushroom stems and pieces, drained
- 1 egg, lightly beaten
- 2 cups (16 ounces) 4% cottage cheese
- 1 package (10 ounces) frozen chopped spinach, thawed and squeezed dry
- 1/4 cup grated Parmesan cheese
- 1/2 teaspoon seasoned salt
- 1/4 teaspoon pepper
- 2 cups (8 ounces) shredded part-skim mozzarella cheese

1 Cook pasta according to package directions. Meanwhile, in a large skillet, cook the sausage, onion and garlic over medium heat until sausage is no longer pink; drain. Stir in spaghetti sauce and mushrooms. Bring to a boil. Reduce heat; cover and cook for 15 minutes or until heated through.

2 Drain pasta. In a large bowl, combine egg, cottage cheese, spinach, Parmesan cheese, salt and pepper. Spread 1 cup sausage mixture in a greased 13-in. x 9-in. baking dish, Top with spaghetti and remaining sausage mixture. Layer with spinach mixture and mozzarella.

3 Cover and bake at 375° for 45 minutes. Uncover; bake 15 minutes longer or until lightly browned and heated through. Let stand for 15 minutes before cutting.

Chicken in Potato Baskets

PREP: 20 MIN. BAKE: 30 MIN. YIELD: 6 SERVINGS

HELEN LAMISON CARNEGIE, PENNSYLVANIA

I like to serve these petite pies for special luncheons. Chock-full of meat and vegetables in a creamy sauce, they're a meal-in-one.

- 4-1/2 cups frozen shredded hash brown potatoes, thawed
- 6 tablespoons butter, melted
- 1-1/2 teaspoons salt
- 1/4 teaspoon pepper

FILLING:
- 1/2 cup chopped onion
- 1/4 cup butter, cubed
- 1/4 cup all-purpose flour
- 2 teaspoons chicken bouillon granules
- 1 teaspoon Worcestershire sauce
- 1/2 teaspoon dried basil
- 2 cups milk
- 3 cups cubed cooked chicken
- 1 cup frozen peas, thawed

1 In a large bowl, combine potatoes, butter, salt and pepper. Press into six greased 10-oz. custard cups; set aside.

2 In a large saucepan, saute onion in butter. Add flour, bouillon, Worcestershire sauce and basil. Stir in milk. Bring to a boil; cook and stir for 2 minutes or until thickened. Add chicken and peas. Spoon into prepared crusts.

3 Bake, uncovered, at 375° for 30-35 minutes or until crust is golden brown.

Chicken and Dumpling Casserole

PREP: 30 MIN. BAKE: 40 MIN. YIELD: 6-8 SERVINGS

SUE MACKEY GALESBURG, ILLINOIS

This savory casserole is one of my husband's favorites. He loves the fluffy dumplings with plenty of gravy.

- 1/2 cup chopped onion
- 1/2 cup chopped celery
- 2 garlic cloves, minced
- 1/4 cup butter, cubed
- 1/2 cup all-purpose flour
- 2 teaspoons sugar
- 1 teaspoon salt
- 1 teaspoon dried basil
- 1/2 teaspoon pepper
- 4 cups chicken broth
- 1 package (10 ounces) frozen green peas
- 4 cups cubed cooked chicken

DUMPLINGS:

- 2 cups biscuit/baking mix
- 2 teaspoons dried basil
- 2/3 cup milk

1. In a large saucepan, saute the onion, celery and garlic in butter until tender. Stir in the flour, sugar, salt, basil and pepper until blended. Gradually add broth; bring to a boil. Cook and stir for 1 minute; reduce heat. Add peas and cook for 5 minutes, stirring constantly. Stir in chicken. Pour into a greased 13-in. x 9-in. baking dish.

2. For dumplings, in a small bowl, combine baking mix and basil. Stir in milk with a fork until moistened. Drop by tablespoonfuls into 12 mounds over chicken mixture.

3. Bake, uncovered, at 350° for 30 minutes. Cover and bake 10 minutes longer or until a toothpick inserted in a dumpling comes out clean.

Four-Cheese Baked Ziti

PREP: 20 MIN. BAKE: 30 MIN. YIELD: 12 SERVINGS

LISA VARNER CHARLESTON, SOUTH CAROLINA

This pasta dish, made with Alfredo sauce, is deliciously different from typical tomato-based recipes. Extra cheesy, it goes together quickly and is always popular at potlucks.

- 1 package (16 ounces) ziti or small tube pasta
- 2 cartons (10 ounces *each*) refrigerated Alfredo sauce
- 1 cup (8 ounces) sour cream
- 2 eggs, lightly beaten
- 1 carton (15 ounces) ricotta cheese
- 1/2 cup grated Parmesan cheese, *divided*
- 1/4 cup grated Romano cheese
- 1/4 cup minced fresh parsley
- 1-3/4 cups shredded part-skim mozzarella cheese

1. Cook pasta according to package directions; drain and return to the pan. Stir in Alfredo sauce and sour cream. Spoon half into a lightly greased 3-qt. baking dish.

2. Combine the eggs, ricotta cheese, 1/4 cup Parmesan cheese, Romano cheese and parsley; spread over pasta. Top with remaining pasta mixture; sprinkle with mozzarella and remaining Parmesan.

3. Cover and bake at 350° for 25 minutes or until a thermometer reads 160°. Uncover; bake 5-10 minutes longer or until bubbly.

Southwest Turkey Casserole

PREP: 20 MIN. BAKE: 20 MIN. YIELD: 2 SERVINGS

MARIA LUISA REYES BASTROP, TEXAS

When I was small, my mother and stepfather—who was head cook for an oil company—made this colorful casserole.

- 1/2 **cup uncooked elbow macaroni**
- 1/4 **cup chopped onion**
- 1/4 **cup chopped sweet red pepper**
- 4-1/2 **teaspoons butter**
- 1 **tablespoon canola oil**
- 1 **tablespoon all-purpose flour**
- 1/2 **teaspoon salt**
- 1/2 **teaspoon ground cumin**

Dash pepper

- 1 **cup 2% milk**
- 1 **cup (4 ounces) shredded cheddar cheese**
- 1 **cup cubed cooked turkey**
- 2/3 **cup canned diced tomatoes and green chilies**
- 1/3 **cup frozen corn**
- 1/3 **cup frozen peas**

1 Cook macaroni according to package directions. Meanwhile, in a large skillet, saute onion and red pepper in butter and oil until tender. Stir in the flour, salt, cumin and pepper until blended; gradually add milk. Bring to a boil; cook and stir for 1-2 minutes or until thickened. Stir in cheese until melted.

2 Drain macaroni; add to cheese mixture. Stir in the turkey, tomatoes, corn and peas. Transfer to a 1-qt. baking dish coated with cooking spray. Bake, uncovered, at 350° for 20-25 minutes or until bubbly.

Three Cheese Enchiladas

PREP: 20 MIN. BAKE: 20 MIN. YIELD: 4 SERVINGS

GRETCHEN MELLBERG HAWARDEN, IOWA

This easy-to-prepare main-dish meal has proven popular with dinner guests of all ages—and especially teenagers. You'll find the Southwest-style enchiladas are not too spicy, just pleasantly flavorful and impressive looking.

- 1-1/2 **cups (6 ounces) shredded Monterey Jack cheese,** *divided*
- 1-1/2 **cups (6 ounces) shredded cheddar cheese,** *divided*
- 1 **package (3 ounces) cream cheese, softened**
- 1 **cup picante sauce,** *divided*
- 1 **medium red** *or* **green bell pepper, diced**
- 1/2 **cup sliced green onions**
- 1 **teaspoon crushed cumin**
- 8 **flour tortillas (7-8 inches)**

Shredded lettuce

Chopped tomato

Sliced ripe olives

Additional picante sauce, optional

1 Combine 1 cup Monterey Jack cheese, 1 cup cheddar cheese, cream cheese, 1/4 cup picante sauce, the bell pepper, onions and cumin; mix well. Spoon 1/4 cup cheese mixture down the center of each tortilla. Roll and place, seam side down, in a 13-in. x 9-in. baking dish. Spoon remaining picante sauce evenly over enchiladas; cover with remaining cheeses.

2 Bake at 350° for 20 minutes or until hot. Top with lettuce, tomato and ripe olives; serve with additional picante sauce if desired.

Turkey Biscuit Potpie

PREP: 30 MIN. BAKE: 20 MIN. YIELD: 6 SERVINGS

SHIRLEY FRANCEY ST. CATHARINES, ONTARIO

My family enjoys this comforting dish that is loaded with chunks of turkey, potatoes, carrots and green beans. Topped with easy-to-make biscuits, it has wonderful down-home flavor.

- 1 large onion, chopped
- 1 garlic clove, minced
- 1-1/2 cups cubed peeled potatoes
- 1-1/2 cups sliced carrots
- 1 cup frozen cut green beans, thawed
- 1 cup reduced-sodium chicken broth
- 4-1/2 teaspoons all-purpose flour
- 1 can (10-3/4 ounces) reduced-fat condensed cream of mushroom soup, undiluted
- 2 cups cubed cooked turkey
- 2 tablespoons minced fresh parsley
- 1/2 teaspoon dried basil
- 1/2 teaspoon dried thyme
- 1/4 teaspoon pepper

BISCUITS:
- 1 cup all-purpose flour
- 2 teaspoons baking powder
- 1/2 teaspoon dried oregano
- 2 tablespoons butter
- 7 tablespoons 1% milk

1 In a large saucepan coated with cooking spray, cook onion and garlic over medium heat until tender. Add the potatoes, carrots, beans and broth; bring to a boil. Reduce heat; cover and simmer for 15-20 minutes or until potatoes are tender.

2 Remove from the heat. Combine the flour and mushroom soup; stir into vegetable mixture. Add the turkey and seasonings. Transfer to a 2-qt. baking dish coated with cooking spray.

3 For biscuits, in a large bowl, combine the flour, baking powder and oregano. Cut in the butter until evenly distributed. Stir in milk. Drop batter in six mounds onto hot turkey mixture.

4 Bake, uncovered, at 400° for 20-25 minutes or until a toothpick inserted in center of biscuits comes out clean and biscuits are golden brown.

Traditional Lasagna

PREP: 30 MIN. + SIMMERING BAKE: 70 MIN. + STANDING
YIELD: 12 SERVINGS

LORRI FOOCKLE GRANVILLE, ILLINOIS

My gang first tasted this rich, classic lasagna at a friend's home on Christmas Eve. We were so impressed with the flavor that it became our own holiday tradition as well. I also prepare it other times of the year. It's requested often by my sister's Italian in-laws, which I consider the highest compliment!

- 1 pound ground beef
- 3/4 pound bulk pork sausage
- 3 cans (8 ounces *each*) tomato sauce
- 2 cans (6 ounces *each*) tomato paste
- 2 garlic cloves, minced
- 2 teaspoons sugar
- 1 teaspoon Italian seasoning
- 1 teaspoon salt
- 1/2 teaspoon pepper
- 3 eggs
- 3 tablespoons minced fresh parsley
- 3 cups (24 ounces) 4% small-curd cottage cheese
- 1 carton (8 ounces) ricotta cheese
- 1/2 cup grated Parmesan cheese
- 9 lasagna noodles, cooked and drained
- 6 slices provolone cheese
- 3 cups (12 ounces) shredded part-skim mozzarella cheese, *divided*

1.   **pound fresh asparagus, cut into 1-inch pieces**
1/4 **cup diced onion**
2   **tablespoons butter**
2   **tablespoons all-purpose flour**
1/2 **teaspoon salt**
1/4 **teaspoon pepper**
1-1/2 **cups milk**
1/2 **cup shredded Swiss cheese**
2   **tablespoons grated Parmesan cheese**
2   **cups diced fully cooked ham**

1 In a large saucepan over medium heat, bring water and butter to a boil. Add flour and salt all at once; stir until a smooth ball forms. Remove from the heat; let stand for 5 minutes. Add eggs, one at a time, beating well after each; beat until smooth. Stir in 3 tablespoons Parmesan cheese.

2 Using 1/4 cupfuls of dough, form a ring around the sides of a greased 10-in. quiche pan or pie plate (mounds should touch). Top with the remaining cheese. Bake at 400° for 35 minutes.

3 Meanwhile, for the filling, cook the asparagus in a small amount of water for 3-4 minutes or until crisp-tender; drain.

4 In a large saucepan, saute onion in butter until tender. Stir in the flour, salt and pepper until blended. Gradually add milk; bring to a boil over medium heat, stirring constantly. Reduce heat; add cheeses and stir until melted.

5 Stir in the ham and asparagus; spoon into the middle of the ring. Serve immediately.

---

1 In a large skillet, cook beef and sausage over medium heat until no longer pink; drain. Add the tomato sauce, tomato paste, garlic, sugar, seasoning, salt and pepper. Bring to a boil. Reduce heat; simmer, uncovered, for 1 hour, stirring occasionally.

2 In a large bowl, combine the eggs and parsley. Stir in the cottage cheese, ricotta and Parmesan.

3 Spread 1 cup of meat sauce in an ungreased 13-in. x 9-in. baking dish. Layer with three noodles, provolone cheese, 2 cups cottage cheese mixture, 1 cup mozzarella, three noodles, 2 cups meat sauce, remaining cottage cheese mixture and 1 cup mozzarella. Top with the remaining noodles, meat sauce and mozzarella (dish will be full).

4 Cover and bake at 375° for 50 minutes. Uncover; bake 20 minutes longer or until heated through. Let stand for 15 minutes before cutting.

Asparagus Puff Ring

PREP: 20 MIN. BAKE: 35 MIN. YIELD: 6 SERVINGS

SHIRLEY DE LANGE BYRON CENTER, MICHIGAN

Every spring when I make this tantalizing entree, I'm struck by how impressive it looks. Ham and asparagus in a creamy sauce are piled high in a cheesy cream puff shell. It's delicious and deceivingly simple to prepare!

3/4 **cup water**
6   **tablespoons butter**
3/4 **cup all-purpose flour**
1/2 **teaspoon salt**
3   **eggs**
1/4 **cup grated Parmesan cheese,** *divided*

onion-beef muffin cups, p. 132

The *enticing aroma* of homemade bread wafting from the oven is *irresistible*. Go ahead and enjoy these *warm, golden* delights today.

breads & rolls

2. For filling, in a small bowl, beat the cream cheese, sugar and egg until smooth. Fold in the berries. Drop a rounded tablespoonful into the center of each muffin.

3. For topping, combine the flour, brown sugar and cinnamon in a small bowl; cut in butter until crumbly. Sprinkle over batter. (Muffin cups will be full.)

4. Bake at 375° for 25-30 minutes or until a toothpick inserted near the center comes out clean. Cool for 5 minutes before removing from pans to wire racks. Serve warm. Refrigerate leftovers.

Berry Cheesecake Muffins

PREP: 30 MIN. BAKE: 25 MIN./BATCH YIELD: 21 MUFFINS

JEANNE BILHIMER MIDLAND, MICHIGAN

I adapted this recipe over the years for my family, and they think it's wonderful. Not only are the muffins delectable, but they're bursting with fantastic color, too.

- 1/3 cup butter, softened
- 3/4 cup sugar
- 2 eggs
- 1/3 cup milk
- 1-1/2 cups all-purpose flour
- 1-1/2 teaspoons baking powder
- 1 teaspoon ground cinnamon

CREAM CHEESE FILLING:
- 2 packages (3 ounces *each*) cream cheese, softened
- 1/3 cup sugar
- 1 egg
- 3/4 cup fresh raspberries
- 3/4 cup fresh blueberries

STREUSEL TOPPING:
- 1/4 cup all-purpose flour
- 2 tablespoons brown sugar
- 1/2 teaspoon ground cinnamon
- 1 tablespoon cold butter

1. In a large bowl, cream butter and sugar until light and fluffy. Add eggs, one at a time, beating well after each addition. Beat in milk. Combine the flour, baking powder and cinnamon; gradually add to creamed mixture just until moistened. Fill greased or paper-lined muffin cups one-third full.

Almond Streusel Rolls

PREP: 40 MIN. + RISING BAKE: 35 MIN. + COOLING
YIELD: 1 DOZEN

PERLENE HOEKEMA LYNDEN, WASHINGTON

These are just wonderful sweet rolls. I've also used them as a deliciously different dessert. Often, the rolls don't even get to cool before the pan is empty!

- 2 packages (1/4 ounce *each*) active dry yeast
- 3/4 cup warm water (110° to 115°)
- 3/4 cup warm milk (110° to 115°)
- 1/4 cup butter, softened
- 1/2 cup sugar
- 2 eggs
- 1 teaspoon salt
- 5-1/4 to 5-1/2 cups all-purpose flour

FILLING:
- 1/2 cup almond paste
- 1/4 cup butter, softened
- 1/2 cup packed brown sugar
- 1/4 teaspoon almond extract

TOPPING:

- 3 tablespoons sugar
- 1 tablespoon all-purpose flour
- 1 tablespoon butter

ICING:

- 1-1/2 cups confectioners' sugar
- 1/4 teaspoon almond extract
- 1 to 2 tablespoons milk

1 In a large bowl, dissolve yeast in warm water. Add the milk, butter, sugar, eggs, salt and 2 cups flour. Beat until smooth. Stir in enough remaining flour to form a soft dough.

2 Turn onto a floured surface; knead until smooth and elastic, about 6-8 minutes. Place in a greased bowl, turning once to grease top. Cover and let rise in a warm place until doubled, about 1 hour.

3 Punch dough down; roll out to a 15-in. x 10-in. rectangle. In a large bowl, beat filling ingredients until smooth. Spread over dough.

4 Roll up jelly-roll style, starting with a short side; seal seams. Cut into 12 slices. Place in a greased 13-in. x 9-in. baking pan. Cover and let rise in a warm place until doubled, about 30 minutes.

5 Combine topping ingredients; sprinkle over rolls. Bake at 350° for 35-40 minutes or until golden brown. Cool on a wire rack.

6 For icing, combine confectioners' sugar, extract and enough milk to achieve drizzling consistency; drizzle over rolls.

Lemon Cheese Braid Bread

PREP: 30 MIN. + RISING BAKE: 25 MIN. YIELD: 12-14 SERVINGS

GRACE DICKEY HILLSBORO, OREGON

This recipe came from my mom, who is an excellent cook. It always gets rave reviews. Although it's fairly simple to make, when you finish, you'll feel a sense of accomplishment because it tastes scrumptious and looks so impressive.

- 1 package (1/4 ounce) active dry yeast
- 3 tablespoons warm water (110° to 115°)
- 1/3 cup milk
- 1/4 cup sugar
- 1/4 cup butter, melted
- 2 eggs
- 1/2 teaspoon salt
- 3 to 3-1/2 cups all-purpose flour

FILLING:

- 2 packages (one 8 ounces, one 3 ounces) cream cheese, softened
- 1/2 cup sugar
- 1 egg
- 1 teaspoon grated lemon peel

ICING:

- 1/2 cup confectioners' sugar
- 1/4 teaspoon vanilla extract
- 2 to 3 teaspoons milk

1 In a large bowl, dissolve yeast in warm water. Add the milk, sugar, butter, eggs, salt and 2 cups flour; beat on low speed for 3 minutes. Stir in enough of remaining flour to form a soft dough.

2 Turn onto a floured surface; knead until smooth and elastic, about 6-8 minutes. Place in a greased bowl, turning once to grease top. Cover and let rise in a warm place until doubled, about 1 hour.

3 Meanwhile, in a small bowl, beat all the filling ingredients until fluffy; set aside.

4 Punch dough down. Turn onto a lightly floured surface; roll into a 14-in. x 12-in. rectangle. Place on a greased baking sheet. Spread filling down center third of rectangle. On each long side, cut 1-in.-wide strips, 3 in. into center. Starting at one end, fold alternating strips at an angle across filling. Seal end. Cover and let rise for 30 minutes.

5 Bake at 375° for 25-30 minutes or until golden brown. Cool on a wire rack. Combine confectioners' sugar, vanilla and enough milk to achieve drizzling consistency; drizzle over bread.

Apple Ladder Loaf

PREP: 70 MIN. + CHILLING   BAKE: 30 MIN.
YIELD: 2 LOAVES (10 SLICES EACH)

NORMA FOSTER COMPTON, ILLINOIS

I first served my family this rich bread with its spicy apple filling years ago. From the very first bite, it was a hit with everyone. Now I bake it often for church groups, potluck dinners and parties with friends. It makes a nice breakfast pastry or dessert with a scoop of ice cream.

        2 packages (1/4 ounce *each*) active dry yeast

    1/4 cup warm water (110° to 115°)

    1/2 cup warm milk (110° to 115°)

    3/4 cup butter, softened, *divided*

    1/3 cup sugar

        4 eggs

        1 teaspoon salt

  4-1/2 to 4-3/4 cups all-purpose flour

FILLING:

    1/3 cup packed brown sugar

        2 tablespoons all-purpose flour

  1-1/4 teaspoons ground cinnamon

    1/2 teaspoon ground nutmeg

    1/8 teaspoon ground allspice

        4 cups thinly sliced peeled tart apples

ICING:

        1 cup confectioners' sugar

        1 to 2 tablespoons orange juice

    1/4 teaspoon vanilla extract

1 In a large bowl, dissolve yeast in water. Add the milk, 1/2 cup butter, sugar, eggs, salt and 2 cups flour. Beat on low speed for 3 minutes. Stir in enough remaining flour to form a soft dough.

2 Turn onto a lightly floured surface; knead until smooth and elastic, about 6-8 minutes. Place in a greased bowl, turning once to grease top. Cover and refrigerate for 1-2 hours; punch dough down. Cover and refrigerate overnight.

3 Punch dough down. Turn onto a lightly floured surface; divide in half. Roll each half into a 12-in. x 9-in. rectangle. Place each on a greased baking sheet. Spread with remaining softened butter. For filling, combine the brown sugar, flour, cinnamon, nutmeg and allspice in a large bowl; add apples and toss to coat. Spread filling down center third of each rectangle.

4 On each long side, cut 1-in. wide strips about 3 in. into center. Starting at one end, fold alternating strips at an angle across filling; seal ends. Cover and let rise until nearly doubled, about 45-60 minutes.

5 Bake at 350° for 30-40 minutes or until golden brown. Combine icing ingredients until smooth; drizzle over warm loaves. Serve warm or at room temperature. Store in the refrigerator.

Onion-Beef Muffin Cups

PREP: 25 MIN. BAKE: 15 MIN. YIELD: 1 LOAF

BARBARA CARLUCCI ORANGE PARK, FLORIDA

A tube of refrigerated biscuits makes these delicious bites so quick and easy! They're one of my tried-and-true, great lunch recipes and always bring raves. In fact, I usually double the recipe just to be sure I have leftovers.

        3 medium onions, thinly sliced

    1/4 cup butter, cubed

        1 boneless beef top sirloin steak (1 inch thick and 6 ounces), cut into 1/8-inch slices

        1 teaspoon all-purpose flour

        1 teaspoon brown sugar

    1/4 teaspoon salt

    1/2 cup beef broth

        1 tube (16.3 ounces) large refrigerated flaky biscuits

    3/4 cup shredded part-skim mozzarella cheese

    1/3 cup grated Parmesan cheese, *divided*

1 In a large skillet, cook onions in butter over medium heat for 10-12 minutes or until very tender. Remove and keep warm. In the same skillet, cook steak for 2-3 minutes or until no longer pink.

1 teaspoon sugar

4 cups warm milk (110° to 115°)

1 cup molasses

1 cup packed brown sugar

1 cup canola oil

1 cup quick-cooking oats

2 tablespoons grated orange peel

1 tablespoon salt

1 teaspoon fennel seed

1 teaspoon aniseed

1 teaspoon caraway seeds

2 cups rye flour

11 to 12 cups all-purpose flour

1 In a large bowl, dissolve yeast in water; stir in sugar and let stand for 5 minutes. Add milk, molasses, brown sugar, oil, oats, orange peel, salt, fennel, aniseed, caraway, rye flour and 6 cups of all-purpose flour. Add enough remaining all-purpose flour to form a soft but sticky dough. Cover and let rise in a warm place overnight.

2 Punch dough down. Turn onto a floured surface; knead until smooth and elastic, about 6-8 minutes. Shape into four loaves. Place in greased 9-in. x 5-in. loaf pans. Cover and let rise until doubled, about 1 hour.

3 Bake at 350° for 35-45 minutes. Remove from the pans to cool on wire racks.

2 Return onions to pan. Stir in the flour, brown sugar and salt until blended; gradually add broth. Bring to a boil; cook and stir for 4-6 minutes or until thickened.

3 Separate biscuits; split each horizontally into three portions. Press onto the bottom and up the sides of eight ungreased muffin cups, overlapping the sides and tops. Fill each with about 2 tablespoons beef mixture.

4 Combine mozzarella cheese and 1/4 cup Parmesan cheese; sprinkle over filling. Fold dough over completely to enclose filling. Sprinkle with remaining Parmesan cheese.

5 Bake at 375° for 12-15 minutes or until golden brown. Let stand for 2 minutes before removing from pan. Serve warm.

Overnight Swedish Rye Bread

PREP: 30 MIN. + RISING BAKE: 35 MIN. YIELD: 4 LOAVES

CAROLINE CARR LYONS, NEBRASKA

I like this recipe because it allows me to bake bread early in the morning, leaving time for other things. We live in a Scandinavian area, so this bread hits the spot with family and friends.

2 packages (1/4 ounce *each*) active dry yeast

1/2 cup warm water (110° to 115°)

2 Turn onto a floured surface; knead until smooth and elastic, about 6-8 minutes. Place in a greased bowl, turning once to grease top. Cover and let rise in a warm place until doubled, about 1 hour.

3 Punch dough down. Turn onto a lightly floured surface; divide into thirds. Roll each portion into a 12-in. circle; spread each with filling. Cut each circle into 12 wedges.

4 Roll up wedges from the wide end and place point side down 2 in. apart on greased baking sheets. Curve ends to form a crescent. Cover and let rise until doubled, about 30 minutes.

5 Bake at 375° for 10-12 minutes or until lightly browned. Remove from pans to wire racks. Serve warm.

Editor's Note: This recipe was tested with Solo brand cake and pastry filling. Look for it in the baking aisle.

Cappuccino Muffins

PREP: 15 MIN. BAKE: 20 MIN.
YIELD: ABOUT 14 MUFFINS (1 CUP SPREAD)

JANICE BASSING RACINE, WISCONSIN

These are my favorite muffins to serve with a cup of coffee or a tall glass of cold milk. Not only are they great for breakfast, they make a tasty dessert or midnight snack. I get lots of recipe requests whenever I serve them. The espresso spread is also super on a bagel.

Almond-Filled Butterhorns

PREP: 30 MIN. + RISING BAKE: 10 MIN./BATCH YIELD: 3 DOZEN

LORAINE MEYER BEND, OREGON

I add potato flakes to make these butterhorns moist and tender. The rolls complement any meal with just the right sweetness to make them a coffee-hour favorite. Remember to hide a few for yourself!

> 3-1/4 teaspoons active dry yeast
> 2 cups warm milk (110° to 115°)
> 4 eggs
> 1 cup mashed potato flakes
> 1 cup butter, softened
> 1/2 cup sugar
> 1-1/8 teaspoons salt
> 7 to 8 cups all-purpose flour
> 1 can (12-1/2 ounces) almond cake and pastry filling

1 In a large bowl, dissolve yeast in milk. Add the eggs, potato flakes, butter, sugar, salt and 4 cups flour. Beat on medium speed for 3 minutes. Beat until smooth. Stir in enough remaining flour to form a soft dough (dough will be sticky).

ESPRESSO SPREAD:

- 4 ounces cream cheese, cubed
- 1 tablespoon sugar
- 1/2 teaspoon instant coffee granules
- 1/2 teaspoon vanilla extract
- 1/4 cup miniature semisweet chocolate chips

MUFFINS:

- 2 cups all-purpose flour
- 3/4 cup sugar
- 2-1/2 teaspoons baking powder
- 1 teaspoon ground cinnamon
- 1/2 teaspoon salt
- 1 cup milk
- 2 tablespoons instant coffee granules
- 1/2 cup butter, melted
- 1 egg
- 1 teaspoon vanilla extract
- 3/4 cup miniature semisweet chocolate chips

1 In a food processor or blender, combine the spread ingredients; cover and process until well blended. Transfer the espresso spread to a small bowl; cover and refrigerate until serving.

2 In a large bowl, combine flour, sugar, baking powder, cinnamon and salt. In another bowl, stir milk and coffee granules until coffee is dissolved. Add butter, egg and vanilla; mix well. Stir into dry ingredients just until moistened. Fold in chocolate chips.

3 Fill greased or paper-lined muffin cups two-thirds full. Bake at 375° for 17-20 minutes or until a toothpick comes out clean. Cool for 5 minutes before removing from pans to wire racks. Serve with espresso spread.

Caramel Pecan Rolls

PREP: 40 MIN. + RISING BAKE: 20 MIN. YIELD: 2 DOZEN

CAROLYN BUSCHKAMP EMMETSBURG, IOWA

These rolls rise nice and high and hold their shape, and the gooey caramel sauce is scrumptious.

- 2 cups milk
- 1/2 cup water
- 1/2 cup sugar
- 1/2 cup butter
- 1/3 cup cornmeal
- 2 teaspoons salt
- 7 to 7-1/2 cups all-purpose flour

- 2 packages (1/4 ounce *each*) active dry yeast
- 2 eggs

TOPPING:

- 2 cups packed brown sugar
- 1/2 cup butter
- 1/2 cup milk
- 1/2 to 1 cup chopped pecans

FILLING:

- 1/4 cup butter, softened
- 1/2 cup sugar
- 2 teaspoons ground cinnamon

1 In a saucepan, combine first six ingredients; bring to a boil, stirring frequently. Set aside to cool to 120°-130°. In a bowl, combine 2 cups flour and yeast. Add cooled cornmeal mixture; beat on low until smooth. Add eggs and 1 cup of flour; mix for 1 minute. Stir in enough remaining flour to form a soft dough.

2 Turn the dough onto a floured board; knead until smooth and elastic, about 6-8 minutes. Place in a greased bowl, turning once to grease top. Cover and let rise in a warm place until doubled, about 1 hour.

3 Combine the first three topping ingredients in a saucepan; bring to a boil, stirring occasionally. Pour into two greased 13-in. x 9-in. baking pans. Sprinkle with pecans; set aside.

4 Punch dough down; divide in half. Roll each into a 12-in. x 15-in. rectangle; spread with butter. Combine sugar and cinnamon; sprinkle over butter. Roll up dough from one long side; pinch seams and turn ends under. Cut each roll into 12 slices. Place 12 slices, cut side down, in each baking pan. Cover and let rise in a warm place until nearly doubled, about 30 minutes.

5 Bake at 375° for 20-25 minutes or until golden brown. Let cool 1 minute; invert onto a serving platter.

Eggnog Bread

PREP: 15 MIN. BAKE: 70 MIN. YIELD: 16 SERVINGS

RUTH BICKEL HICKORY, NORTH CAROLINA

Someone always asks for the recipe when I make this rich bread for the holidays or give it as gifts. It's a cinch to make and quite delicious. The bread is a traditional part of the season at my home here in the foothills of the Blue Ridge Mountains.

- 1/4 **cup butter, melted**
- 3/4 **cup sugar**
-   2 **eggs, beaten**
- 2-1/4 **cups all-purpose flour**
-   2 **teaspoons baking powder**
-   1 **teaspoon salt**
-   1 **cup eggnog**
- 1/2 **cup chopped pecans**
- 1/2 **cup raisins**
- 1/2 **cup chopped red and green candied cherries**

1   In a large bowl, combine butter, sugar and eggs; mix well. Combine the flour, baking powder and salt. Stir into butter mixture alternately with eggnog; mix only until dry ingredients are moistened. Fold in pecans, raisins and cherries.

2   Spoon into a greased 8-in. x 4-in. loaf pan. Bake at 350° for 70 minutes or until bread tests done.

Cream Cheese Coils

PREP: 30 MIN. + CHILLING BAKE: 10 MIN. YIELD: 1-1/2 DOZEN

SUSAN PECK REPUBLIC, MISSOURI

These are my absolute favorite sweet rolls! They never last long around my family. They're easy to make but look like you spent a lot of time on them.

- 3-3/4 **to 4-1/4 cups all-purpose flour**
- 3/4 **cup sugar, *divided***
-   2 **packages (1/4 ounce *each*) active dry yeast**
- 1-1/2 **teaspoons salt**
- 3/4 **cup milk**
- 1/2 **cup water**
- 1/2 **cup butter, cubed**
-   1 **egg**
-   1 **package (8 ounces) cream cheese, softened**
-   1 **egg yolk**
- 1/2 **teaspoon vanilla extract**

GLAZE:
-   1 **cup confectioners' sugar**
- 1/2 **teaspoon vanilla extract**
-   3 **to 4 teaspoons water**

1   In a large bowl, combine 1 cup flour, 1/2 cup sugar, yeast and salt. In a small saucepan, heat the milk, water and butter to 120°-130°. Add to the dry ingredients; beat on medium speed for 2 minutes. Add egg and 1/2 cup flour; beat on high for 2 minutes. Stir in enough remaining flour to form a stiff dough. Cover and refrigerate for 2 hours.

2   Turn dough onto a lightly floured surface; divide into 18 pieces. Shape each piece into a ball; roll each into a 15-in. rope. Holding one end of the rope, loosely wrap dough around, forming a coil. Tuck the end under; pinch to seal.

3 Place coils 2 in. apart on greased baking sheets. Cover and let rise until doubled, about 1 hour.

4 In a small bowl, beat the cream cheese, egg yolk, vanilla and remaining sugar until smooth. Using the back of a spoon, make a 1-in.-wide indentation in the center of each coil; spoon a round tablespoon of cream cheese mixture into each indentation.

5 Bake at 400° for 10-12 minutes or until lightly browned. Remove from pans to wire racks to cool.

6 In a small bowl, combine the confectioners' sugar, vanilla and enough water to achieve drizzling consistency. Drizzle over cooled rolls. Store in the refrigerator.

Marmalade Monkey Bread

PREP: 15 MIN. BAKE: 30 MIN. YIELD: 8 SERVINGS

DELIA KENNEDY DEER PARK, WASHINGTON

We love this pretty pull-apart bread, and company just raves about it. Because it uses refrigerated biscuits, it's so simple and quick to fix. You can try whatever jam you have on hand in place of the marmalade.

> 2/3 cup orange marmalade
> 1/2 cup chopped pecans *or* walnuts
> 1/4 cup honey
> 2 tablespoons butter, melted
> 2 tubes (7-1/2 ounces *each*) refrigerated buttermilk biscuits

1 In a small bowl, combine the marmalade, pecans, honey and butter. Cut each biscuit into four pieces. Layer half of the pieces in a greased 10-in. tube pan; top with half of the marmalade mixture. Repeat.

2 Bake at 375° for 27-30 minutes or until golden brown. Cool in pan for 5 minutes before inverting onto a serving plate. Serve warm.

Buttermilk Pan Rolls

PREP: 20 MIN. + RISING BAKE: 20 MIN. YIELD: 2 DOZEN

PATRICIA YOUNG BELLA VISTA, ARKANSAS

These wonderful rolls can be made very quickly. Hot, fresh rolls go well with just about any meal.

> 2 packages (1/4 ounce *each*) active dry yeast
> 1/4 cup warm water (110° to 115°)
> 1-1/2 cups warm buttermilk (110° to 115°)
> 1/2 cup canola oil
> 3 tablespoons sugar
> 4-1/2 cups all-purpose flour
> 1 teaspoon baking soda
> 1/2 teaspoon salt

1 In a large bowl, dissolve yeast in warm water. Add the buttermilk, oil and sugar. Combine the flour, baking soda and salt; add to yeast mixture and beat until smooth. Do not knead. Let stand for 10 minutes.

2 Turn dough onto a lightly floured surface; punch down. Shape into 24 balls and place in two greased 9-in. square baking pans. Cover and let rise in a warm place until doubled, about 30 minutes.

3 Bake at 400° for 20 minutes or until golden brown. Remove from pans to wire racks to cool.

Editor's Note: Warmed buttermilk will appear curdled.

 Yeast can be purchased in three ways. It can come dry in individual packets, in bulk or in cake (also known as fresh) form. Each 1/4-ounce package of active dry yeast equals 2-1/4 teaspoons, or one .6-ounce cake of fresh yeast.

Finnish Bread

PREP: 20 MIN. + RISING BAKE: 40 MIN.
YIELD: 2 LOAVES (12 SLICES EACH)

ARTHUR LUAMA RED LODGE, MONTANA

This recipe was brought over from Finland by pioneers who settled the area. We make this bread for a local festival that features foods from different countries.

    1 package (1/4 ounce) active dry yeast
    2 cups warm water (110° to 115°)
    1 cup whole wheat flour
  1/4 cup butter, melted, *divided*
    1 tablespoon brown sugar
    2 teaspoons salt
4-1/2 to 5 cups all-purpose flour

1   In a large bowl, dissolve yeast in water. Add whole wheat flour, 2 tablespoons of butter, brown sugar, salt and 2 cups of flour; beat until smooth. Add enough remaining flour to form a soft dough.

2   Turn onto a floured surface; knead until smooth and elastic, about 6-8 minutes. Place in a greased bowl, turning once to grease top. Cover and let rise in a warm place until doubled, about 1 hour.

3   Punch the dough down. Shape into two 6-in. rounds; place on a greased baking sheet. Cut slashes in top with a knife. Cover and let rise in a warm place until doubled, about 40 minutes.

4   Bake at 400° for 40-45 minutes or until golden brown. Brush with remaining butter.

Apple Streusel Muffins

PREP: 20 MIN. BAKE: 15 MIN. YIELD: 6 MUFFINS

ELIZABETH CALABRESE YUCAIPA, CALIFORNIA

I was looking for something warm to make for my daughter before school on a rainy morning. So I jazzed up a boxed muffin mix with a chopped apple, walnuts, brown sugar and a fast-to-fix vanilla glaze. The tasty results really hit the spot.

    1 package (6-1/2 ounces) apple cinnamon muffin mix
    1 large tart apple, peeled and diced
  1/3 cup chopped walnuts
    3 tablespoons brown sugar
4-1/2 teaspoons all-purpose flour
    1 tablespoon butter, melted

GLAZE:
  3/4 cup confectioners' sugar
  1/2 teaspoon vanilla extract
    1 to 2 tablespoons milk

1   Prepare muffin mix according to package directions; fold in apple. Fill greased muffin cups three-fourths full. In a small bowl, combine the walnuts, brown sugar, flour and butter; sprinkle over batter.

2   Bake at 400° for 15-20 minutes or until a toothpick comes out clean. Cool for 5 minutes before removing from pan to a wire rack.

3   In a small bowl, combine the confectioners' sugar, vanilla and enough milk to achieve desired consistency; drizzle over warm muffins. Serve warm.

Editor's Note: This recipe was tested with Betty Crocker apple cinnamon muffin mix.

LORI JAMESON
WALLA WALLA,
WASHINGTON

Its pretty braided shape and pleasant dill flavor distinguish this golden brown loaf from other yeast breads. My family loves to eat it alongside soup, roast beef or pot roast. I almost always make two loaves because one just isn't enough!

Dill Seed Braid

PREP: 25 MIN. + RISING BAKE: 35 MIN. YIELD: 1 LOAF

1 package (1/4 ounce)
  active dry yeast

1/4 cup warm water
  (110° to 115°)

1 cup plain yogurt

1 small onion, finely
  chopped

1/4 cup sugar

2 tablespoons butter,
  softened

1 egg

1 tablespoon dill seed

1 teaspoon salt

3 to 3-1/2 cups all-purpose
  flour

1 In a large bowl, dissolve yeast in warm water. Add the yogurt, onion, sugar, butter, egg, dill seed, salt and 1 cup flour. Beat until smooth. Stir in enough remaining flour to form a soft dough.

2 Turn onto a floured surface; knead until smooth and elastic, about 6-8 minutes. Place in a greased bowl, turning once to grease top. Cover and let rise in a warm place until doubled, about 1 hour.

3 Punch dough down. Turn onto a lightly floured surface; divide into thirds. Shape each portion into a 20-in. rope. Place ropes on a large greased baking sheet and braid; pinch ends to seal and tuck under. Cover and let rise until doubled, about 30 minutes.

4 Bake at 350° for 35-40 minutes or until golden brown. Remove from pan to a wire rack to cool.

Parmesan Herb Loaf

PREP: 15 MIN. BAKE: 30 MIN. YIELD: 1 LOAF (4 WEDGES)

DIANNE CULLEY NESBIT, MISSISSIPPI

This moist loaf is one of my very best quick bread recipes. I like to serve slices accompanied by individual ramekins filled with extra virgin olive oil infused with herbs for dipping.

1-1/4	cups all-purpose flour
3	tablespoons plus 1 teaspoon grated Parmesan cheese, *divided*
1-1/2	teaspoons sugar
1-1/2	teaspoons dried minced onion
1-1/4	teaspoons Italian seasoning, *divided*
1/2	teaspoon baking soda
1/4	teaspoon salt
1/2	cup sour cream
2	tablespoons plus 2 teaspoons 2% milk
4-1/2	teaspoons butter, melted
1	egg white, lightly beaten

1   In a small bowl, combine the flour, 3 tablespoons Parmesan cheese, sugar, onion, 1 teaspoon Italian seasoning, baking soda and salt. In another bowl, combine the sour cream, milk and butter. Stir into dry ingredients just until moistened.

2   Turn onto a floured surface; knead for 1 minute. Shape into a round loaf; place on a baking sheet coated with cooking spray. With scissors, cut a 1/4-in.-deep cross in top of loaf.

3   Brush with egg white. Sprinkle with remaining cheese and Italian seasoning. Bake at 350° for 30-35 minutes or until golden brown. Serve warm.

Cardamom Braids

PREP: 25 MIN. + RISING BAKE: 25 MIN.
YIELD: 2 LOAVES (16 SLICES EACH)

WALTER DUST RAPID CITY, MICHIGAN

This is an old recipe that I like to make for breakfast. The bread is great for dunking in a cup of coffee.

1	package (1/4 ounce) active dry yeast
1-1/2	cups warm milk (110° to 115°), *divided*
1	cup sugar, *divided*
3	eggs yolks, lightly beaten
1/2	cup butter, softened
1	tablespoon ground cardamom
1/2	teaspoon salt
5	to 6 cups all-purpose flour
2	tablespoons milk

1   In a large bowl, dissolve yeast in 1/2 cup warm milk. Add 3/4 cup sugar, egg yolks, butter, cardamom, salt, 3 cups of flour and remaining warm milk; beat until smooth. Stir in enough remaining flour to form a soft dough.

2   Turn onto a floured surface; knead until smooth and elastic, about 6-8 minutes. Place in a greased bowl, turning once to grease top. Cover and let rise in a warm place until doubled, about 1-1/4 hours.

3   Punch dough down; divide into six pieces. Shape each piece into a 16-in. rope. Place three ropes on a greased baking sheet; braid. Pinch ends firmly and tuck under. Repeat with remaining three ropes on another baking sheet. Cover and let rise until doubled, about 45 minutes.

4   Brush braids with milk and sprinkle with remaining sugar. Bake at 350° for 25-30 minutes or until golden brown. Remove to wire racks to cool.

Herbed Dinner Rolls

PREP: 20 MIN. + RISING BAKE: 15 MIN. YIELD: 16 ROLLS

DANA LOWRY HICKORY, NORTH CAROLINA

After I had my sixth child, a friend dropped off dinner and these rolls, which start in a bread machine. They were so delicious that I quickly bought my own machine so I could make them myself.

- 1 cup water (70° to 80°)
- 2 tablespoons butter, softened
- 1 egg
- 1/4 cup sugar
- 1 teaspoon salt
- 1/2 teaspoon *each* dried basil, oregano, thyme and rosemary, crushed
- 3-1/4 cups bread flour
- 2-1/4 teaspoons active dry yeast

Additional butter, melted

Coarse salt, optional

1 In a bread machine pan, place the water, butter, egg, sugar, salt, seasonings, flour and yeast in order suggested by manufacturer. Select dough setting (check dough after 5 minutes of mixing; add 1 to 2 tablespoons of water or flour if needed).

2 When cycle is completed, turn dough onto a lightly floured surface. Divide dough into 16 portions; shape each into a ball. Place 2 in. apart on greased baking sheets. Cover and let rise in a warm place until doubled, about 30 minutes.

3 Bake at 375° for 12-15 minutes or until golden brown. If desired, brush with butter and sprinkle with coarse salt. Remove from pans to wire racks.

Editor's Note: We recommend you do not use a bread machine's time-delay feature for this recipe.

Italian Parmesan Bread

PREP: 20 MIN. + RISING BAKE: 35 MIN. YIELD: 1 LOAF

FRANCES POSTE WALL, SOUTH DAKOTA

When my grown children come home for visits, they ask me to make this bread and their favorite spaghetti dinner.

- 1 package (1/4 ounce) active dry yeast
- 1 cup warm water (110° to 115°)
- 3 cups all-purpose flour, *divided*
- 1/4 cup butter, softened
- 1 egg, beaten
- 2 tablespoons sugar
- 1 teaspoon salt
- 1-1/2 teaspoons dried minced onion
- 1/2 teaspoon Italian seasoning
- 1/2 teaspoon garlic salt
- 1/2 cup grated Parmesan cheese, *divided*

Additional butter, melted

1 In a large bowl, dissolve yeast in warm water. Add 2 cups flour, 1/4 cup butter, egg, sugar, salt and seasonings. Beat at low speed until mixed, about 30 seconds; increase speed to medium and continue beating for 2 minutes. Stir in remaining flour and 1/3 cup cheese; beat until smooth.

2 Cover bowl and let rise in a warm place until doubled, about 1 hour. Stir batter 25 strokes. Spread batter into a greased, round 1-1/2-qt. casserole dish; brush with melted butter and sprinkle with the remaining cheese. Cover and let rise until doubled, about 30 minutes.

3 Bake at 350° for 35 minutes or until golden brown. Cool on wire rack 10 minutes before removing from dish.

Multigrain Bread

PREP: 10 MIN. BAKE: 3-4 HOURS YIELD: 1 LOAF (2 POUNDS)

MICHELE MACKINLAY MADOC, ONTARIO

It's hard to get a good whole grain bread where I live, so my bread machine comes in very handy when making this hearty loaf. I adapted it from an old recipe, and I've been enjoying it ever since. Cornmeal and wheat germ give it a wonderful texture and nutty flavor I love.

- 1 cup water (70° to 80°)
- 2 tablespoons canola oil
- 2 egg yolks
- 1/4 cup molasses
- 1 teaspoon salt
- 1-1/2 cups bread flour
- 1 cup whole wheat flour
- 1/2 cup rye flour
- 1/2 cup nonfat dry milk powder
- 1/4 cup quick-cooking oats
- 1/4 cup toasted wheat germ
- 1/4 cup cornmeal
- 2-1/4 teaspoons active dry yeast

1 In bread machine pan, place all ingredients in order suggested by manufacturer. Select basic bread setting. Choose crust color and loaf size if available.

2 Bake according to bread machine directions (check dough after 5 minutes of mixing; add 1 to 2 tablespoons water or flour if needed).

Editor's Note: We recommend you do not use a bread machine's time-delay feature for this recipe.

Pumpkin Chip Muffins

PREP: 10 MIN. BAKE: 15 MIN. + COOLING
YIELD: ABOUT 2 DOZEN MUFFINS

CINDY MIDDLETON CHAMPION, ALBERTA

I started cooking and baking at a young age, just like my sisters and brothers. Our mother was a great teacher in the kitchen. Now, I've passed on the same lessons to my kids!

- 4 eggs
- 2 cups sugar
- 1 can (15 ounces) solid-pack pumpkin
- 1-1/2 cups canola oil
- 3 cups all-purpose flour
- 2 teaspoons baking soda
- 1 teaspoon baking powder
- 1 teaspoon ground cinnamon
- 1 teaspoon salt
- 2 cups (12 ounces) semisweet chocolate chips

1 In a large bowl, beat the eggs, sugar, pumpkin and oil until smooth. Combine the flour, baking soda, baking powder, cinnamon and salt; gradually add to pumpkin mixture and mix well. Fold in chocolate chips. Fill greased or paper-lined muffin cups three-fourths full.

2 Bake at 400° for 15-18 minutes or until a toothpick inserted near the center comes out clean. Cool in pan 10 minutes before removing to a wire rack.

Surprise Sausage Bundles

PREP: 45 MIN. + RISING BAKE: 20 MIN. YIELD: 16 SERVINGS

BARB RUIS GRANDVILLE, MICHIGAN

Kielbasa and sauerkraut star in a tasty filling for these scrumptious stuffed rolls, which make a great dinner with soup or salad.

- 6 bacon strips, diced
- 1 cup chopped onion
- 1 can (16 ounces) sauerkraut, rinsed and well drained
- 1/2 pound smoked kielbasa *or* Polish sausage, coarsely chopped
- 2 tablespoons brown sugar
- 1/2 teaspoon garlic salt
- 1/4 teaspoon caraway seeds
- 1/8 teaspoon pepper
- 1 package (16 ounces) hot roll mix
- 2 eggs
- 1 cup warm water (120° to 130°)
- 2 tablespoons butter, softened

Poppy seeds

1. In a large skillet, cook bacon until crisp; remove to paper towels. Reserve 2 tablespoons drippings. Saute onion in drippings until tender. Stir in the sauerkraut, sausage, brown sugar, garlic salt, caraway and pepper. Cook and stir for 5 minutes. Remove from the heat; add bacon. Set aside to cool.

2. In a large bowl, combine contents of the roll mix and yeast packets. Stir in one egg, water and butter to form a soft dough. Turn onto a floured surface; knead until smooth and elastic, about 5 minutes. Cover dough with a large bowl; let stand for 5 minutes.

3. Divide dough into 16 pieces. On a floured surface, roll out each piece into a 4-in. circle. Top each with 1/4 cup filling. Fold dough around filling, forming a ball; pinch edges to seal. Place seam side down on greased baking sheets. Cover loosely with plastic wrap that has been coated with cooking spray. Let rise in a warm place for 15 minutes.

4. Beat remaining egg; brush over bundles. Sprinkle with poppy seeds. Bake at 350° for 16-17 minutes or until golden brown. Serve warm.

Maple Oatmeal Bread

PREP: 20 MIN. + RISING BAKE: 40 MIN. YIELD: 2 LOAVES

MARIAN TOBIN UNDERHILL, VERMONT

This is one of my favorite recipes, especially since it features maple syrup. Vermont produces more maple syrup than any other state.

- 1 cup hot brewed coffee
- 3/4 cup boiling water
- 1/2 cup maple syrup
- 1/3 cup canola oil
- 1 cup old-fashioned oats
- 1/2 cup sugar
- 2 teaspoons salt
- 2 packages (1/4 ounce *each*) active dry yeast
- 1/4 cup warm water (110° to 115°)
- 2 eggs, lightly beaten
- 5-1/2 to 6 cups bread flour

1. In a bowl, combine the first seven ingredients. Cool to 110°-115°.

2. In a large bowl, dissolve yeast in warm water. Add the oat mixture, eggs and 2 cups flour; mix well. Stir in enough remaining flour to form a soft dough.

3. Turn onto a floured surface; knead until smooth and elastic, about 6-8 minutes. Place in a greased bowl, turning once to grease top. Cover and let rise in a warm place until doubled, about 1 hour.

4. Punch dough down. Turn onto a lightly floured surface; divide in half. Shape into loaves. Place in two greased 9-in. x 5-in. loaf pans. Cover and let rise until doubled, about 30 minutes.

5. Bake at 350° for 40-45 minutes or until golden brown. Remove from pans to wire racks to cool.

Savory Italian Rounds

PREP/TOTAL TIME: 30 MIN. YIELD: 10 SERVINGS

DONNA EBERT RICHFIELD, WISCONSIN

A friend gave me the recipe for these cheesy golden rounds years ago. She said her dad used to make them for her when she was little. Because they're a snap to put together, I frequently fix them for my family during the week…and for company on the weekends.

> 2/3 cup grated Parmesan cheese
> 1/2 cup mayonnaise
> 1/4 teaspoon dried basil
> 1/8 teaspoon garlic powder
> 1/8 teaspoon garlic salt
> 1/8 teaspoon dried oregano

Dash onion salt

> 1 tube (12 ounces) refrigerated buttermilk biscuits

1 In a small bowl, combine the first seven ingredients. Separate biscuits and place on two ungreased baking sheets. Let stand for 5 minutes.

2 Flatten biscuits into 4-in. circles. Spread about 1 tablespoon mayonnaise mixture over each circle to within 1/2 in. of edge.

3 Bake at 400° for 10-13 minutes or until golden brown. Serve warm.

Editor's Note: Reduced-fat or fat-free mayonnaise is not recommended for this recipe.

Creole Corn Bread

PREP: 15 MIN. BAKE: 45 MIN. YIELD: 12 SERVINGS

ENID HEBERT LAFAYETTE, LOUISIANA

Corn bread is a staple of Cajun and Creole cuisine. This is an old favorite that I found in the bottom of my recipe drawer, and it really tastes wonderful.

> 2 cups cooked rice
> 1 cup yellow cornmeal
> 1/2 cup chopped onion
> 1 to 2 tablespoons seeded chopped jalapeno pepper
> 1 teaspoon salt
> 1/2 teaspoon baking soda
> 2 eggs
> 1 cup milk
> 1/4 cup canola oil
> 1 can (16-1/2 ounces) cream-style corn
> 3 cups (12 ounces) shredded cheddar cheese

Additional cornmeal

1 In a large bowl, combine rice, cornmeal, onion, jalapeno, salt and baking soda.

2 In another bowl, beat eggs, milk and oil. Add corn; mix well. Stir into rice mixture until blended. Fold in cheese. Sprinkle a well-greased 10-in. ovenproof skillet with cornmeal. Pour batter into skillet.

3 Bake at 350° for 45-50 minutes or until bread tests done. Cut into wedges and serve warm.

Editor's Note: When cutting hot peppers, disposable gloves are recommended. Avoid touching your face.

Pecan Pie Mini Muffins

PREP: 10 MIN. BAKE: 25 MIN. YIELD: ABOUT 2-1/2 DOZEN

PAT SCHRAND ENTERPRISE, ALABAMA

While these are delicious year-round, you could easily turn them into an edible Christmas gift. They look festive on a decorative tray wrapped in red or green cellophane or tucked into a cookie plate. And don't forget to include the recipe so your recipient can enjoy this treat over and over again.

    1 cup packed brown sugar
  1/2 cup all-purpose flour
    1 cup chopped pecans
  2/3 cup butter, melted
    2 eggs, lightly beaten

1 In a large bowl, combine the brown sugar, flour and pecans; set aside. Combine butter and eggs. Stir into brown sugar mixture.

2 Fill greased and floured miniature muffin cups two-thirds full. Bake at 350° for 22-25 minutes or until a toothpick inserted near the center comes out clean. Immediately remove from pans to wire racks to cool.

Bacon-Onion Crescent Buns

PREP: 40 MIN. + RISING BAKE: 15 MIN. YIELD: 4 DOZEN

HELEN WILSON SAN BENITO, TEXAS

These savory crescents are a hit with everyone. They're very tasty served alongside many main dishes as well as for brunch. I like them warm with soft butter.

4-3/4 to 5-1/4 cups all-purpose flour
  1/2 cup sugar

---

    1 package (1/4 ounce) active dry yeast
  1/2 teaspoon salt
    1 cup milk
  1/2 cup butter, cubed
  1/2 teaspoon caraway seeds
    3 eggs
    1 pound sliced bacon, diced
    1 small onion, finely chopped
  1/8 teaspoon white pepper
    2 tablespoons water

1 In a large bowl, combine 2 cups flour, sugar, yeast and salt. In a small saucepan, heat the milk and butter to 120°-130°. Add to dry ingredients; beat on medium speed for 2 minutes. Add caraway seeds and 2 eggs; beat until smooth. Stir in enough remaining flour to form a stiff dough.

2 Turn onto a floured surface; knead until smooth and elastic, about 6-8 minutes. Place in a greased bowl, turning once to grease top. Cover and let rise in a warm place until doubled, about 1 hour.

3 Meanwhile, in a large skillet, cook bacon over medium heat until crisp. Remove with a slotted spoon to paper towels. Saute onion in the drippings; remove onion with a slotted spoon and set aside. When cool, combine the bacon, onion and pepper; set aside.

4 Punch dough down. Turn onto a lightly floured surface; divided into four portions. Roll each into a 12-in. circle; cut into 12 wedges. Sprinkle a heaping teaspoonful of bacon mixture over each wedge. Roll up from the wide end. Place point end down 2 in. part on greased baking sheets. Cover and let rise, about 30 minutes.

5 In a small bowl, beat water and remaining egg; brush over rolls. Bake at 350° for 12-14 minutes or until golden brown. Refrigerate leftovers.

Garlic Parmesan Breadsticks

PREP: 25 MIN. + RISING BAKE: 20 MIN. YIELD: 4 DOZEN

BARBARA GROSS WARDEN, WASHINGTON

I receive many compliments when I make these delicious breadsticks. I've passed the recipe on to a number of family members and friends.

- 1 tablespoon active dry yeast
- 1-1/2 cups warm water (110° to 115°)
- 2 tablespoons sugar
- 3/4 cup butter, melted, *divided*
- 1/2 teaspoon salt
- 4-1/2 cups all-purpose flour

Garlic salt

Grated Parmesan cheese

Marinara *or* spaghetti sauce, warmed, optional

1. In a bowl, dissolve yeast in water. Add sugar; let stand for 5 minutes. Add 1/2 cup butter, salt and 2 cups flour; beat until smooth. Stir in enough remaining flour to form a soft dough. Turn onto a floured surface; knead until smooth and elastic, about 6-8 minutes. Place in a greased bowl, turning once to grease top. Cover and let rise in a warm place until doubled, about 45 minutes.

2. Punch dough down. Turn onto a lightly floured surface; roll into a 24-in. x 10-in. rectangle. Cut dough in half lengthwise, then into 5-in. x 1-in. strips. Twist each strip and place 2 in. apart on greased baking sheets.

3. Brush strips with remaining butter; sprinkle with garlic salt and Parmesan cheese. Cover and let rise in a warm place until doubled, about 20 minutes.

4. Bake at 350° for 20 minutes or until golden brown. Remove from pans to wire racks. If desired, serve with marinara or spaghetti sauce for dipping.

Pizza Loaf

PREP: 20 MIN. BAKE: 35 MIN. YIELD: 10-12 SLICES

JENNY BROWN WEST LAFAYETTE, INDIANA

This savory stromboli relies on frozen bread dough, so it comes together in no time. The golden loaf is stuffed with cheese, pepperoni, mushrooms, peppers and olives. I often add a few slices of ham, too. It's tasty served with warm pizza sauce for dipping.

- 1 loaf (1 pound) frozen bread dough, thawed
- 2 eggs, *separated*
- 1 tablespoon grated Parmesan cheese
- 1 tablespoon olive oil
- 1 teaspoon minced fresh parsley
- 1 teaspoon dried oregano
- 1/2 teaspoon garlic powder
- 1/4 teaspoon pepper
- 8 ounces sliced pepperoni
- 2 cups (8 ounces) shredded part-skim mozzarella cheese
- 1 can (4 ounces) mushroom stems and pieces, drained
- 1/4 to 1/2 cup pickled pepper rings
- 1 medium green pepper, diced
- 1 can (2-1/4 ounces) sliced ripe olives
- 1 can (15 ounces) pizza sauce

1. On a greased baking sheet, roll out dough into a 15-in. x 10-in. rectangle. In a small bowl, combine the egg yolks, Parmesan cheese, oil, parsley, oregano, garlic powder and pepper. Brush over the dough.

2. Sprinkle with the pepperoni, mozzarella cheese, mushrooms, pepper rings, green pepper and olives. Roll up jelly-roll style, starting with a long side; pinch seam to seal and tuck ends under.

3. Place seam side down; brush with egg whites. Do not let rise. Bake at 350° for 35-40 minutes or until golden brown. Warm the pizza sauce; serve with sliced loaf.

PB&J Spirals

PREP/TOTAL TIME: 30 MIN. YIELD: 8 SERVINGS

LISA RENSHAW KANSAS CITY, MISSOURI

Kids young and old love these peanut butter and jelly treats. Using refrigerated crescent roll dough, they're a fun snack for hungry youngsters to assemble. Parents just have to help with the baking. Plus, they're easy to vary using different jelly flavors and nuts to suit each child's taste.

- 1 tube (8 ounces) refrigerated crescent rolls
- 8 teaspoons creamy peanut butter
- 8 teaspoons grape jelly
- 1/4 cup chopped unsalted peanuts
- 2 tablespoons confectioners' sugar

1. Unroll crescent dough; separate into triangles. Spread 1 teaspoon each of peanut butter and jelly on the wide end of each triangle; sprinkle with peanuts. Roll up from the wide end and place point side down 2 in. apart on an ungreased baking sheet. Curve ends to form a crescent shape.

2. Bake at 375° for 11-13 minutes or until lightly browned. Dust with confectioners' sugar. Serve warm.

Southern Banana Nut Bread

PREP: 15 MIN. BAKE: 45 MIN. + COOLING YIELD: 2 LOAVES

VIVA FORMAN TALLAHASSEE, FLORIDA

One day I had two ripe bananas and decided to make banana bread. I found this recipe in an old church recipe book. It really is good with pecans in the bread and in the topping, which makes it unique.

- 1/2 cup butter-flavored shortening
- 1-1/2 cups sugar
- 2 eggs
- 1 cup mashed ripe bananas (about 2 medium)
- 1 teaspoon vanilla extract
- 2 cups self-rising flour
- 1/2 cup buttermilk
- 3/4 cup chopped pecans

TOPPING:
- 1/4 to 1/3 cup mashed ripe bananas
- 1-1/4 cups confectioners' sugar
- 1 teaspoon lemon juice

Additional chopped pecans

1. In a large bowl, cream shortening and sugar until light and fluffy. Beat in eggs. Blend in bananas and vanilla. Add flour alternately with buttermilk, beating well after each addition. Fold in pecans.

2. Pour into two greased 8-in. x 4-in. loaf pans. Bake at 350° for 45-55 minutes or until a toothpick inserted near the center comes out clean. Cool in pan for 10 minutes before removing to a wire rack; cool completely.

3. For topping, combine the banana, confectioners' sugar and lemon juice; spread over loaves. Sprinkle with pecans.

Editor's Note: As a substitute for each cup of self-rising flour, place 1-1/2 teaspoons baking powder and 1/2 teaspoon salt in a measuring cup. Add all-purpose flour to measure 1 cup.

zucchini crescent pie, p. 154

Bright, cheerful mornings are the perfect reason to make these home-spun breakfasts. You'll find everything from rich and filling hot dishes to baked goods.

breakfast & brunch

2. Knead on a floured surface until smooth, about 6-8 minutes. Place in a bowl coated with cooking spray; turn once to coat top. Cover and let rise until doubled, about 1 hour.

3. Combine the walnuts, cherries, brown sugar and cinnamon; set aside. Punch dough down; roll into an 18-in. x 12-in. rectangle. Brush with butter; sprinkle with nut mixture to within 1/2 in. of edges. Roll up tightly, jelly-roll style, starting with a long side; seal ends.

4. Place seam side down on a 14-in. pizza pan coated with cooking spray; pinch ends together to form a ring. With scissors, cut from outside edge two-thirds of the way toward center of ring at scant 1-in. intervals. Separate strips slightly; twist so filling shows. Cover and let rise until doubled, about 40 minutes.

5. Bake at 400° for 20-25 minutes or until golden brown. Cool on a wire rack. Combine icing ingredients; drizzle over ring.

Swedish Tea Ring

PREP: 30 MIN. + RISING BAKE: 20 MIN. + COOLING
YIELD: 1 RING (24 SLICES)

ELSIE EPP NEWTON, KANSAS

My mother used to prepare this delightful tea ring in the 1940s, and it's still a favorite today. Maraschino cherries add a festive touch.

- 1 tablespoon active dry yeast
- 1-1/2 cups warm water (110° to 115°)
- 1/4 cup sugar
- 1/4 cup canola oil
- 2 egg whites, lightly beaten
- 1-1/4 teaspoons salt
- 5-1/2 to 6 cups all-purpose flour
- 1/2 cup chopped walnuts
- 1/2 cup chopped maraschino cherries, patted dry
- 1/4 cup packed brown sugar
- 1 teaspoon ground cinnamon
- 2 tablespoons butter, melted

ICING:
- 1 cup confectioners' sugar
- 1 to 2 tablespoons fat-free milk

1. In a large bowl, dissolve the yeast in warm water. Add the sugar, oil, egg whites, salt and 1 cup flour; beat until smooth. Stir in enough remaining flour to form a soft dough.

Pumpkin Scones With Berry Butter

PREP: 25 MIN. + CHILLING BAKE: 15 MIN.
YIELD: 8 SCONES (ABOUT 1/2 CUP BERRY BUTTER)

JUDY WILSON SUN CITY WEST, ARIZONA

These delightful scones are perfect on a cold winter day with a steaming hot cup of coffee. They also make a wonderful hostess gift arranged in a basket.

- 2 tablespoons dried cranberries
- 1/2 cup boiling water
- 1/2 cup butter, softened
- 3 tablespoons confectioners' sugar

DOUGH:

- 2-1/4 cups all-purpose flour
- 1/4 cup packed brown sugar
- 2 teaspoons baking powder
- 1-1/2 teaspoons pumpkin pie spice
- 1/4 teaspoon salt
- 1/4 teaspoon baking soda
- 1/2 cup cold butter
- 1 egg
- 1/2 cup canned pumpkin
- 1/3 cup milk
- 2 tablespoons chopped pecans, optional

1 Place cranberries in a small bowl; add boiling water. Let stand for 5 minutes; drain and chop. In a small bowl, beat butter until light and fluffy. Add confectioners' sugar and cranberries; mix well. Cover and refrigerate for at least 1 hour.

2 In a large bowl, combine the flour, brown sugar, baking powder, pie spice, salt and baking soda. Cut in butter until mixture resembles coarse crumbs. In a small bowl, whisk the egg, pumpkin and milk; add to crumb mixture just until moistened. Stir in pecans if desired.

3 Turn dough onto a floured surface; knead 10 times. Pat into an 8-in. circle. Cut into eight wedges; separate wedges and place on a greased baking sheet.

4 Bake at 400° for 12-15 minutes or until golden brown. Serve warm with berry butter.

Strawberry Rhubarb Coffee Cake

PREP: 45 MIN. BAKE: 40 MIN. YIELD: 16-20 SERVINGS

DOROTHY MOREHOUSE MASSENA, NEW YORK

Although my coffee cake makes a large pan, it never lasts very long! It's great for a Sunday brunch after church and nice to bring to family reunions, too.

FILLING:

- 3 cups sliced fresh *or* frozen rhubarb (1-inch pieces)
- 1 quart fresh strawberries, mashed
- 2 tablespoons lemon juice
- 1 cup sugar
- 1/3 cup cornstarch

CAKE:

- 3 cups all-purpose flour
- 1 cup sugar

- 1 teaspoon baking powder
- 1 teaspoon baking soda
- 1/2 teaspoon salt
- 1 cup butter, cut into pieces
- 1-1/2 cups buttermilk
- 2 eggs
- 1 teaspoon vanilla extract

TOPPING:

- 1/4 cup butter
- 3/4 cup all-purpose flour
- 3/4 cup sugar

1 In a large saucepan, combine rhubarb, strawberries and lemon juice. Cover and cook over medium heat about 5 minutes. Combine sugar and cornstarch; stir into saucepan. Bring to a boil, cook and stir for 2 minutes or until thickened. Remove from the heat and set aside.

2 For cake, in a large bowl, combine flour, sugar, baking powder, baking soda and salt. Cut in butter until mixture resembles coarse crumbs. Beat buttermilk, eggs and vanilla; stir into crumb mixture.

3 Spread half of the batter evenly into a greased 13-in. x 9-in. baking dish. Carefully spread filling on top. Drop remaining batter by tablespoonfuls over filling.

4 For topping, melt butter in a saucepan over low heat. Remove from heat; stir in flour and sugar until mixture resembles coarse crumbs. Sprinkle over batter. Lay foil on lower rack to catch any juice fruit spillovers.

5 Place coffee cake on middle rack; bake at 350° for 40-45 minutes. Cool in pan. Cut into squares.

Apple-Bacon Egg Bake

PREP: 15 MIN. BAKE: 30 MIN. YIELD: 2 SERVINGS

NANCY MILLER BETTENDORF, IOWA

I wanted an inexpensive, healthy egg dish for Sunday brunch, so I came up with this recipe. It's hearty and delicious, and the apples give it a slight sweetness.

- 3 eggs
- 1 small apple, diced
- 3/4 cup frozen O'Brien potatoes, thawed
- 1/3 cup 2% milk
- 1/3 cup sour cream
- 1/3 cup shredded cheddar cheese, *divided*
- 3 bacon strips, cooked and crumbled, *divided*

Dash salt and pepper

1. In a small bowl, beat the eggs. Stir in the apple, hash browns, milk, sour cream, 3 tablespoons cheese, 1 tablespoon bacon, salt and pepper.

2. Pour into two 2-cup baking dishes coated with cooking spray. Sprinkle with remaining cheese and bacon.

3. Bake, uncovered, at 350° for 30-35 minutes or until a knife inserted near the center comes out clean.

Asparagus Sausage Crepes

PREP: 20 MIN. BAKE: 20 MIN. YIELD: 8 SERVINGS

LISA HANSON GLENVIEW, ILLINOIS

This was my favorite recipe when I was growing up in western Michigan, where asparagus is a big spring crop. With its sausage-and-cheese filling, tender asparagus and rich sour cream topping, this pretty dish will impress guests.

- 1 pound bulk pork sausage
- 1 small onion, chopped
- 1 package (3 ounces) cream cheese, cubed
- 1/2 cup shredded Monterey Jack cheese
- 1/4 teaspoon dried marjoram
- 1 cup milk
- 3 eggs
- 1 tablespoon canola oil
- 1 cup all-purpose flour
- 1/2 teaspoon salt
- 32 fresh asparagus spears (about 1 pound), trimmed

TOPPING:
- 1/4 cup butter, softened
- 1/2 cup sour cream

1. In a large skillet, cook sausage and onion over medium heat until sausage is no longer pink; drain. Stir in the cream cheese, Monterey Jack cheese and marjoram; set aside.

2. In a large bowl, combine the milk, eggs and oil. Combine flour and salt; add to milk mixture and mix well. Cover and refrigerate for 1 hour.

3. Heat a lightly greased 8-in. nonstick skillet over medium heat; pour 2 tablespoons batter into the center of skillet. Lift and tilt pan to coat bottom evenly. Cook until top

appears dry; turn and cook 15-20 seconds longer. Remove to a wire rack. Repeat with remaining batter, greasing skillet as needed. When cool, stack crepes with waxed paper or paper towels in between.

4   Spoon 2 tablespoons of the sausage mixture onto the center of each crepe. Top with two asparagus spears. Roll up; place in two greased 13-in. x 9-in. baking dishes.

5   Cover and bake at 375° for 15 minutes. Combine the butter and sour cream; spoon over crepes. Bake 5 minutes longer or until heated through.

Pull-Apart Caramel Coffee Cake

PREP: 10 MIN. BAKE: 25 MIN. YIELD: 12 SERVINGS

JAIME KEELING KEIZER, OREGON

The first time I made this delightful breakfast treat for a brunch party, it was a huge hit. Now I get requests every time family or friends do anything around the breakfast hour! I always keep the four simple ingredients on hand.

  2   tubes (12 ounces *each*) refrigerated flaky buttermilk biscuits
  1   cup packed brown sugar
1/2   cup heavy whipping cream
  1   teaspoon ground cinnamon

1   Cut each biscuit into four pieces; arrange evenly in a 10-in. fluted tube pan coated with cooking spray. Combine the brown sugar, cream and cinnamon; pour over biscuits.

2   Bake at 350° for 25-30 minutes or until golden brown. Cool for 5 minutes before inverting onto a serving platter.

Sausage Spinach Bake

PREP: 20 MIN. BAKE: 35 MIN. YIELD: 12 SERVINGS

KATHLEEN GRANT SWAN LAKE, MONTANA

This delicious recipe, which uses a packaged stuffing mix, was given to me some years ago by a friend. It is perfect for a brunch, but so versatile, it can also be served as a filling lunch or dinner.

    1   package (6 ounces) savory herb-flavored stuffing mix
  1/2   pound bulk pork sausage
  1/4   cup chopped green onions
  1/2   teaspoon minced garlic
    1   package (10 ounces) frozen chopped spinach, thawed and squeezed dry
1-1/2   cups (6 ounces) shredded Monterey Jack cheese
1-1/2   cups half-and-half cream
    3   eggs
    2   tablespoons grated Parmesan cheese

1   Prepare stuffing according to package directions. Meanwhile, crumble sausage into a large skillet; add onions; cook over medium heat until meat is no longer pink. Add garlic; cook 1 minute longer. Drain.

2   In a large bowl, combine the stuffing, sausage mixture and spinach. Transfer to a greased 13-in. x 9-in. baking dish; sprinkle with Monterey Jack cheese. In a small bowl, combine cream and eggs; pour over sausage mixture.

3   Bake at 400° for 30 minutes or until a thermometer reads 160°. Sprinkle with Parmesan cheese; bake 5 minutes longer or until bubbly.

Zucchini Crescent Pie

PREP: 25 MIN. BAKE: 20 MIN. YIELD: 6 SERVINGS

SUSAN DAVIS ANN ARBOR, MICHIGAN

This is one of my mother's many recipes that was designed to take advantage of bountiful zucchini. This tasty pie is affordable, nutritious, tasty, filling and super easy.

  1 package (8 ounces) refrigerated crescent rolls
  2 medium zucchini, sliced lengthwise and quartered
1/2 cup chopped onion
1/4 cup butter, cubed
  2 teaspoons minced fresh parsley
1/2 teaspoon salt
1/2 teaspoon garlic powder
1/2 teaspoon pepper
1/4 teaspoon dried basil
1/4 teaspoon dried oregano
  2 eggs, lightly beaten
  2 cups (8 ounces) shredded part-skim mozzarella cheese
3/4 cup cubed fully cooked ham
  1 medium Roma tomato, thinly sliced

1 Separate crescent dough into eight triangles; place in a greased 9-in. pie plate with points toward the center. Press onto the bottom and up the sides to form a crust; seal seams and perforations. Bake at 375° for 5-8 minutes or until lightly browned.

2 Meanwhile, in a large skillet, saute zucchini and onion in butter until tender; stir in seasonings. Spoon into crust. Combine the eggs, cheese and ham; pour over zucchini mixture. Top with tomato slices.

3 Bake at 375° for 20-25 minutes or until a knife inserted near the center comes out clean. Let stand for 5 minutes before cutting.

Cherry Chip Scones

PREP: 15 MIN. BAKE: 20 MIN. YIELD: 8 SERVINGS

PAMELA BROOKS SOUTH BERWICK, MAINE

These buttery scones, dotted with dried cherries and vanilla chips, are so sweet and flaky that I even serve them for dessert. Sometimes I bake a double batch and give them out as a house-warming or hostess gift.

    3 cups all-purpose flour
  1/2 cup sugar
2-1/2 teaspoons baking powder
  1/2 teaspoon baking soda
    6 tablespoons cold butter
    1 cup (8 ounces) vanilla yogurt
  1/4 cup plus 2 tablespoons milk, *divided*
1-1/3 cups dried cherries
  2/3 cup vanilla *or* white chips

1 In a large bowl, combine the flour, sugar, baking powder and baking soda. Cut in the butter until the mixture resembles coarse crumbs. Combine the yogurt and 1/4 cup milk; stir into the crumb mixture just until moistened. Knead in the dried cherries and vanilla chips.

2 On a greased baking sheet, pat the dough into a 9-in. circle. Cut into eight wedges; separate wedges. Brush with the remaining milk. Bake at 400° for 20-25 minutes or until golden brown. Serve warm.

NELLIE GRIMES
JACKSONVILLE, TEXAS

A comforting combination of cranberries, apples and walnuts makes this tea ring a lovely addition to brunch. Invite friends and family over to enjoy a few slices over coffee.

Cran-Apple Tea Ring

PREP: 45 MIN. + RISING BAKE: 20 MIN. + COOLING YIELD: 16 SERVINGS

1 package (1/4 ounce) active dry yeast

1/4 cup warm water (110° to 115°)

1/2 cup warm fat-free milk (110° to 115°)

1 egg

2 tablespoons butter, softened

1 tablespoon grated orange peel

1 teaspoon salt

3 tablespoons plus 1/2 cup sugar, *divided*

2-3/4 to 3-1/4 cups all-purpose flour

1 cup thinly sliced peeled apple

1 cup dried cranberries

1/2 cup chopped walnuts, toasted

1-1/2 teaspoons ground cinnamon

1 egg white

1 tablespoon water

1/2 cup confectioners' sugar

1 tablespoon orange juice

1 In a large bowl, dissolve yeast in warm water. Add milk, egg, butter, orange peel, salt, 3 tablespoons sugar and 1 cup flour; beat until smooth. Stir in enough remaining flour to form a soft dough.

2 Turn onto a floured surface; knead until smooth and elastic, about 6-8 minutes. Place in a bowl coated with cooking spray; turn once to coat top. Cover and let rise in a warm place for 1 hour.

3 In a bowl, toss apple, cranberries, walnuts, cinnamon and remaining sugar; set aside. Punch dough down; turn onto a lightly floured surface. Roll into a 20-in. x 10-in. rectangle. Combine egg white and water; chill 3 tablespoons. Brush remaining mixture over dough. Spoon fruit mixture to within 1 in. of edges. Roll up tightly jelly-roll style, starting with a long side; seal ends.

4 Place seam side down in a 15-in. x 10-in. x 1-in. baking pan coated with cooking spray; pinch ends to form a ring. With scissors, cut from outside edge two-thirds of the way toward center of ring at 1-in. intervals. Separate strips slightly; twist so filling shows. Cover and let rise until doubled, about 40 minutes.

5 Brush with reserved egg white mixture. Bake at 375° for 20-25 minutes or until golden brown (cover with foil during the last 10 minutes). Remove to a wire rack to cool. Combine the confectioners' sugar and orange juice; drizzle over ring.

Raspberry Streusel Coffee Cake

PREP: 25 MIN. + COOLING BAKE: 40 MIN. YIELD: 12-16 SERVINGS

AMY MITCHELL SABETHA, KANSAS

One of my mother's friends used to bring this over at the holidays, and it never lasted long. With the tangy raspberry filling, tender cake and crunchy topping, it has become a favorite at our house.

3-1/2 cups unsweetened raspberries

1 cup water

2 tablespoons lemon juice

1-1/4 cups sugar

1/3 cup cornstarch

BATTER:

3 cups all-purpose flour

1 cup sugar

1 teaspoon baking powder

1 teaspoon baking soda

1 cup cold butter, cubed

2 eggs, lightly beaten

1 cup (8 ounces) sour cream

1 teaspoon vanilla extract

TOPPING:

1/2 cup all-purpose flour

1/2 cup sugar

1/4 cup butter, softened

1/2 cup chopped pecans

GLAZE:

1/2 cup confectioners' sugar

2 teaspoons milk

1/2 teaspoon vanilla extract

1 In a large saucepan, cook raspberries and water over medium heat for 5 minutes. Add lemon juice. Combine sugar and cornstarch; stir into fruit mixture. Bring to a boil; cook and stir for 2 minutes or until thickened. Cool.

2 For batter, in a large bowl, combine the flour, sugar, baking powder and baking soda. Cut in butter until mixture resembles coarse crumbs. Stir in eggs, sour cream and vanilla (batter will be stiff).

3 Spread half into a greased 13-in. x 9-in. baking dish. Spread raspberry filling over batter; spoon remaining batter over filling. Combine topping ingredients; sprinkle over top.

4 Bake at 350° for 40-45 minutes or until golden brown. Combine the glaze ingredients; drizzle over warm cake.

Florence-Inspired Souffle

PREP: 35 MIN. BAKE: 35 MIN. YIELD: 4 SERVINGS

JENNY FLAKE GILBERT, ARIZONA

This souffle is not only absolutely delicious, but light and beautiful. Your guests will be impressed every time this brunch dish is served. So grab your fork and dig in to this little taste of Florence!

6 egg whites

3/4 cup onion and garlic salad croutons

1 small onion, finely chopped

1/4 cup finely chopped sweet red pepper

2 ounces thinly sliced prosciutto, chopped

2 teaspoons olive oil

1 garlic clove, minced

2 cups fresh baby spinach

1/3 cup all-purpose flour

1/2 teaspoon salt

1/4 teaspoon pepper

1-1/4 cups fat-free milk

1 egg yolk, lightly beaten

1/4 teaspoon cream of tartar

1/4 cup shredded Italian cheese blend

1 Let egg whites stand at room temperature for 30 minutes. Place croutons in a food processor; cover and process until ground. Sprinkle evenly onto the bottom and 1 in. up the sides of a 2-qt. baking dish coated with cooking spray; set aside.

2 In a large saucepan, saute the onion, red pepper and prosciutto in oil for 3-5 minutes or until vegetables are crisp-tender; add garlic, cook 1 minute longer. Add spinach; cook just until wilted.

3 Combine the flour, salt and pepper. Stir into pan until blended; gradually add milk. Bring to a boil; cook and stir for 2 minutes or until thickened. Transfer to a large bowl.

4 Stir a small amount of hot mixture into egg yolk; return all to the bowl, stirring constantly. Allow to cool slightly.

5 In a large bowl, beat egg whites and cream of tartar until stiff peaks form. Fold into vegetable mixture.

6 Transfer to prepared dish; sprinkle with cheese. Bake at 350° for 35-40 minutes or until the top is puffed and center appears set. Serve immediately.

Almond Bear Claws

PREP: 45 MIN. + RISING BAKE: 15 MIN. YIELD: 1-1/2 DOZEN

ANETA KISH LA CROSSE, WISCONSIN

These bear claws are absolutely melt-in-your-mouth delicious! It's impossible to resist the delicate pastry, rich almond filling and pretty fanned tops sprinkled with sugar and almonds. I made yummy treats like this when I worked in a bakery years ago.

1-1/2 cups cold butter, cut into 1/2-inch pieces

5 cups all-purpose flour, *divided*

1 package (1/4 ounce) active dry yeast

1-1/4 cups half-and-half cream

1/4 cup sugar

1/4 teaspoon salt

2 eggs

1 egg white

3/4 cup confectioners' sugar

1/2 cup almond paste, cubed

1 tablespoon water

Coarse *or* granulated sugar

Sliced almonds

1 In a bowl, toss butter with 3 cups flour until well coated; refrigerate. In a large bowl, combine yeast and remaining flour.

2 In a saucepan, heat cream, sugar and salt to 120°-130°. Add to yeast mixture with 1 egg. Beat until smooth. Stir in butter mixture just until moistened.

3 Place dough onto a well floured surface; roll into a 21-in. x 12-in. rectangle. Starting at a short side, fold dough in thirds, forming a 12-in. x 7-in. rectangle. Give dough a quarter turn; roll into a 21-in. x 12-in. rectangle. Fold into thirds, starting with a short side. Repeat, flouring surface as needed. (Do not chill dough between each rolling and folding.) Cover and chill for 4 to 24 hours or until firm.

4 For filling, in a small bowl, beat egg white until foamy. Gradually add confectioners' sugar and almond paste; beat until smooth. Cut dough in half widthwise. Roll each portion into a 12-in. square; cut each square into three 12-in. x 4-in. strips. Spread about 2 tablespoons filling down center of each strip. Fold long edges together; seal edges and ends. Cut into three pieces.

5 Place on greased baking sheets with folded edge facing away from you. With scissors, cut strips four times to within 1/2 in. of folded edge; separate slightly. Repeat with remaining dough and filling. Cover and let rise in a warm place until doubled, about 1 hour.

6 Lightly beat water and remaining egg; brush over dough. Sprinkle with sugar and almonds. Bake at 375° for 15 minutes or until golden brown. Remove from pans to wire racks to cool.

2 Remove from the heat. Gently stir in vanilla and ice cream until the ice cream is melted. Place plastic wrap over the surface of the sauce; cool.

3 For berry sauce, combine raspberries and sugar in a saucepan. Simmer, uncovered, for 2-3 minutes. Remove from the heat; set aside.

4 For the French toast, in a shallow bowl, beat the eggs. Dip both sides of the croissants in the egg mixture. On a griddle, brown the croissants on both sides in the butter. Serve the French toast with the vanilla and berry sauces.

Florentine Egg Bake

PREP: 30 MIN. BAKE: 50 MIN. + STANDING YIELD: 8 SERVINGS

PATRICIA HARMON BADEN, PENNSYLVANIA

This flavorful breakfast bake comes together quickly using handy convenience foods, including refrigerated hash browns, biscuit mix and store-bought pesto. For an elegant seafood variation of the same dish, I like to replace the ham with crabmeat.

1 package (20 ounces) refrigerated shredded hash brown potatoes
1 tablespoon olive oil
1 package (10 ounces) frozen chopped spinach, thawed and squeezed dry

Croissant French Toast

PREP/TOTAL TIME: 30 MIN. YIELD: 4 SERVINGS

JUNE DICKERSON PHILIPPI, WEST VIRGINIA

More like a scrumptious dessert than a main dish, this rich French toast is topped with a tangy raspberry sauce and a vanilla sauce that includes ice cream.

1/2 cup sugar
1 tablespoon all-purpose flour
2 cups heavy whipping cream
4 egg yolks
1 tablespoon vanilla extract
2 scoops vanilla ice cream

BERRY SAUCE:
2 cups fresh raspberries *or* frozen unsweetened raspberries
2 tablespoons sugar

FRENCH TOAST:
3 eggs
4 croissants, split
2 tablespoons butter

1 In a large saucepan, combine the sugar and flour. Stir in cream until smooth. Cook and stir over medium-high heat until thickened and bubbly. Reduce heat; cook and stir 2 minutes longer. Remove from the heat. Stir a small amount of hot filling into egg yolks; return all to the pan, stirring constantly. Cook and stir until mixture reaches 160°.

- 4 ounces Swiss cheese, cubed
- 4 ounces thinly sliced deli ham, coarsely chopped
- 8 eggs
- 1/2 cup buttermilk
- 1 tablespoon prepared pesto
- 1 cup biscuit/baking mix
- 1/4 teaspoon salt
- 1/8 teaspoon pepper
- 1-1/2 cups shredded Asiago cheese
- 2 tablespoons minced fresh basil

1 In a large bowl, combine the hash browns and oil. Press into a 13-in. x 9-in. baking dish coated with cooking spray. Bake at 350° for 25-30 minutes or until edges are golden brown.

2 Combine the spinach and Swiss cheese; sprinkle over crust. Top with ham. In a large bowl, whisk the eggs, buttermilk and pesto. Combine the biscuit mix, salt and pepper; add to egg mixture. Stir in the Asiago cheese. Pour over ham.

3 Bake, uncovered, for 25-30 minutes or until a thermometer reads 160°. Let stand for 10-15 minutes before cutting. Sprinkle with basil.

Creamy Rhubarb Crepes

PREP: 15 MIN. + STANDING COOK: 20 MIN. YIELD: 10 CREPES

STASHA WAMPLER GATE CITY, VIRGINIA

Fixing rhubarb this way brings a spring "zing" to the table. I adapted this crepe recipe, which originally featured strawberry jelly, from one I loved as a child. My husband declared it a "winner." He even came up with its name.

- 3 eggs
- 1 cup milk
- 5 tablespoons butter, melted
- 1/4 cup sugar
- 1/4 teaspoon salt
- 1 cup all-purpose flour

Additional butter

SAUCE/FILLING:
- 1 cup sugar
- 1 tablespoon cornstarch
- 1/4 teaspoon ground cinnamon
- 2 cups thinly sliced fresh *or* frozen rhubarb, thawed
- 1 package (8 ounces) cream cheese, softened

Confectioners' sugar

1 In a large bowl, whisk the eggs, milk, melted butter, sugar and salt. Beat in the flour until smooth; let stand for 30 minutes.

2 Melt 1/2 teaspoon butter in an 8-in. nonstick skillet. Pour 1/4 cup batter into the center of skillet; lift and turn pan to cover bottom. Cook until lightly browned; turn and brown the other side. Remove to a wire rack; cover with paper towel. Repeat with remaining batter, adding butter to skillet as needed.

3 Meanwhile, for sauce, combine the sugar, cornstarch and cinnamon in a saucepan. Stir in rhubarb. Bring to a boil over medium heat; cook and stir for 2 minutes or until slightly thickened and rhubarb is tender. Remove from the heat; cool slightly.

4 For filling, in a bowl, beat cream cheese and 1/4 cup of the rhubarb sauce until smooth and creamy. Place a rounded tablespoonful on each crepe; fold in half and in half again, forming a triangle. Dust with confectioners' sugar. Serve with remaining sauce.

Editor's Note: If using frozen rhubarb, measure rhubarb while still frozen, then thaw completely. Drain in a colander, but do not press liquid out.

 Look for rhubarb stalks that are crisp and brightly colored. Tightly wrap in a plastic bag and store in the refrigerator for up to 3 days. Wash the stalks and remove the poisonous leaves before using. One pound of rhubarb yields about 3 cups chopped. When rhubarb is out of season, substitute an equal amount of tart apples.

ELLY TOWNSEND
SUMMERFIELD, FLORIDA

Several years ago, I had to come up with an appetizer to serve at a pool party, and this colorful quiche was a hit. It's great on an antipasto tray, cut into wedges.

Pepperoni Spinach Quiche

PREP: 25 MIN. BAKE: 25 MIN. YIELD: 8 SERVINGS

1 tube (8 ounces) refrigerated crescent rolls

1 large sweet red pepper, chopped

1 tablespoon olive oil

1 garlic clove, minced

5 eggs, lightly beaten

1/2 cup shredded part-skim mozzarella cheese

1/2 cup frozen chopped spinach, thawed and squeezed dry

1/4 cup sliced pepperoni, cut into strips

1/4 cup half-and-half cream

2 tablespoons grated Parmesan cheese

1 tablespoon minced fresh parsley

1 tablespoon minced fresh basil *or* 1 teaspoon dried basil

Dash pepper

1 Separate crescent dough into eight triangles; place in an ungreased 9-in. fluted tart pan with removable bottom with points toward the center. Press onto the bottom and up the sides to form a crust; seal seams. Set aside.

2 In a small skillet, saute red pepper in oil until tender. Add garlic; cook 1 minute longer. Remove from the heat.

3 In another small bowl, combine the remaining ingredients; stir in red pepper mixture. Pour into crust.

4 Bake at 375° for 25-30 minutes or until a knife inserted near the center comes out clean. Let stand for 5 minutes before cutting.

Dried herbs don't spoil, but they do lose flavor and potency over time. For maximum flavor in your cooking, you may want to replace herbs that are over a year old. Store dried herbs in airtight containers away from heat and light.

It's best to crush herbs and spices just before using them. If you don't have a mortar and pestle, use the back of a metal spoon to crush them against the side of a glass bowl.

Rich Cranberry Coffee Cake

PREP: 10 MIN. BAKE: 65 MIN. + COOLING
YIELD: ABOUT 16 SERVINGS

MILDRED SCHWARTZENTRUBER TAVISTOCK, ONTARIO

When our children come home for the holidays, I make sure to bake this coffee cake. I always use fresh berries in season, then put a few bags in the freezer for later on. That way, we can enjoy this moist cake anytime we want!

- 1 package (8 ounces) cream cheese, softened
- 1 cup butter, softened
- 1-1/2 cups sugar
- 1-1/2 teaspoons vanilla extract
- 4 eggs
- 2-1/4 cups all-purpose flour, *divided*
- 1-1/2 teaspoons baking powder
- 1/2 teaspoon salt
- 2 cups fresh *or* frozen cranberries, patted dry
- 1/2 cup chopped pecans *or* walnuts

Confectioners' sugar

1 In a bowl, beat cream cheese, butter, sugar and vanilla until smooth. Add eggs, one at a time, mixing well after each addition.

2 Combine 2 cups flour, baking powder and salt; gradually add to butter mixture. Mix remaining flour with cranberries and nuts; fold into batter. Batter will be very thick. Spoon into a greased 10-in. fluted tube pan.

3 Bake at 350° for 65-70 minutes or until cake tests done. Let stand 5 minutes before removing from the pan. Cool on a wire rack. Before serving, dust with confectioners' sugar.

Southwest Sausage Bake

PREP: 15 MIN. + CHILLING BAKE: 1 HOUR + STANDING
YIELD: 12 SERVINGS

BARBARA WADDEL LINCOLN, NEBRASKA

This layered tortilla dish is not only delicious, but it's a real time-saver because it's put together the night before. The tomato slices provide a nice touch of color. I like to serve this crowd-pleasing casserole with muffins and fresh fruit.

- 6 flour tortillas (10 inches), cut into 1/2-inch strips
- 4 cans (4 ounces *each*) chopped green chilies, drained
- 1 pound bulk pork sausage, cooked and drained
- 2 cups (8 ounces) shredded Monterey Jack cheese
- 10 eggs
- 1/2 cup milk
- 1/2 teaspoon *each* salt, garlic salt, onion salt, pepper and ground cumin

Paprika

- 2 medium tomatoes, sliced

Sour cream and salsa

1 In a greased 13-in. x 9-in. baking dish, layer half of the tortilla strips, green chilies, sausage and cheese. Repeat layers.

2 In a bowl, beat the eggs, milk and seasonings; pour over cheese. Sprinkle with paprika. Cover and refrigerate overnight.

3 Remove from the refrigerator 30 minutes before baking. Bake, uncovered, at 350° for 50 minutes. Arrange tomato slices over the top. Bake 10-15 minutes longer or until a knife inserted near the center comes out clean. Let stand for 10 minutes before cutting. Serve with sour cream and salsa.

Scrambled Egg Casserole

PREP: 20 MIN. + CHILLING BAKE: 30 MIN. YIELD: 10-12 SERVINGS

MARY ANNE MCWHIRTER PEARLAND, TEXAS

This has become the brunch dish I'm known for. The recipe combines the favorite flavors of hearty, old-time country breakfasts with the ease of a modern, make-ahead dish. Try it—you'll enjoy it!

CHEESE SAUCE:
- 2 **tablespoons butter**
- 7-1/2 **teaspoons all-purpose flour**
- 2 **cups milk**
- 1/2 **teaspoon salt**
- 1/8 **teaspoon pepper**
- 1 **cup process cheese (Velveeta), shredded**
- 1 **cup cubed fully cooked ham**
- 1/4 **cup chopped green onions**
- 3 **tablespoons butter, melted**
- 12 **eggs, beaten**
- 1 **can (4 ounces) mushroom stems and pieces, drained**

TOPPING:
- 1/4 **cup melted butter**
- 2-1/4 **cups soft bread crumbs**

1 To make cheese sauce, melt butter, blend in flour and cook for 1 minute. Gradually stir in milk; cook until thick. Add salt, pepper and cheese; stir until cheese melts. Set aside.

2 Saute ham and green onions in 3 tablespoons melted butter until onions are tender. Add eggs and cook over medium heat until eggs are set; stir in the mushrooms and cheese sauce.

3 Spoon eggs into greased 13-in. x 9-in. baking pan. Combine topping ingredients; spread evenly over egg mixture. Cover; chill overnight. Uncover; bake at 350° for 30 minutes.

Grilled Ham and Egg Salad Sandwiches

PREP/TOTAL TIME: 25 MIN. YIELD: 6 SERVINGS

BEVERLY STIGER HELENA, MONTANA

An aunt shared this wonderful recipe with me years ago when I was looking for some low-budget meals. The hearty ham and toasted bread make it a deliciously different kind of egg salad sandwich.

- 6 **hard-cooked eggs, chopped**
- 1 **cup diced fully cooked ham**
- 1/2 **cup finely chopped celery**
- 1 **tablespoon finely chopped onion**
- 1/2 **cup mayonnaise**
- 2 **teaspoons prepared mustard**
- 1/2 **teaspoon salt**
- 1/4 **teaspoon pepper**
- 12 **slices whole wheat** *or* **white bread**

Canola oil

BATTER:
- 1/2 **cup cornmeal**
- 1/2 **cup all-purpose flour**
- 1 **teaspoon baking powder**
- 1 **teaspoon salt**
- 2 **cups milk**
- 2 **eggs, lightly beaten**

1 Combine eggs, ham, celery, onion, mayonnaise, mustard, salt and pepper; spread on six slices of bread. Top with remaining bread and set aside.

2 Heat about 1/2 in. of oil in a large deep skillet. Meanwhile, in a bowl, whisk batter ingredients until well blended. Dip sandwiches into batter. Fry in hot oil for 3 minutes on each side or until golden brown. Drain on paper towels.

Italian Sausage Strata

PREP: 20 MIN. + CHILLING BAKE: 1 HOUR YIELD: 12 SERVINGS

AMANDA REID OAKVILLE, IOWA

When our family sits down for breakfast on days when this do-ahead dish is on the menu, I can relax and join them.

- 1/2 cup butter, softened, *divided*
- 12 to 16 slices day-old bread, crusts removed
- 1/2 pound fresh mushrooms, sliced
- 2 cups sliced onions

Salt and pepper to taste
- 1 pound bulk Italian sausage, cooked and drained
- 3 cups (12 ounces) shredded cheddar cheese
- 5 eggs
- 2-1/2 cups milk
- 1 tablespoon Dijon mustard
- 1 teaspoon ground nutmeg
- 1 teaspoon ground mustard
- 2 tablespoons minced fresh parsley

1 Using 1/4 cup butter, spread one side of each bread slice with butter. Place half of the bread, butter side down, in a greased 13-in. x 9-in. baking dish.

2 In a large skillet, saute mushrooms and onions in remaining butter; sprinkle with salt and pepper. Spoon half of mushroom mixture over bread in prepared pan. Top with half of sausage and cheese. Layer with the remaining bread, mushroom mixture, sausage and cheese. Combine eggs, milk, Dijon mustard, nutmeg and ground mustard. Pour over cheese. Cover; refrigerate overnight.

3 Remove from the refrigerator 30 minutes before baking. Bake, covered, at 350° for 50 minutes. Uncover; bake 10-15 minutes longer or until a knife inserted near the center comes out clean. Sprinkle with parsley.

Broccoli-Ham Puff Pancake

PREP: 20 MIN. BAKE: 25 MIN. YIELD: 6 SERVINGS

EDNA HOFFMAN HEBRON, INDIANA

You won't have to pay a pretty penny to prepare this special-looking Sunday supper. The golden brown puff pancake makes a tasty main dish for brunch, lunch or dinner when filled with a creamy ham and broccoli mixture.

- 1/4 cup butter, cubed
- 1 cup all-purpose flour
- 4 eggs
- 1 cup milk

FILLING:
- 3 tablespoons butter
- 3 tablespoons all-purpose flour
- 1 cup plus 2 tablespoons milk
- 1 package (16 ounces) frozen chopped broccoli, thawed
- 1-1/2 cups cubed fully cooked ham
- 1/3 cup sour cream
- 1-1/2 teaspoons lemon juice
- 1/8 teaspoon hot pepper sauce

1 Place butter in a 10-in. ovenproof skillet; melt in a 425° oven for 3-4 minutes or until melted. In a small bowl, beat the flour, eggs and milk until smooth. Pour into prepared skillet. Bake at 425° for 22-25 minutes or until puffed and golden brown.

2 Meanwhile, for filling, in a large saucepan, melt butter. Stir in flour until smooth; gradually add milk. Bring to a boil; cook and stir for 2 minutes or until thickened. Reduce heat; add the remaining filling ingredients. Cook for 10 minutes or until heated through.

3 Spoon into center of puff pancake. Cut into wedges; serve immediately.

Breakfast Pockets

PREP: 35 MIN. + RISING BAKE: 15 MIN. YIELD: 14 SERVINGS

DOLORES JANTZEN PLYMOUTH, NEBRASKA

With these, I like being able to serve a complete breakfast inside a tidy pocket of dough. Just add fresh fruit, juice or fruit-flavored gelatin on the side.

　2　packages (1/4 ounce *each*) active dry yeast
1/2　cup warm water (110° to 115°)
3/4　cup warm evaporated milk (110° to 115°)
1/2　cup canola oil
1/4　cup sugar
　1　egg
　1　teaspoon salt
　3　to 4 cups all-purpose flour

FILLING:
　1　pound bulk pork sausage
1/2　cup chopped onion
2-1/2　cups frozen shredded hash brown potatoes, thawed
　7　eggs, lightly beaten
　3　tablespoons milk
1/2　teaspoon salt
1/2　teaspoon pepper
1/2　teaspoon garlic salt
Pinch cayenne pepper
　3　cups (12 ounces) shredded cheddar cheese

1　In a bowl, dissolve yeast in water. Add evaporated milk, oil, sugar, egg, salt and 2 cups flour; beat until smooth. Add enough remaining flour to form a soft dough (do not knead). Cover and let rise in a warm place until doubled, about 1 hour.

2　Meanwhile, for filling, in a skillet, cook the sausage and onion over medium heat until sausage is no longer pink; drain. Add hash browns, eggs, milk and seasonings. Cook and stir until the eggs are completely set. Sprinkle with cheese; keep warm.

3　Punch dough down; divide into 14 pieces. On a floured surface, roll out dough into 7-in. circles. Top each with about 1/3 cup filling; fold dough over filling and pinch the edges to seal. Place on greased baking sheets.

4　Bake at 350° for 15-20 minutes or until golden brown.

Best-of-Show Tomato Quiche

PREP: 20 MIN. + CHILLING BAKE: 50 MIN. + STANDING
YIELD: 6-8 SERVINGS

DOROTHY SWANSON ST. LOUIS, MISSOURI

I knew this delicious recipe was a "keeper" when I first tried it in the 1970s as a new bride. It impressed my in-laws when I made it for them! Now I sometimes substitute Mexican or Cajun seasoning for the basil. No matter how it's seasoned, it's wonderful.

3/4　cup all-purpose flour
1/2　cup cornmeal
1/2　teaspoon salt
1/8　teaspoon pepper
1/3　cup shortening
　4　to 5 tablespoons cold water

FILLING:

- 2 cups chopped plum tomatoes
- 1 teaspoon salt
- 1/2 teaspoon dried basil
- 1/8 teaspoon pepper
- 1/2 cup chopped green onions
- 1/2 cup shredded cheddar cheese
- 1/2 cup shredded Swiss cheese
- 2 tablespoons all-purpose flour
- 2 eggs
- 1 cup evaporated milk

1   In a small bowl, combine the first four ingredients. Cut in the shortening until crumbly. Add water, tossing with a fork until the dough forms a ball. Refrigerate for 30 minutes.

2   On a lightly floured surface, roll out dough to fit a 9-in. pie plate; transfer pastry to plate. Trim to 1/2 in. beyond edge of plate; flute edges. Bake at 375° for 10 minutes. Cool completely.

3   For filling, place tomatoes in the crust; sprinkle with salt, basil, pepper, onions and cheeses. In a small bowl, whisk the flour, eggs and milk until smooth. Pour into the crust, over vegetables, seasonings and cheese.

4   Bake at 375° for 40-45 minutes or until a knife inserted near the center comes out clean. Let stand for 10 minutes before cutting. Refrigerate leftovers.

Blueberry French Toast

PREP: 30 MIN. + CHILLING   BAKE: 55 MIN.
YIELD: 6-8 SERVINGS (1-3/4 CUPS SAUCE)

PATRICIA AXELSEN AURORA, MINNESOTA

This is the best breakfast dish I've ever tasted. With luscious blueberries inside and in a sauce, it's almost more like a dessert. The recipe was shared with me by a local blueberry grower.

- 12 slices day-old white bread, crusts removed
- 2 packages (8 ounces *each*) cream cheese
- 1 cup fresh *or* frozen blueberries
- 12 eggs
- 2 cups milk
- 1/3 cup maple syrup *or* honey

SAUCE:

- 1 cup sugar
- 2 tablespoons cornstarch
- 1 cup water

- 1 cup fresh *or* frozen blueberries
- 1 tablespoon butter

1   Cut bread into 1-in. cubes; place half in a greased 13-in. x 9-in. baking dish. Cut cream cheese into 1-in. cubes; place over bread. Top with blueberries and remaining bread cubes.

2   In a large bowl, beat eggs. Add milk and syrup; mix well. Pour over bread mixture. Cover and refrigerate for 8 hours or overnight.

3   Remove from the refrigerator 30 minutes before baking. Cover and bake at 350° for 30 minutes. Uncover; bake 25-30 minutes longer or until golden brown and center is set.

4   For sauce, in a small saucepan, combine sugar, cornstarch and water until smooth. Bring to a boil over medium heat; cook and stir for 3 minutes. Stir in blueberries; reduce heat. Simmer for 8-10 minutes or until berries have burst. Stir in butter until melted. Serve with French toast.

 Frozen blueberries are perfect for many baked items. They are especially nice in pancakes, muffins, pies, cobblers, coffee cakes, tea breads and many other baked desserts. For best results, do not defrost frozen blueberries before adding them to the recipe.

chocolate coconut candies, p. 171

Sweet, scrumptious treats will always put a smile on your face. These heavenly bites are deliciously rich, irresistible and wonderfully fun.

cookies, bars & candies

3 Bake at 400° for 7-9 minutes or until edges are lightly browned. Cool for 1 minute before removing to wire racks.

4 In a small bowl, whisk together the confectioners' sugar, almond extract and enough water to achieve glaze consistency. Tint with food coloring if desired; drizzle over cookies. Sprinkle with almonds.

Maple Peanut Delights

PREP: 30 MIN. + CHILLING   YIELD: ABOUT 8 DOZEN

KATIE STUTZMAN   GOSHEN, INDIANA

This wonderful candy recipe makes a big batch—enough to fill several Christmas gift boxes and still have treats left for my husband and our grandchildren. One of our daughters-in-law shared the recipe a few years ago.

 1 package (8 ounces) cream cheese, softened
1/2 cup butter, softened
 6 cups confectioners' sugar
 1 teaspoon maple flavoring
 2 pounds dark chocolate candy coating, coarsely chopped
 1 cup chopped peanuts

1 In a large bowl, beat the cream cheese, butter, confectioners' sugar and flavoring until smooth. Cover and refrigerate for 1 hour.

2 Shape into 1-in. balls. In a microwave, melt candy coating, stirring often. Dip balls in coating; sprinkle with peanuts. Place on waxed paper-lined baking sheets. Refrigerate.

Almond Sugar Cookies

PREP/TOTAL TIME: 30 MIN.   YIELD: ABOUT 4 DOZEN

LISA HUMMELL   PHILLIPSBURG, NEW JERSEY

It's a tradition in our house to start baking Christmas cookies early in the season and try new recipes every year. This nutty, glazed and irresistible cookie is one of my favorites.

 1 cup butter, softened
3/4 cup sugar
 1 teaspoon almond extract
 2 cups all-purpose flour
1/2 teaspoon baking powder
1/4 teaspoon salt

Additional sugar

GLAZE:
 1 cup confectioners' sugar
1-1/2 teaspoons almond extract
 2 to 3 teaspoons water

Green food coloring, optional

Sliced almonds, toasted

1 In a large bowl, cream butter and sugar until light and fluffy. Beat in almond extract. Combine the flour, baking powder and salt; gradually add to creamed mixture and mix well. Roll into 1-in. balls.

2 Place 2 in. apart on ungreased baking sheets. Coat bottom of a glass with cooking spray; dip in sugar. Flatten cookies with prepared glass, dipping glass in sugar again as needed.

Very Chocolate Brownies

PREP: 20 MIN. + CHILLING BAKE: 25 MIN. + COOLING
YIELD: 3 DOZEN

ARLENE KAY BUTLER OGDEN, UTAH

I've spent years trying different recipes in search of the perfect brownie…and this scrumptious version might be it. The fluffy melt-in-your-mouth top layer is absolutely heavenly. Try them and see for yourself!

- 4 ounces unsweetened chocolate, chopped
- 3/4 cup butter
- 2 cups sugar
- 3 eggs
- 1 teaspoon vanilla extract
- 1 cup all-purpose flour
- 1 cup coarsely chopped walnuts

TOPPING:
- 1 cup (6 ounces) semisweet chocolate chips
- 1/4 cup water
- 2 tablespoons butter
- 1 cup heavy whipping cream, whipped

1 In a microwave or double boiler, melt chocolate and butter; cool for 10 minutes. Add sugar; mix well. Stir in eggs and vanilla. Add flour; mix well. Stir in the walnuts.

2 Line a 13-in. x 9-in. baking pan with foil and grease the foil. Pour batter into pan. Bake at 350° for 25-30 minutes or until a toothpick inserted near the center comes out with moist crumbs (do not overbake). Cool completely.

3 For topping, melt chocolate chips, water and butter in a microwave or double boiler; stir until smooth. Cool to room temperature. Fold in whipped cream. Spread over brownies. Chill before cutting. Store leftovers in the refrigerator.

Swedish Butter Cookies

PREP: 10 MIN. BAKE: 25 MIN. YIELD: ABOUT 6 DOZEN

SUE SODERLAND ELGIN, ILLINOIS

It's impossible to eat just one of these treats. Naturally, they're a tradition with my Swedish husband and children, but anyone with a sweet tooth will appreciate them. My recipe is "well-traveled" among our friends and neighbors.

- 1 cup butter, softened
- 1 cup sugar
- 2 teaspoons maple syrup
- 2 cups all-purpose flour
- 1 teaspoon baking soda

Confectioners' sugar

1 In a large bowl, cream butter and sugar until light and fluffy. Add syrup. Combine flour and baking soda; gradually add to creamed mixture and mix well. Divide dough into eight portions. Roll each portion into a 9-in. log.

2 Place 3 in. apart on ungreased baking sheets. Bake at 300° for 25 minutes or until lightly browned. Cut into 1-in. slices. Remove to wire racks to cool. Dust with confectioners' sugar.

Ultimate Double Chocolate Brownies

PREP: 15 MIN. BAKE: 35 MIN. YIELD: 3 DOZEN

CAROL PREWETT CHEYENNE, WYOMING

We live in the city–but, within just a block of our house, we can see cattle grazing in a grassy green pasture. It's a sight that I never tire of.

- 3/4 **cup baking cocoa**
- 1/2 **teaspoon baking soda**
- 2/3 **cup butter, melted,** *divided*
- 1/2 **cup boiling water**
- 2 **cups sugar**
- 2 **eggs**
- 1-1/3 **cups all-purpose flour**
- 1 **teaspoon vanilla extract**
- 1/4 **teaspoon salt**
- 1/2 **cup coarsely chopped pecans**
- 2 **cups (12 ounces) semisweet chocolate chunks**

1 In a large bowl, combine cocoa and baking soda; stir in 1/3 cup melted butter. Add boiling water; stir until well blended. Stir in sugar, eggs and remaining butter. Add the flour, vanilla and salt. Stir in the pecans and chocolate chunks.

2 Pour into a greased 13-in. x 9-in. baking pan. Bake at 350° for 35-40 minutes or until brownies begin to pull away from sides of pan. Cool.

Cookie Dough Truffles

PREP: 1 HOUR + CHILLING YIELD: 5-1/2 DOZEN

LANITA DEDON SLAUGHTER, LOUISIANA

The flavorful filling at the center of these yummy candies tastes like genuine chocolate chip cookie dough...without the worry of raw eggs. That's what makes them so appealing. Plus, they're simple to prepare.

- 1/2 **cup butter, softened**
- 3/4 **cup packed brown sugar**
- 1 **teaspoon vanilla extract**
- 2 **cups all-purpose flour**
- 1 **can (14 ounces) sweetened condensed milk**
- 1/2 **cup miniature semisweet chocolate chips**
- 1/2 **cup chopped walnuts**
- 1-1/2 **pounds dark chocolate candy coating, coarsely chopped**

1 In a large bowl, cream the butter and brown sugar until light and fluffy. Beat in vanilla. Gradually add flour, alternately with milk, beating well after each addition. Stir in the chocolate chips and walnuts. Shape into 1-in. balls; place on waxed paper-lined baking sheets. Loosely cover and refrigerate for 2 hours or until firm.

2 In a microwave-safe bowl, melt candy coating; stir until smooth. Dip balls in coating, allowing excess to drip off; place on waxed paper-lined baking sheets. Refrigerate until firm, about 15 minutes. If desired, remelt remaining candy coating and drizzle over candies. Store in the refrigerator.

Apricot Bars

PREP: 15 MIN. BAKE: 30 MIN. + COOLING YIELD: 3 DOZEN

JILL MORITZ IRVINE, CALIFORNIA

This recipe is down-home baking at its best. It's won blue ribbons at county fairs and cookie contests in several states! This treat is easy to make, and it's perfect for potluck suppers, bake sales, lunch boxes or just plain snacking. Bake a batch tonight.

- 3/4 cup butter, softened
- 1 cup sugar
- 1/2 teaspoon vanilla extract
- 1 egg
- 2 cups all-purpose flour
- 1/4 teaspoon baking powder
- 1-1/3 cups flaked coconut
- 1/2 cup chopped walnuts
- 1 jar (10 to 12 ounces) apricot preserves

1 In a large bowl, cream butter, sugar and vanilla. Add egg; mix well. Combine flour and baking powder. Gradually add to creamed mixture. Fold in coconut and walnuts.

2 Press two-thirds of dough into a greased 13-in. x 9-in. baking pan. Spread with preserves; crumble remaining dough over preserves. Bake at 350° for 30-35 minutes or until golden brown. Cool in pan on wire rack. Cut into bars.

Chocolate Coconut Candies

PREP: 30 MIN. + CHILLING YIELD: 2-1/2 DOZEN

MARY ANN MARINO WEST PITTSBURG, PENNSYLVANIA

These candies disappear just as fast as I put them out. They're a snap to whip up and are beautiful on any holiday cookie plate. I mound them high and sprinkle with coconut…then watch them vanish!

- 1-3/4 cups confectioners' sugar
- 1-3/4 cups flaked coconut
- 1 cup chopped almonds
- 1/2 cup sweetened condensed milk
- 2 cups (12 ounces) semisweet chocolate chips
- 2 tablespoons shortening

1 In a large bowl, combine the confectioners' sugar, coconut, almonds and milk. Shape into 1-in. balls. Refrigerate until firm, about 20 minutes.

2 In a microwave, melt semisweet chips and shortening on high for about 1 minute; stir. Microwave at additional 10- to 20-second intervals, stirring until smooth.

3 Dip balls in chocolate; allow excess to drip off. Place on waxed paper; let stand until set. Store in an airtight container.

Dipped Peanut Butter Cookies

PREP: 30 MIN. + CHILLING BAKE: 15 MIN. YIELD: ABOUT 5 DOZEN

STEPHANIE DELOACH MAGNOLIA, ARKANSAS

A baking mix makes these soft, moist cookies a snap to make, yet they're pretty enough for parties. I'm often asked to bring them to wedding and baby showers, and they're popular around the holidays, too. I sometimes mix the dough the day before and chill it until I have time to bake the cookies.

> 1 **cup peanut butter**
>
> 1 **can (14 ounces) sweetened condensed milk**
>
> 1 **egg**
>
> 1 **teaspoon vanilla extract**
>
> 2 **cups biscuit/baking mix**
>
> 3/4 **to 1 pound milk chocolate candy coating, coarsely chopped**
>
> 1 **tablespoon shortening**

1 In a large bowl, combine the peanut butter, milk, egg and vanilla; beat until smooth. Gradually stir in biscuit mix and mix well. Cover and refrigerate for 1 hour.

2 Shape into 1-in. balls and place 1 in. apart on ungreased baking sheets. Flatten each ball with the bottom of a glass. Bake at 350° for 8-10 minutes or until golden brown. Cool on wire racks.

3 In a microwave, melt candy coating and shortening; stir until smooth. Dip each cookie halfway into chocolate; shake off excess. Place on waxed paper-lined baking sheets; let stand until set.

Editor's Note: Milk chocolate confectionery coating is found in the baking section of most grocery stores. It is sometimes labeled "candy coating" and is often sold in bulk packages of 1 to 1-1/2 pounds.

Pecan Toffee Fudge

PREP: 20 MIN. + CHILLING YIELD: 2-1/2 POUNDS

DIANE WILLEY BOZMAN, MARYLAND

This quick fudge is always well-liked wherever it shows up and makes great gifts for loved ones and friends. People love the creaminess and toffee bits. And it's so easy, even young children can help make it—with a little supervision!

> 1 **teaspoon butter**
>
> 1 **package (8 ounces) cream cheese, softened**
>
> 3-3/4 **cups confectioners' sugar**
>
> 6 **ounces unsweetened chocolate, melted and cooled**
>
> 1/4 **teaspoon almond extract**
>
> **Dash salt**
>
> 1/4 **cup coarsely chopped pecans**
>
> 1/4 **cup English toffee bits**

1 Line a 9-in. square pan with foil and grease the foil with butter; set aside. In a large bowl, beat cream cheese until fluffy. Gradually beat in confectioners' sugar. Add the melted chocolate, extract and salt; mix well. Stir in pecans and toffee bits.

2 Spread into prepared pan. Cover and refrigerate overnight or until firm. Using foil, lift fudge out of pan. Gently peel off foil; cut fudge into 1-in. squares. Store in an airtight container in the refrigerator.

JEANNETTE NORD
SAN JUAN CAPISTRANO,
CALIFORNIA

When I take this crowd-pleasing treat to a potluck, I come home with an empty pan every time. Cooking and baking come naturally for me—as a farm girl, I helped my mother feed my 10 siblings.

Pear Custard Bars

PREP: 20 MIN. + CHILLING BAKE: 50 MIN. + COOLING YIELD: 16 BARS

1/2 **cup butter, softened**

1/3 **cup sugar**

1/4 **teaspoon vanilla extract**

3/4 **cup all-purpose flour**

2/3 **cup chopped macadamia nuts**

FILLING/TOPPING:

1 **package (8 ounces) cream cheese, softened**

1/2 **cup sugar**

1 **egg**

1/2 **teaspoon vanilla extract**

1 **can (15-1/4 ounces) pear halves, drained**

1/2 **teaspoon sugar**

1/2 **teaspoon ground cinnamon**

1 In a large bowl, cream butter and sugar until light and fluffy. Beat in vanilla. Gradually add flour to creamed mixture. Stir in the nuts.

2 Press into a greased 8-in. square baking pan. Bake at 350° for 20 minutes or until lightly browned. Cool on a wire rack.

3 For filling, in a small bowl, beat cream cheese until smooth. Beat in the sugar, egg and vanilla. Pour over crust.

4 Cut pears into 1/8-in. slices; arrange in a single layer over filling. Combine sugar and cinnamon; sprinkle over pears. Bake at 375° for 28-30 minutes (center will be soft-set and will become firmer upon cooling). Cool on a wire rack for 45 minutes.

5 Cover and refrigerate for at least 2 hours before cutting. Store in the refrigerator.

Aunt Rose's Fantastic Butter Toffee

PREP/TOTAL TIME: 30 MIN. YIELD: ABOUT 2 POUNDS

KATHY DORMAN SNOVER, MICHIGAN

I don't live in the country, but I love everything about it, especially good old-fashioned home cooking! Every year, you'll find me at our County Fair, entering a different recipe contest. I find new recipes everywhere–especially in my large cookbook collection. This toffee, however, comes from the heart. It's been a favorite in my family since I was a little girl!

  2 cups whole unblanched almonds (about 10 ounces), *divided*

 11 ounces milk chocolate, *divided*

  2 sticks sweet butter

  1 cup sugar

  3 tablespoons cold water

1 Spread almonds in a pan and toast in 350° oven for about 10 minutes, shaking pan occasionally. Cool nuts. Grind milk chocolate fine in food processor–do not overprocess. Set aside.

2 Chop nuts coarse in food processor. Sprinkle 1 cup nuts over bottom of greased 15-in. x 10-in. x 1-in. jelly roll pan. Sprinkle 1 cup ground chocolate over nuts. Set aside.

3 In heavy saucepan, combine butter, sugar and water; cook over medium heat, stirring occasionally, until the mixture reaches 290° (soft-crack stage).

4 Very quickly pour mixture over nuts and chocolate. Sprinkle remaining chocolate over toffee; top with remaining nuts. Chill and break into pieces.

Editor's Note: We recommend that you test your candy thermometer before each use by bringing water to a boil; the thermometer should read 212°. Adjust your recipe temperature up or down based on your test.

Rustic Nut Bars

PREP: 20 MIN. BAKE: 35 MIN. + COOLING YIELD: ABOUT 3 DOZEN

BARBARA DRISCOLL WEST ALLIS, WISCONSIN

Everyone will crunch with joy when they bite into these chewy, gooey bars. They'll love the shortbread-like crust and the wildly nutty topping.

      1 tablespoon plus 3/4 cup cold butter, *divided*

 2-1/3 cups all-purpose flour

    1/2 cup sugar

    1/2 teaspoon baking powder

    1/2 teaspoon salt

      1 egg, lightly beaten

TOPPING:

    2/3 cup honey

    1/2 cup packed brown sugar

    1/4 teaspoon salt

      6 tablespoons butter, cubed

      2 tablespoons heavy whipping cream

      1 cup chopped hazelnuts, toasted

      1 cup roasted salted almonds

      1 cup salted cashews, toasted

      1 cup pistachios, toasted

1 Line a 13-in. x 9-in. baking pan with foil; grease the foil with 1 tablespoon butter. Set aside.

2 In a large bowl, combine the flour, sugar, baking powder and salt; cut in remaining butter until mixture resembles coarse crumbs. Stir in egg until blended (mixture will be dry).

3 Press firmly onto the bottom of prepared pan. Bake at 375° for 18-20 minutes or until edges are golden brown. Cool on a wire rack.

4 For topping, in a large heavy saucepan, bring the honey, brown sugar and salt to a boil over medium

CARAMEL DRIZZLE:
- 1/2 cup packed brown sugar
- 1/4 cup heavy whipping cream
- 1/2 cup confectioners' sugar

CHOCOLATE DRIZZLE:
- 1 square (1 ounce) semisweet chocolate
- 1 tablespoon butter

1. In a large bowl, cream butter and brown sugar until light and fluffy. Beat in egg and vanilla. Combine the flour, baking powder and salt; gradually add to creamed mixture and mix well.

2. Shape dough into 1-in. balls; roll in pecans. Place 2 in. apart on ungreased baking sheets; flatten slightly. Bake at 350° for 8-10 minutes or until lightly browned. Cool for 2 minutes before removing to wire racks to cool completely.

3. In a small saucepan, bring brown sugar and cream to a boil. Remove from the heat; whisk in confectioners' sugar. Immediately drizzle over cookies.

4. In a small microwave-safe bowl, melt chocolate and butter; stir until smooth. Drizzle over cookies. Let stand until set. Store in an airtight container.

heat until sugar is smooth; stirring often. Boil without stirring for 2 minutes. Add butter and cream. Bring to a boil; cook and stir for 1 minute or until smooth. Remove from the heat; stir in the hazelnuts, almonds, cashews and pistachios. Spread over crust.

5. Bake at 375° for 15-20 minutes or until topping is bubbly. Cool completely on a wire rack. Using foil, lift bars out of pan. Discard foil; cut into squares.

Double-Drizzle Pecan Cookies

PREP: 25 MIN. **BAKE:** 10 MIN./BATCH + COOLING
YIELD: ABOUT 3-1/2 DOZEN

PAULA MARCHESI LENHARTSVILLE, PENNSYLVANIA

These chewy, toasted pecan treats are a must with my cookie munchers every holiday. The caramel and chocolate drizzles make them doubly delicious and pretty. You can't go wrong with these delights!

- 1/2 cup butter, softened
- 1-1/2 cups packed brown sugar
- 1 egg
- 1 teaspoon vanilla extract
- 1-1/2 cups all-purpose flour
- 1-1/2 teaspoons baking powder
- 1/4 teaspoon salt
- 1-1/4 cups chopped pecans, toasted

STACY ABELL
OLATHE, KANSAS

Nothing compares to the melt-in-your-mouth flavor of these truffles...or to the simplicity of the recipe. Whenever I make them for my family or friends, they're quickly devoured. No one has to know how easy they are to prepare!

Mocha Truffles

PREP: 25 MIN. + CHILLING YIELD: ABOUT 5-1/2 DOZEN

- **2 packages (12 ounces *each*) semisweet chocolate chips**
- **1 package (8 ounces) cream cheese, softened**
- **3 tablespoons instant coffee granules**
- **2 teaspoons water**
- **1 pound dark chocolate candy coating, coarsely chopped**

White candy coating, optional

1 In a microwave, melt chocolate chips; stir until smooth. Add cream cheese, coffee and water. Chill until firm enough to shape. Shape into 1-in. balls and place on waxed paper-lined baking sheet. Chill for 1-2 hours or until firm.

2 In a microwave, melt chocolate coating; stir until smooth. Dip balls in chocolate; allow excess to drip off. Place on waxed paper; let stand until set. Melt white coating and drizzle over truffles if desired.

Editor's Note: Dark, white or milk chocolate confectionery coating is found in the baking section of most grocery stores. It is sometimes labeled "almond bark" or "candy coating" and is often sold in bulk packages (1 to 1-1/2 pounds). It is the product used for dipping chocolate. A substitute for 6 ounces chocolate coating would be 1 cup (6 ounces) semisweet, dark or white chocolate chips and 1 tablespoon shortening melted together. Truffles can be frozen for several months before dipping in chocolate. Thaw in the refrigerator before dipping.

Chocolate Malted Cookies

PREP/TOTAL TIME: 30 MIN. YIELD: ABOUT 1-1/2 DOZEN

TERI RASEY CADILLAC, MICHIGAN

These yummy cookies are the next best thing to a good old-fashioned malted milk shake. With malted milk powder, chocolate syrup plus chocolate chips and chunks, these are the best cookies I've ever tasted...and with six kids, I've made a lot of cookies over the years.

- 1 cup butter-flavored shortening
- 1-1/4 cups packed brown sugar
- 1/2 cup malted milk powder
- 2 tablespoons chocolate syrup
- 1 tablespoon vanilla extract
- 1 egg
- 2 cups all-purpose flour
- 1 teaspoon baking soda
- 1/2 teaspoon salt
- 1-1/2 cups semisweet chocolate chunks
- 1 cup milk chocolate chips

1 In a large bowl, beat the shortening, brown sugar, malted milk powder, chocolate syrup and vanilla for 2 minutes. Add egg.

2 Combine the flour, baking soda and salt; gradually add to creamed mixture, mixing well after each addition. Stir in chocolate chunks and chips.

3 Shape into 2-in. balls; place 3 in. apart on ungreased baking sheets. Bake at 375° for 12-14 minutes or until golden brown. Cool for 2 minutes before removing to a wire rack.

Sour Cream Raisin Squares

PREP: 25 MIN. BAKE: 30 MIN. YIELD: 12-16 SERVINGS

LEONA EASH MCCONNELSVILLE, OHIO

My aunt shared this recipe with me, and my family has always enjoyed it. I love to make these bars for friends who visit or give them away as gifts.

- 1 cup butter, softened
- 1 cup packed brown sugar
- 2 cups all-purpose flour
- 2 cups quick-cooking oats
- 1 teaspoon baking powder
- 1 teaspoon baking soda
- 1/8 teaspoon salt

FILLING:

- 4 egg yolks
- 2 cups (16 ounces) sour cream
- 1-1/2 cups raisins
- 1 cup sugar
- 1 tablespoon cornstarch

1 In a large bowl, cream the butter and brown sugar until light and fluffy. Combine the flour, oats, baking powder, baking soda and salt; gradually add to creamed mixture (mixture will be crumbly).

2 Set aside 2 cups; pat remaining crumbs into a greased 13-in. x 9-in. baking pan. Bake at 350° for 15 minutes. Cool.

3 Meanwhile, in a small saucepan, combine filling ingredients. Bring to a boil; cook and stir for 5-8 minutes. Pour over crust; sprinkle with reserved crumbs. Bake 15 minutes longer.

3   For sauce, combine syrup and butter in a saucepan. Bring to a boil; cook and stir for 3 minutes. Remove from the heat; stir in milk. Cut brownies into squares; cut in half if desired.

4   Place on dessert plates with a scoop of ice cream. Top with sauce; sprinkle with pecans.

Frosted Fudge Brownies

PREP: 10 MIN. + COOLING BAKE: 25 MIN. + COOLING
YIELD: 2 DOZEN

SUE SODERLUND ELGIN, ILLINOIS

A neighbor brought over a pan of these delicious brownies along with the recipe when I came home from the hospital with our baby daughter many years ago. I've made them ever since for family occasions, potlucks and parties at work.

        1   cup plus 3 tablespoons butter, cubed
    3/4   cup baking cocoa
        4   eggs
        2   cups sugar
1-1/2   cups all-purpose flour
        1   teaspoon baking powder
        1   teaspoon salt
        1   teaspoon vanilla extract

Blond Brownies a la Mode

PREP: 25 MIN. BAKE: 25 MIN. + COOLING YIELD: 20 SERVINGS

PAT PARKER CHESTER, SOUTH CAROLINA

We have a lot of church socials, and I'm always looking for something new and different to prepare. These brownies, drizzled with a sweet maple sauce, are a sure hit...with or without the ice cream.

    3/4   cup butter, softened
        2   cups packed brown sugar
        4   eggs
        2   teaspoons vanilla extract
        2   cups all-purpose flour
        2   teaspoons baking powder
        1   teaspoon salt
1-1/2   cups chopped pecans

MAPLE CREAM SAUCE:
        1   cup maple syrup
        2   tablespoons butter
    1/4   cup evaporated milk
Vanilla ice cream and chopped pecans

1   In a large bowl, cream butter and brown sugar until light and fluffy. Add eggs, one at a time, beating well after each addition. Beat in vanilla. Combine the flour, baking powder and salt; gradually add to creamed mixture. Stir in pecans.

2   Spread into a greased 13-in. x 9-in. baking pan. Bake at 350° for 25-30 minutes or until a toothpick inserted near the center comes out clean. Cool on a wire rack.

FROSTING:

- **6 tablespoons butter, softened**
- **2-2/3 cups confectioners' sugar**
- **1/2 cup baking cocoa**
- **1 teaspoon vanilla extract**
- **1/4 to 1/3 cup milk**

1. In a saucepan, melt butter. Remove from the heat. Stir in cocoa; cool. In a large bowl, beat eggs and sugar until blended. Combine flour, baking powder and salt; gradually add to egg mixture. Stir in vanilla and the cooled chocolate mixture until well blended.

2. Spread into a greased 13-in. x 9-in. baking pan. Bake at 350° for 25-28 minutes or until a toothpick inserted near the center comes out clean (do not overbake). Cool on a wire rack.

3. For frosting, in a large bowl, cream butter and confectioners' sugar until light and fluffy. Beat in cocoa and vanilla. Add enough milk until the frosting achieves spreading consistency. Spread over brownies. Cut into bars.

Three-Chip English Toffee

PREP: 15 MIN. + CHILLING COOK: 30 MIN.
YIELD: ABOUT 2-1/2 POUNDS

LANA PETFIELD RICHMOND, VIRGINIA

With its melt-in-your-mouth texture and scrumptiously rich flavor, this is the ultimate toffee! Drizzled on top are three different kinds of melted chips, plus a sprinkling of walnuts. Packaged in colorful tins, these pretty pieces make great gifts. They're also easy to transport in the pan and are great for bake sales.

- **1/2 teaspoon plus 2 cups butter, *divided***
- **2 cups sugar**
- **1 cup slivered almonds**
- **1 cup milk chocolate chips**
- **1 cup chopped walnuts**
- **1/2 cup semisweet chocolate chips**
- **1/2 cup vanilla *or* white chips**
- **1-1/2 teaspoons shortening**

1. Butter a 15-in. x 10-in. x 1-in. pan with 1/2 teaspoon butter. In a heavy saucepan over medium-low heat, bring sugar and remaining butter to a boil, stirring constantly. Cover and cook for 2-3 minutes.

2. Uncover; add almonds. Cook and stir with a clean spoon until a candy thermometer reads 300° (hard-crack stage) and mixture is golden brown.

3. Pour into prepared pan (do not scrape sides of saucepan). Surface will be buttery. Cool for 1-2 minutes. Sprinkle with milk chocolate chips. Let stand for 1-2 minutes; spread chocolate over the top. Sprinkle with walnuts; press down gently with the back of a spoon. Chill for 10 minutes.

4. In a microwave, melt semisweet chips; stir until smooth. Drizzle over walnuts. Refrigerate for 10 minutes. Melt vanilla chips and shortening; stir until smooth. Drizzle over walnuts. Cover and refrigerate for 1-2 hours. Break into pieces.

Editor's Note: We recommend that you test your candy thermometer before each use by bringing water to a boil; the thermometer should read 212°. Adjust your recipe temperature up or down based on your test. If the toffee separates during cooking, add 1/2 cup hot water and stir vigorously. Bring the temperature back up to 300° and proceed as recipe directs.

 When making toffee or candy from scratch, measure all ingredients for a recipe before beginning. Use heavy-gauge saucepans that are deep enough to allow candy mixtures to boil freely without boiling over and use wooden spoons with long handles to stir.

Apple Pie Bars

PREP: 30 MIN. BAKE: 45 MIN. + COOLING
YIELD: ABOUT 2 DOZEN

JANET ENGLISH PITTSBURGH, PENNSYLVANIA

These delicious bars, with their flaky crust and scrumptious fruit filling, are perfect for serving apple pie to a crowd.

- 4 cups all-purpose flour
- 1 teaspoon salt
- 1 teaspoon baking powder
- 1 cup shortening
- 4 egg yolks
- 2 tablespoons lemon juice
- 8 to 10 tablespoons cold water

FILLING:

- 7 cups finely chopped peeled apples
- 2 cups sugar
- 1/4 cup all-purpose flour
- 2 teaspoons ground cinnamon

Dash ground nutmeg

Water *or* milk

GLAZE:

- 1 cup confectioners' sugar
- 1 tablespoon milk
- 1 tablespoon lemon juice

1 In a large bowl, combine flour, salt and baking powder. Cut in shortening until mixture resembles coarse crumbs. Whisk egg yolks, lemon juice and water; gradually add to flour mixture, tossing with a fork until dough forms a ball. Divide in half. Chill for 30 minutes.

2 Roll out one portion of the dough between two large sheets of waxed paper into a 17-in. x 12-in. rectangle. Transfer dough to an ungreased 15-in. x 10-in. x 1-in. baking pan. Press the pastry onto the bottom and up the sides of the pan; trim the pastry so it is even with top edge of the pan.

3 For filling, in a large bowl, toss the apples, sugar, flour, ground cinnamon and nutmeg; spread over crust. Roll out the remaining pastry to fit the top of the pan; place over the filling. Trim edges and brush with water or milk; pinch the edges together to seal. Cut slits in top.

4 Bake at 375° for 45-50 minutes or until golden brown. Cool on a wire rack. Combine glaze ingredients until smooth; drizzle over bars before cutting.

S'more Sandwich Cookies

PREP: 25 MIN. BAKE: 10 MIN. + COOLING YIELD: ABOUT 2 DOZEN

ABBY METZGER LARCHWOOD, IOWA

Capture the taste of campfire s'mores in your kitchen. Graham cracker crumbs added to chocolate chip cookie dough bring out the flavor of the fireside favorite. Melting the cookies' marshmallow centers in the microwave makes them simple to assemble. The treats are a delicious way to experience the great outdoors!

- 3/4 cup butter, softened
- 1/2 cup sugar
- 1/2 cup packed brown sugar
- 1 egg
- 2 tablespoons milk
- 1 teaspoon vanilla extract
- 1-1/4 cups all-purpose flour
- 1-1/4 cups graham cracker crumbs (about 20 squares)
- 1/2 teaspoon baking soda
- 1/4 teaspoon salt
- 1/8 teaspoon ground cinnamon
- 2 cups (12 ounces) semisweet chocolate chips
- 24 to 28 large marshmallows

1 In a large bowl, cream butter and sugars until light and fluffy. Beat in the egg, milk and vanilla. Combine the flour, graham cracker crumbs, baking soda, salt and cinnamon; gradually add to creamed mixture and mix well. Stir in chocolate chips.

2 Drop by tablespoonfuls 2 in. apart onto ungreased baking sheets. Bake at 375° for 8-10 minutes or until golden brown. Remove to wire racks to cool.

2 Place almond paste in a large bowl; break up with a fork. Cream with butter, sugar and egg yolks until light, fluffy and smooth. Stir in flour. In another bowl, beat egg whites until soft peaks form. Fold into dough, mixing until thoroughly blended.

3 Divide dough into three portions (about 1-1/3 cups each). Color one portion with red food coloring and one with green; leave the remaining portion uncolored. Spread each portion into the prepared pans. Bake at 350° for 10-12 minutes or until edges are light golden brown.

4 Invert onto wire racks; remove waxed paper. Place another wire rack on top and turn over. Cool completely.

5 Place green layer on a large piece of plastic wrap. Spread evenly with raspberry jam. Top with uncolored layer and spread with apricot jam. Top with pink layer. Bring plastic wrap over layers. Slide onto a baking sheet and set a cutting board or heavy, flat pan on top to compress layers. Refrigerate overnight.

6 The next day, melt chocolate in a double boiler. Spread over top layer; allow to harden. With a sharp knife, trim edges. Cut into 1/2-in. strips across the width; then cut each strip into 4-5 pieces. Store in airtight containers.

3 Place four cookies bottom side up on a microwave-safe plate; top each with a marshmallow. Microwave, uncovered, on high for 10-15 seconds or until marshmallows begin to puff (do not overcook). Top each with another cookie. Repeat.

Rainbow Cookies

PREP: 50 MIN. + CHILLING BAKE: 10 MIN. + COOLING
YIELD: ABOUT 8 DOZEN

MARY ANN LEE MARCO ISLAND, FLORIDA

I always bake my Rainbow Cookies two weeks ahead. That allows them enough time to mellow, leaving them moist and full of almond flavor!

  1 can (8 ounces) almond paste

  1 cup butter, softened

  1 cup sugar

  4 eggs, *separated*

  2 cups all-purpose flour

  6 to 8 drops red food coloring

  6 to 8 drops green food coloring

1/4 cup seedless red raspberry jam

1/4 cup apricot jam

  1 cup (6 ounces) semisweet chocolate chips

1 Grease the bottoms of three matching 13-in. x 9-in. baking pans (or reuse one pan). Line the pans with waxed paper; grease the paper.

Chunky Peanut Brittle

PREP: 10 MIN. COOK: 20 MIN. + COOLING YIELD: 2-1/2 POUNDS

JANET GONOLA EAST MCKEESPORT, PENNSYLVANIA

As a farm girl, I often made Christmas goodies with my mother for our family of eight candy-loving kids. Now, my own children and grandkids say the season wouldn't be the same without a tray filled with this chocolaty peanut brittle.

1-1/2 teaspoons plus 1-1/2 cups butter, *divided*
   2 cups peanut butter chips, *divided*
1-3/4 cups sugar
   3 tablespoons light corn syrup
   3 tablespoons water
1-1/2 cups salted peanuts, coarsely chopped
  1/2 cup semisweet chocolate chips

1 Butter the bottom and sides of a 15-in. x 10-in. x 1-in. pan with 1-1/2 teaspoons of butter. Sprinkle with 1 cup peanut butter chips; set aside.

2 In a heavy saucepan, bring sugar, corn syrup, water and remaining butter to a boil over medium heat, stirring constantly. Cook and stir until butter is melted. Cook, without stirring, until a candy thermometer reads 300° (hard-cracked stage).

3 Remove from the heat; stir in peanuts. Quickly pour onto prepared pan; sprinkle with chocolate chips and remaining peanut butter chips. With a knife, gently swirl softened chips over top of brittle. Cool before breaking into pieces. Store in an airtight container.

Editor's Note: We recommend that you test your candy thermometer before each use by bringing water to a boil; the thermometer should read 212°. Adjust your recipe temperature up or down based on your test.

Coffee Shop Fudge

PREP: 15 MIN. + CHILLING YIELD: 2 POUNDS

BETH OSBORNE SKINNER BRISTOL, TENNESSEE

This recipe is one that my son, Jackson, and I worked on together. After several efforts, we decided this version was a winner. It is smooth, creamy and has an irresistible crunch from pecans. The coffee and cinnamon blend nicely to provide subtle flavor.

   1 cup chopped pecans
   3 cups (18 ounces) semisweet chocolate chips
   1 can (14 ounces) sweetened condensed milk
   2 tablespoons strong brewed coffee, room temperature
   1 teaspoon ground cinnamon
1/8 teaspoon salt
   1 teaspoon vanilla extract

1 Line an 8-in. square pan with foil and butter the foil; set aside. Place pecans in a microwave-safe pie plate. Microwave, uncovered, on high for 3 minutes, stirring after each minute; set aside.

2 In a 2-qt. microwave-safe bowl, combine the chocolate chips, milk, coffee, cinnamon and salt. Microwave, uncovered, on high for 1 minute. Stir until smooth. Stir in vanilla and pecans. Immediately spread into the prepared pan.

3 Cover and refrigerate until firm, about 2 hours. Remove from pan; cut into 1-in. squares. Cover and store at room temperature (70°-80°).

PRISCILLA
ANDERSON
SALT LAKE CITY, UTAH

These pretzel-shaped buttery chocolate cookies are covered in a rich mocha glaze and drizzled with white chocolate. My family goes wild over their chocolaty crunch. They're beautiful to serve and to give as gifts.

Chocolate Pretzel Cookies

PREP: 30 MIN. + CHILLING BAKE: 5 MIN./BATCH + COOLING YIELD: 4 DOZEN

1/2 cup butter, softened

2/3 cup sugar

1 egg

2 ounces unsweetened chocolate, melted and cooled

2 teaspoons vanilla extract

1-3/4 cups all-purpose flour

1/2 teaspoon salt

MOCHA GLAZE:

1 cup (6 ounces) semisweet chocolate chips

1 teaspoon shortening

1 teaspoon light corn syrup

1 cup confectioners' sugar

4 to 5 tablespoons strong brewed coffee

2 ounces white baking chocolate

1 In a large bowl, cream butter and sugar until light and fluffy. Add the egg, chocolate and vanilla; mix well. Combine flour and salt; gradually add to creamed mixture and mix well. Cover and refrigerate for 1 hour or until firm.

2 Divide dough into fourths; form each portion into a 6-in. roll. Cut each roll into 1/2-in. slices; roll each into a 9-in. rope. Place ropes on greased baking sheets; form into pretzel shapes and space 2 in. apart. Bake at 400° for 5-7 minutes or until firm. Cool 1 minute before removing to wire racks to cool completely.

3 For glaze, melt the chocolate chips and shortening with corn syrup in a heavy saucepan or microwave; stir until smooth. Stir in confectioners' sugar and enough coffee to make a smooth glaze. Dip pretzels; place on waxed paper until set. Melt white chocolate; drizzle with white chocolate; let stand until chocolate is completely set. Store in an airtight container.

When creaming butter, it should be softened (a table knife should be able to glide through the butter). When butter is cut into a mixture, it should be cold from the refrigerator.

sour cream-lemon pie, p. 201

This chapter has home-spun sweets of lovely cakes and tempting pies that are chock-full of scrumptious fillings, fruits and nuts.

cakes & pies

1. In a large bowl, beat the eggs, coffee, oil, vinegar and vanilla until well blended. In a small bowl, combine the flour, sugar, cocoa, baking soda and salt; gradually beat into coffee mixture until blended.

2. Fill paper-lined muffin cups three-fourths full. Bake at 350° for 20-25 minutes or until a toothpick comes out clean. Cool for 10 minutes before removing from pan to a wire rack to cool.

3. For frosting, in a microwave, melt chips and butter; stir until smooth. Transfer to a large bowl. Gradually beat in confectioners' sugar and coffee until smooth. Pipe frosting onto cupcakes. Top with sprinkles and gently press down.

Lemon Chiffon Cake

PREP: 25 MIN. BAKE: 50 MIN. + COOLING YIELD: 12-16 SERVINGS

TRISHA KAMMERS CLARKSTON, WASHINGTON

This moist, airy cake was my dad's favorite. My mom revamped the original recipe to include lemons. I'm not much of a baker, so I don't make it very often. But it is well worth the effort.

- 7 eggs, *separated*
- 2 cups all-purpose flour
- 1-1/2 cups sugar
- 3 teaspoons baking powder
- 1 teaspoon salt
- 3/4 cup water
- 1/2 cup canola oil
- 4 teaspoons grated lemon peel

Special Mocha Cupcakes

PREP: 25 MIN. BAKE: 20 MIN. + COOLING YIELD: 1 DOZEN

MARY BILYEU ANN ARBOR, MICHIGAN

Topped with a fluffy frosting and chocolate sprinkles, these extra-rich, extra-delicious cupcakes smell wonderful while baking—and taste even better!

- 2 eggs
- 1/2 cup cold brewed coffee
- 1/2 cup canola oil
- 3 teaspoons cider vinegar
- 3 teaspoons vanilla extract
- 1-1/2 cups all-purpose flour
- 1 cup sugar
- 1/3 cup baking cocoa
- 1 teaspoon baking soda
- 1/2 teaspoon salt

MOCHA FROSTING:
- 3 tablespoons milk chocolate chips
- 3 tablespoons semisweet chocolate chips
- 1/3 cup butter, softened
- 2 cups confectioners' sugar
- 1 to 2 tablespoons brewed coffee
- 1/2 cup chocolate sprinkles

2 teaspoons vanilla extract

1/2 teaspoon cream of tartar

LEMON FROSTING:

1/3 cup butter, softened

3 cups confectioners' sugar

4-1/2 teaspoons grated lemon peel

Dash salt

1/4 cup lemon juice

1 Let eggs stand at room temperature for 30 minutes. In a large bowl, combine the flour, sugar, baking powder and salt. In another bowl, whisk the egg yolks, water, oil, lemon peel and vanilla; add to dry ingredients. Beat until well blended.

2 In another large bowl, beat egg whites and cream of tartar on medium speed until soft peaks form; fold into batter. Gently spoon into an ungreased 10-in. tube pan. Cut through batter with a knife to remove air pockets.

3 Bake on the lowest oven rack at 325° for 50-55 minutes or until top springs back when lightly touched. Immediately invert the pan; cool completely, about 1 hour.

4 Run a knife around side and center tube of pan. Remove cake to a serving plate. In a small bowl, combine frosting ingredients; beat until smooth. Spread over top of cake.

Chocolate Chip Banana Cream Pie

PREP: 25 MIN. BAKE: 10 MIN. + CHILLING YIELD: 6-8 SERVINGS

TAYLOR CARROLL PARKESBURG, PENNSYLVANIA

This rich treat is a hit every time I serve it. Brimming with bananas, the chilled filling is refreshing, and the cookie crust provides a chocolaty crunch. Even a small slice will satisfy the biggest sweet tooth.

1 tube (16-1/2 ounces) refrigerated chocolate chip cookie dough

1/3 cup sugar

1/4 cup cornstarch

1/8 teaspoon salt

2-1/3 cups milk

5 egg yolks, lightly beaten

2 tablespoons butter

2 teaspoons vanilla extract, *divided*

3 medium firm bananas

1-1/2 cups heavy whipping cream

3 tablespoons confectioners' sugar

1 Cut the cookie dough in half widthwise. Let one portion stand at room temperature for 5-10 minutes to soften (return the other half to the refrigerator for another use).

2 Press dough onto the bottom and up the sides of an ungreased 9-in. pie plate. Bake at 375° for 11-12 minutes or until lightly browned. Cool on a wire rack.

3 In a large saucepan, combine the sugar, cornstarch and salt. Stir in milk until smooth. Cook and stir over medium-high heat until thickened and bubbly. Reduce heat; cook and stir 2 minutes longer. Remove from the heat. Stir a small amount of hot filling into egg yolks; return all to the pan, stirring constantly. Bring to a gentle boil; cook and stir 2 minutes longer. Remove from the heat; stir in butter and 1 teaspoon vanilla.

4 Spread 1 cup filling into prepared crust. Slice bananas; arrange over filling. Pour remaining filling over bananas. Refrigerate for 2 hours or until set.

5 In a large bowl, beat cream until it begins to thicken. Add confectioners' sugar and remaining vanilla; beat until stiff peaks form. Spread over pie. Refrigerate for 1 hour or until chilled. Refrigerate leftovers.

When making a cream pie with egg yolks, the hot liquid needs to be added carefully to the egg yolks. Remove about 1 cup of the hot mixture and stir into the yolks. Return mixture to pan. Proceed with recipe as directed.

Chocolate Mocha Torte

PREP: 50 MIN. BAKE: 35 MIN. + COOLING YIELD: 16 SERVINGS

ABBY SLAVINGS BUCHANAN, MICHIGAN

A mocha filling is spread between the layers of this decadent chocolate cake that's piled high with flavor.

CAKE:
- 1/2 cup baking cocoa
- 1/2 cup boiling water
- 2-1/2 cups all-purpose flour
- 1-1/2 teaspoons baking soda
- 1/2 teaspoon salt
- 2/3 cup butter, softened
- 1-3/4 cups sugar
- 2 eggs
- 1 teaspoon vanilla extract
- 1 cup buttermilk

FILLING:
- 5 tablespoons all-purpose flour
- 1 cup milk
- 1 cup butter, softened
- 1 cup sugar
- 1/2 teaspoon instant coffee granules
- 2 teaspoons water
- 2 teaspoons baking cocoa
- 1 teaspoon vanilla extract
- 1 cup chopped pecans

FROSTING:
- 1/2 cup shortening
- 1/4 cup butter, softened
- 2 tablespoons plus 1-1/2 teaspoons evaporated milk
- 1 tablespoon boiling water
- 1-1/2 teaspoons vanilla extract
- Dash salt
- 3-3/4 cups confectioners' sugar, *divided*
- Pecan halves, optional

1 For cake, make a paste of cocoa and water; cool and set aside. Sift together the flour, baking soda and salt; set aside. In a large bowl, cream butter and sugar until light and fluffy. Add eggs, one at a time, beating well after each addition. Beat in vanilla. Blend in cocoa mixture. Add dry ingredients to the creamed mixture alternately with buttermilk, beating well after each addition.

2 Pour into two greased and floured 9-in. round baking pans. Bake at 350° for 35 minutes or until a toothpick inserted near the center comes out clean. Cool for 10 minutes before removing from pans to wire racks to cool completely.

3 For filling, in a saucepan, combine the flour and milk until smooth. Bring to a boil over low heat; cook and stir for 1-2 minutes or until thickened. Remove from the heat; cool.

4 Meanwhile, cream butter and sugar until light and fluffy. Dissolve coffee in water; add to creamed mixture along with cocoa, vanilla and cooled milk mixture. Beat until fluffy, about 5 minutes. Fold in nuts.

5 Split each cake into two horizontal layers. Place bottom layer on a serving plate; top with a third of the filling. Repeat layers twice. Top with remaining cake layer.

6 For frosting, in a large bowl, cream shortening and butter until light and fluffy. Add the milk, water, vanilla, salt and half of confectioners' sugar; mix well. Beat in the remaining confectioners' sugar until smooth and fluffy. Spread frosting between layers and over the top and sides of cake. Garnish with pecan halves if desired.

Chunky Apple Cake

PREP: 20 MIN. BAKE: 40 MIN. + COOLING YIELD: 12-14 SERVINGS

DEBI BENSON BAKERSFIELD, CALIFORNIA

This tender cake is full of old-fashioned comfort, and the yummy brown-sugar sauce makes it special. For a festive occasion, top with a dollop of whipped cream.

- 1/2 cup butter, softened
- 2 cups sugar
- 2 eggs
- 1/2 teaspoon vanilla extract

1 package (18-1/4 ounces) lemon cake mix
1-1/3 cups water
3/4 cup egg substitute
1/3 cup unsweetened applesauce
3 tablespoons poppy seeds

FILLING:
1 package (8 ounces) reduced-fat cream cheese
1/2 cup confectioners' sugar
1 can (15-3/4 ounces) lemon pie filling

TOPPING:
1/3 cup packed brown sugar
1/4 cup chopped pecans
3 tablespoons all-purpose flour
4-1/2 teaspoons butter, melted
1/2 teaspoon ground cinnamon
1/8 teaspoon vanilla extract

GLAZE:
1/2 cup confectioners' sugar
4 teaspoons lemon juice

1 In a large bowl, combine the first five ingredients; beat on low speed for 30 seconds. Beat on medium for 2 minutes. Coat a 13-in. x 9-in. baking pan with cooking spray and dust with flour; spread half of the batter into pan.

2 For filling, in a large bowl, beat cream cheese and confectioners' sugar until smooth. Stir in pie filling. Drop by teaspoonfuls and gently spread over batter. Top with remaining batter. Combine topping ingredients; sprinkle over batter.

3 Bake at 350° for 40-45 minutes or until a toothpick inserted near the center comes out clean. Cool on a wire rack. Combine glaze ingredients; drizzle over cake. Refrigerate leftovers.

---

2 cups all-purpose flour
1-1/2 teaspoons ground cinnamon
1 teaspoon ground nutmeg
1/2 teaspoon salt
1/2 teaspoon baking soda
6 cups chopped peeled tart apples

BUTTERSCOTCH SAUCE:
1/2 cup packed brown sugar
1/4 cup butter, cubed
1/2 cup heavy whipping cream

1 In a large bowl, cream butter and sugar until light and fluffy. Add eggs, one at a time, beating well after each addition. Beat in vanilla. Combine the flour, cinnamon, nutmeg, salt and baking soda; gradually add to creamed mixture and mix well (batter will be stiff). Stir in apples until well combined.

2 Spread into a greased 13-in. x 9-in. baking dish. Bake at 350° for 40-45 minutes or until top is lightly browned and springs back when lightly touched. Cool for 30 minutes before serving.

3 For sauce, meanwhile, in a small saucepan, combine brown sugar and butter. Cook over medium heat until butter is melted. Gradually add cream. Bring to a slow boil over medium heat, stirring constantly. Remove from the heat. Serve with cake.

Lemon Delight Cake

PREP: 35 MIN. **BAKE:** 40 MIN. + COOLING **YIELD:** 18 SERVINGS

LYDIA MASON BRAINERD, MINNESOTA

When I needed to bring a treat to work, I combined four different recipes into this moist cake. A boxed mix makes it easy, but the creamy filling and buttery topping make it memorable.

Zucchini Cupcakes

PREP: 20 MIN. BAKE: 20 MIN. + COOLING
YIELD: 1-1/2 TO 2 DOZEN

VIRGINIA BREITMEYER CRAFTSBURY, VERMONT

I asked my grandmother for this recipe after trying these irresistible spice cupcakes at her home. I love their creamy caramel frosting. They're such a scrumptious dessert; you actually forget you're eating your vegetables, too!

> 3 eggs
> 1-1/3 cups sugar
> 1/2 cup canola oil
> 1/2 cup orange juice
> 1 teaspoon almond extract
> 2-1/2 cups all-purpose flour
> 2 teaspoons ground cinnamon
> 2 teaspoons baking powder
> 1 teaspoon baking soda
> 1 teaspoon salt
> 1/2 teaspoon ground cloves
> 1-1/2 cups shredded zucchini

CARAMEL FROSTING:
> 1 cup packed brown sugar
> 1/2 cup butter
> 1/4 cup milk
> 1 teaspoon vanilla extract
> 1-1/2 to 2 cups confectioners' sugar

1 In a large bowl, beat the eggs, sugar, oil, orange juice and extract. Combine dry ingredients; gradually add to egg mixture and mix well. Stir in zucchini.

2 Fill paper-lined muffin cups two-thirds full. Bake at 350° for 20-25 minutes or until toothpick comes out clean. Cool for 10 minutes before removing to a wire rack.

3 For frosting, combine brown sugar, butter and milk in a saucepan. Bring to a boil over medium heat; cook and stir for 2 minutes or until thickened. Remove from the heat; stir in vanilla. Cool to lukewarm.

4 Gradually beat in confectioners' sugar until frosting reaches spreading consistency. Frost cupcakes.

Coffee Ice Cream Pie

PREP: 30 MIN. + FREEZING YIELD: 8 SERVINGS

VELMA BROWN TURNER STATION, KENTUCKY

While coffee ice cream is great, I sometimes vary the flavor of this family favorite. It's one dreamy summertime treat that's always high on requests for dessert.

> 2 ounces unsweetened chocolate
> 1/4 cup butter, cubed
> 1 can (5 ounces) evaporated milk
> 1/2 cup sugar
> 1 pint coffee ice cream, softened
> 1 chocolate crumb crust (8 inches)
> 1 carton (8 ounces) frozen whipped topping, thawed
> 1/4 cup chopped pecans

1 In a heavy saucepan, melt chocolate and butter over low heat. Stir in milk and sugar. Bring to a boil over medium heat, stirring constantly. Cook and stir for 3-4 minutes or until thickened. Remove from the heat; cool completely.

2 Spoon ice cream into crust. Stir sauce; spread over ice cream. Top with whipped topping; sprinkle with pecans. Freeze until firm. Remove from the freezer 15 minutes before serving.

HELEN TOULANTIS
WANTAGH, NEW YORK

When our family is invited to holiday gatherings, this pie usually comes with us. The recipe is very versatile. You can make it with a double crust or replace the pears with baking apples. Serve it with ice cream or even whipped topping.

Cranberry Pear Pie

PREP: 20 MIN. BAKE: 50 MIN. + COOLING YIELD: 6-8 SERVINGS

Pastry for single-crust pie (9 inches)

- 2 **tablespoons all-purpose flour**
- 1/2 **cup maple syrup**
- 2 **tablespoons butter, melted**
- 5 **cups sliced peeled fresh pears**
- 1 **cup fresh *or* frozen cranberries**

TOPPING:

- 1/2 **cup all-purpose flour**
- 1/4 **cup packed brown sugar**
- 1 **teaspoon ground cinnamon**
- 1/3 **cup cold butter, cubed**
- 1/2 **cup chopped walnuts**

1 Line a 9-in. pie plate with pastry; trim and flute edges. Set aside. In a large bowl, combine the flour, syrup and butter until smooth. Add the pears and cranberries; toss to coat. Spoon into crust. For topping, combine the flour, brown sugar and cinnamon; cut in butter until crumbly. Stir in walnuts. Sprinkle over filling.

2 Cover the edges of the crust loosely with foil to prevent overbrowning. Bake at 400° for 15 minutes. Reduce heat to 350°. Remove the foil; bake 35-40 minutes longer or until crust is golden brown and filling is bubbly. Cool on a wire rack.

To core a fresh pear, insert an apple corer into the bottom of the pear to within 1 in. of its top. Twist the corer to cut around the core, then slowly pull the corer out. If you don't have an apple corer, use a sharp knife or vegetable peeler to cut the core from the bottom of the pear.

Cream-Filled Pumpkin Cupcakes

PREP: 35 MIN. BAKE: 20 MIN. + COOLING
YIELD: ABOUT 1-3/4 DOZEN

ALI JOHNSON PETERSBURG, PENNSYLVANIA

Here's a deliciously different use for pumpkin. Bursting with flavor and plenty of eye-catching appeal, these sweet and spicy filled cupcakes are bound to dazzle your family any time of the year.

- 2 cups sugar
- 3/4 cup canola oil
- 1 can (15 ounces) solid-pack pumpkin
- 4 eggs
- 2 cups all-purpose flour
- 2 teaspoons baking soda
- 1 teaspoon salt
- 1 teaspoon baking powder
- 1 teaspoon ground cinnamon

FILLING:
- 1 tablespoon cornstarch
- 1 cup milk
- 1/2 cup shortening
- 1/4 cup butter, softened
- 2 cups confectioners' sugar
- 1/2 teaspoon vanilla extract, optional

1 In a large bowl, combine the sugar, oil, pumpkin and eggs. Combine the flour, baking soda, salt, baking powder and cinnamon; gradually add to pumpkin mixture and beat until well mixed.

2 Fill paper-lined muffin cups two-thirds full. Bake at 350° for 18-22 minutes or until a toothpick comes out clean. Cool for 10 minutes before removing from pans to wire racks to cool completely.

3 For filling, combine cornstarch and milk in a small saucepan until smooth. Bring to a boil, stirring constantly. Remove from the heat; cool to room temperature.

4 In a large bowl, cream the shortening, butter and confectioners' sugar. Beat in vanilla if desired. Gradually add the cornstarch mixture, beating until light and fluffy.

5 Using a sharp knife, cut a 1-in. circle 1 in. deep in the top of each cupcake. Carefully remove the tops and set aside. Spoon or pipe the filling into cupcakes. Replace tops.

Blueberry Pie With Lemon Crust

PREP: 30 MIN. + CHILLING BAKE: 40 MIN. YIELD: 6-8 SERVINGS

SARA WEST BROKEN ARROW, OKLAHOMA

I've never entered a cooking contest before, but when "Country Woman" magazine requested blueberry recipes, I had to send in this tasty pie. Mom and I have a lot of fun making it together, and I hope one day to be a great baker like she is. I think that the zesty lemon peel pairs well with the sweet blueberries.

- 2 cups all-purpose flour
- 1 teaspoon salt
- 1/2 teaspoon grated lemon peel
- 2/3 cup shortening
- 1 tablespoon lemon juice
- 4 to 6 tablespoons cold water

FILLING:
- 4 cups fresh blueberries
- 3/4 cup sugar
- 3 tablespoons all-purpose flour
- 1/2 teaspoon grated lemon peel

Dash salt
- 1 to 2 teaspoons lemon juice
- 1 tablespoon butter

1. In a large bowl, combine the flour, salt and lemon peel. Cut in shortening until crumbly. Add lemon juice. Gradually add water, tossing with a fork until a ball forms. Cover and refrigerate for 1 hour.

2. Divide dough in half. On a lightly floured surface, roll out one portion to fit a 9-in. pie plate. Transfer pastry to pie plate; trim to 1 in. beyond edge of plate.

3. For filling, in a large bowl, combine the blueberries, sugar, flour, lemon peel and salt; spoon into crust. Drizzle with lemon juice; dot with butter. Roll out remaining pastry; place over filling. Seal and flute edges. Cut slits in top crust.

4. Bake at 400° for 40-45 minutes or until crust is golden brown and filling is bubbly. Cool on a wire rack. Store in refrigerator.

White Chocolate Banana Cake

PREP: 30 MIN. BAKE: 25 MIN. + COOLING YIELD: 12-16 SERVINGS

YVONNE ARTZ GREENVILLE, OHIO

When I mentioned a recipe contest to my husband, he immediately suggested I enter this extra-special cake. The batter is packed with ripe bananas and white chocolate, and it tastes wonderful even without the frosting.

  1/2 cup shortening
    2 cups sugar
    2 eggs
1-1/2 cups mashed ripe bananas (about 3 medium)
    3 teaspoons vanilla extract
    3 cups all-purpose flour
    1 teaspoon baking powder

  1/2 teaspoon baking soda
  1/2 teaspoon salt
    1 cup buttermilk
    4 squares (1 ounce *each*) white baking chocolate, melted and cooled

CREAM CHEESE FROSTING:
    1 package (8 ounces) cream cheese, softened
  3/4 cup butter, softened
    1 teaspoon vanilla extract
    5 cups confectioners' sugar
  1/2 cup finely chopped pecans, toasted

1. In a large bowl, cream shortening and sugar until light and fluffy. Add eggs, one at a time, beating well after each addition. Beat in bananas and vanilla. Combine the flour, baking powder, baking soda and salt; add to creamed mixture alternately with buttermilk, beating well after each addition. Fold in chocolate.

2. Pour into three greased and floured 9-in. round baking pan. Bake at 350° for 25-30 minutes or until a toothpick inserted near the center comes out clean. Cool for 10 minutes before removing cake from pans to wire racks to cool completely.

3. For frosting, in a large bowl, beat the cream cheese, butter and vanilla until smooth. Gradually beat in confectioners' sugar. Spread between layers and over top and sides of cake. Sprinkle with pecans. Store in the refrigerator.

Chocolate Whipping Cream Torte

PREP: 45 MIN. BAKE: 20 MIN. YIELD: 22 SERVINGS

RITA FUTRAL STARKVILLE, MISSISSIPPI

This recipe is a trio of decadent flavors, including tender chocolate cake, layered with a sweet vanilla filling, and topped with a rich chocolate icing. The cake is made with unsweetened chocolate, which also goes by the names of baking or bitter chocolate.

- 1/2 cup butter, cubed
- 3 ounces unsweetened chocolate
- 1-1/2 cups heavy whipping cream
- 4 eggs, lightly beaten
- 1 teaspoon vanilla extract
- 2 cups all-purpose flour
- 1-1/2 cups sugar
- 2 teaspoons baking powder
- 1/2 teaspoon salt

FILLING:
- 1 cup heavy whipping cream
- 1 package (8 ounces) cream cheese, softened
- 1 cup confectioners' sugar
- 1 teaspoon vanilla extract

ICING:
- 1/4 cup butter
- 2 ounces unsweetened chocolate
- 1/2 cup heavy whipping cream
- 1 teaspoon vanilla extract
- 3 cups confectioners' sugar, sifted

Fresh whole strawberries, optional

1 In heavy saucepan or microwave, melt butter and chocolate; stir until smooth. Cool. In a chilled large bowl, beat cream until soft peaks form. Add the eggs, vanilla and cooled chocolate mixture; beat on low speed just until combined. Combine the flour, sugar, baking powder and salt. With mixer on low speed, add dry ingredients to creamed mixture until just combined.

2 Pour into three greased and floured 8-in. or 9-in. round baking pans. Bake at 350° for 20-25 minutes or a toothpick inserted near the center comes clean. Cool for 10 minutes before removing from pans to wire racks to cool completely.

3 For filling, beat cream in a chilled small bowl until soft peaks form; set aside. In a large bowl, beat cream cheese until smooth. Beat in confectioners' sugar and vanilla. Add whipped cream, beat until smooth.

4 Split each cake into two horizontal layers. Place one layer on a serving plate; top with about 1/2 cup filling. Repeat four times. Top with remaining cake layer. Cover and refrigerate.

5 For icing, melt butter and chocolate in a heavy saucepan or microwave; stir until smooth. Cool to room temperature; transfer to a large bowl. Add cream and vanilla; mix well. Beat in confectioners' sugar. Spread over top and sides of cake. Garnish with strawberries if desired. Store in the refrigerator.

Butter Pecan Pumpkin Pie

PREP: 20 MIN. + FREEZING YIELD: 6-8 SERVINGS

ARLETTA SLOCUM VENICE, FLORIDA

This pie is so easy to assemble. It's handy to have in the freezer when unexpected company stops in.

1 quart butter pecan ice cream, softened

1 pastry shell (9 inches), baked

1 cup canned pumpkin

1/2 cup sugar

1/4 teaspoon *each* ground cinnamon, ginger and nutmeg

1 cup heavy whipping cream, whipped

1/2 cup caramel ice cream topping

1/2 cup chocolate ice cream topping, optional

Additional whipped cream

1 Spread ice cream into the crust; freeze for 2 hours or until firm. In a small bowl, combine the pumpkin, sugar, cinnamon, ginger and nutmeg; fold in whipped cream. Spread over ice cream. Cover and freeze for 2 hours or until firm. May be frozen for up to 2 months.

2 Remove from the freezer 15 minutes before slicing. Drizzle with caramel ice cream topping. Drizzle with chocolate ice cream topping if desired. Dollop with whipped cream.

Tunnel of Berries Cake

PREP: 30 MIN. BAKE: 1 HOUR + COOLING YIELD: 12 SERVINGS

SHIRLEY NOE LEBANON JUNCTION, KENTUCKY

This cake is not overly sweet or heavy. If your family does not care for strawberries, try using peaches instead.

6 eggs, *separated*

2-1/4 cups cake flour

2 cups sugar, *divided*

1 tablespoon baking powder

1 teaspoon ground cinnamon

3/4 teaspoon salt

3/4 cup water

1/2 cup canola oil

1-1/2 teaspoons vanilla extract, *divided*

1/4 teaspoon cream of tartar

4 cups fresh whole strawberries, *divided*

2-1/2 cups heavy whipping cream

1 Let the eggs stand at room temperature for 30 minutes. In a large bowl, combine flour, 1 cup sugar, baking powder, ground cinnamon and salt. In a bowl, whisk yolks, water, oil and 1 teaspoon vanilla; add to dry ingredients. Beat until well blended. In another large bowl and with clean beaters, beat egg whites and cream of tartar on medium speed until soft peaks form. Fold into the yolk mixture.

2 Gently spoon batter into an ungreased 10-in. tube pan. Cut through the batter with a knife to remove air pockets. Bake at 325° for 60-70 minutes or until top springs back when lightly touched and cracks feel dry. Immediately invert pan; cool completely. Run a knife around sides and center tube of pan. Invert cake onto a serving plate.

3 Slice off the top 1/2 in. of cake; set aside. With a knife, cut a tunnel about 1-1/2 in. deep in top of cake, leaving a 3/4-in. shell. Remove cake from tunnel and save for another use. Chop half of the strawberries; set aside. In a chilled large bowl, beat whipping cream until it begins to thicken. Gradually add remaining sugar and vanilla, beating until stiff peaks form. Combine 1-1/2 cups cream mixture and chopped berries.

4 Fill the tunnel with strawberry mixture. Replace cake top. Frost cake with the remaining cream mixture. Refrigerate. Just before serving, cut the remaining strawberries in half and use to garnish the cake. Refrigerate leftovers.

To stabilize whipped cream, add gelatin. Soften 1/2 teaspoon unflavored gelatin in 1 tablespoon cold water in a heatproof glass measuring cup; let stand for 5 minutes. Heat gelatin (in the cup) in a pan of simmering water, or microwave until melted. Cool slightly (mixture will be warm). Beat 1 cup whipping cream until soft peaks form. Add gelatin mixture and some sugar; beat until thickened.

Strawberry Lover's Pie

PREP: 25 MIN. + CHILLING YIELD: 6-8 SERVINGS

LAURETHA ROWE SCRANTON, KANSAS

The second question people ask when I serve them this pie is, "What's your recipe?" It comes right after their first question, "May I have another slice?"

3	ounces semisweet chocolate, *divided*
1	tablespoon butter
1	pastry shell (9 inches), baked
2	packages (3 ounces *each*) cream cheese, softened
1/2	cup sour cream
3	tablespoons sugar
1/2	teaspoon vanilla extract
3 to 4	cups fresh strawberries, hulled
1/3	cup strawberry jam, melted

1 In a large saucepan, melt 2 oz. chocolate and butter over low heat, stirring constantly; spread or brush over the bottom and up the sides of pastry shell. Chill.

2 Meanwhile, in a large bowl, beat the cream cheese, sour cream, sugar and vanilla until smooth. Spread over chocolate layer; cover and chill for 2 hours.

3 Arrange strawberries over the filling; brush with jam. Melt the remaining chocolate and drizzle over the top.

White Chocolate Mousse Cherry Pie

PREP: 1 HOUR BAKE: 15 MIN. + CHILLING YIELD: 8-10 SERVINGS

BERNICE JANOWSKI STEVENS POINT, WISCONSIN

A cookie crust is topped with a cherry-almond filling and light-as-air mousse in this delectable dessert. It makes any dinner extra special.

14	cream-filled chocolate sandwich cookies
3/4	cup chopped macadamia nuts
2	tablespoons butter, melted

FILLING:

1	tablespoon cornstarch
2	tablespoons water
1	can (21 ounces) cherry pie filling
1/2	teaspoon almond extract

WHITE CHOCOLATE MOUSSE:

1	cup cold milk
1	package (3.3 ounces) instant white chocolate pudding mix
1	envelope unflavored gelatin
3	cups heavy whipping cream, *divided*
1/4	cup sugar
1/4	teaspoon almond extract

Chocolate curls and drizzle, optional

1 In a food processor, combine the cookies and nuts; cover and process until cookies are finely chopped. Add butter; cover and pulse until mixture resembles coarse crumbs.

2 Press onto the bottom and up the sides of an ungreased 9-in. deep-dish pie plate. Bake at 350° for 8-10 minutes or until set. Cool on a wire rack.

3 For filling, combine the cornstarch and water in a small saucepan until smooth. Stir in pie filling. Bring to a boil; cook and stir for 1 minute or until slightly thickened. Remove from the heat; stir in the extract. Cool completely.

4 For mousse, in a large bowl, whisk milk and pudding mix for 2 minutes. Let stand for 2 minutes or until soft-set; set aside. In a small saucepan, sprinkle gelatin over 1/2 cup cream; let stand for 1 minute. Heat over low heat, stirring until gelatin is completely dissolved. Remove from the heat.

5 In a large bowl, beat remaining cream until it begins to thicken. Add sugar and extract; beat until soft peaks form. Gradually beat in gelatin mixture. Fold into pudding. Refrigerate until slightly firm, about 30 minutes.

6 Spread cooled filling into crust; top with mousse. Refrigerate for 2 hours or until firm. Garnish with chocolate curls and drizzle if desired.

Carrot Layer Cake

PREP: 55 MIN. BAKE: 35 MIN. + COOLING YIELD: 16-20 SERVINGS

LINDA VAN HOLLAND INNISFAIL, ALBERTA

My sister gave me this recipe for what she called "the ultimate carrot cake." It really lives up to the name! When people cut into it, they're bowled over by the moist, not-too-sweet cake with a decadent pecan filling. It's a dessert that turns any meal into a special occasion.

FILLING:
  1 cup sugar
  2 tablespoons all-purpose flour
1/4 teaspoon salt
  1 cup heavy whipping cream
1/2 cup butter
  1 cup chopped pecans
  1 teaspoon vanilla extract

CAKE:
1-1/4 cups canola oil
  2 cups sugar
  2 cups all-purpose flour
  2 teaspoons ground cinnamon
  2 teaspoons baking powder
  1 teaspoon baking soda

  1 teaspoon salt
  4 eggs
  4 cups finely shredded carrots
  1 cup raisins
  1 cup chopped pecans

FROSTING:
3/4 cup butter, softened
  2 packages (3 ounces *each*) cream cheese, softened
  1 teaspoon vanilla extract
  3 cups confectioners' sugar

1 For filling, in a large heavy saucepan, combine sugar, flour and salt. Stir in cream; add butter. Cook and stir over medium heat until the butter is melted; bring to a boil. Reduce heat. Simmer, uncovered, for 30 minutes, stirring occasionally. Stir in nuts and vanilla. Cool and set aside.

2 For cake, in a large bowl, beat oil and sugar until well blended. Combine the flour, cinnamon, baking powder, baking soda and salt; add to the creamed mixture alternately with eggs, beating well after each addition. Stir in the carrots, raisins and nuts.

3 Pour into three greased and floured 9-in. round baking pans. Bake at 350° for 35-40 minutes or until a toothpick inserted near the center comes out clean. Cool in pans 10 minutes before removing to wire racks to cool completely.

4 For frosting, in a small bowl, beat the butter, cream cheese and vanilla until fluffy. Gradually beat in sugar until smooth. Spread filling between cake layers. Frost the sides and top of cake. Store in the refrigerator.

Pecan Cake Roll

PREP: 20 MIN. + CHILLING BAKE: 10 MIN. + COOLING
YIELD: 10-12 SERVINGS

SHIRLEY AWALD WALKERTON, INDIANA

Like my husband, I'm a retired teacher. This dessert is one that always went over big as a snack whenever I'd take it to share in the teachers' lounge! However, it's rich and elegant enough to be used for a special occasion. For a boost of flavor, toast the pecans before grinding them.

   4 **eggs,** *separated*
   1 **cup confectioners' sugar**
   2 **cups ground pecans**
   1 **cup heavy whipping cream**
   3 **tablespoons sugar**
   2 **teaspoons baking cocoa**
   1/2 **teaspoon vanilla extract**

Chocolate shavings and additional confectioners' sugar, optional

1   Let eggs stand at room temperature for 30 minutes. Line a greased 15-in. x 10-in. x 1-in. baking pan with waxed paper; grease and flour paper and set aside.

2   In a large bowl, beat egg yolks and confectioners' sugar until thick and lemon-colored, about 5 minutes. In another bowl, beat whites until soft peaks form; fold into yolk mixture. Fold in pecans until well blended (batter will be thin).

3   Spread batter into prepared pan. Bake at 375° for 10-15 minutes or until cake springs back when lightly touched. Cool in pan for 5 minutes. Turn onto a linen towel dusted with confectioners' sugar. Gently peel off waxed paper. Roll cake up in towel, starting with short end. Cool completely on wire rack.

4   Meanwhile, beat the cream, sugar, cocoa and vanilla in a bowl until soft peaks form. Carefully unroll cake. Spread filling over cake to within 1/2 in. of edges. Roll up again. Cover and refrigerate for 1 hour before serving. If desired, garnish with chocolate shavings and confectioners' sugar. Refrigerate leftovers.

Chocolate-Cherry Ice Cream Pie

PREP: 15 MIN. + FREEZING YIELD: 6 SERVINGS

KIMBERLY WEST PRAIRIEVILLE, LOUISIANA

No one would ever dream that the fancy taste and look of this luscious freezer pie could come from only five simple ingredients! This makes an unbelievably easy dessert.

   1 **bottle (7-1/4 ounces) chocolate hard-shell ice cream topping,** *divided*
   1 **graham cracker crust (9 inches)**
   1 **jar (10 ounces) maraschino cherries, drained**
   1 **quart vanilla ice cream, softened**
   2 **packages (1-1/2 ounces** *each***) peanut butter cups, chopped**

1   Following package directions, drizzle half of the ice cream topping over crust; gently spread to coat bottom and sides. Freeze until firm.

2   Meanwhile, set aside six cherries for garnish; chop remaining cherries. In a large bowl, combine ice cream and chopped cherries. Spread into prepared crust. Sprinkle with peanut butter cups; drizzle with remaining ice cream topping.

3   Garnish with reserved cherries. Cover and freeze for 2 hours or until firm. Remove from the freezer 15 minutes before serving.

Raspberry Meringue Pie

PREP: 30 MIN. BAKE: 15 MIN. + CHILLING YIELD: 8-10 SERVINGS

KAREN REMPEL ARTHUR WAINFLEET, ONTARIO

Whether my husband and I are hosting a barbecue or a formal dinner, we love treating guests to this raspberry pie.

- 1/3 **cup plus 1/4 cup sugar,** *divided*
- 3 **tablespoons cornstarch**
- 1-1/2 **cups milk**
- 4 **eggs,** *separated*
- 1 **teaspoon butter**
- 1/4 **teaspoon almond extract**
- 1 **extra-servings-size graham cracker crust (9 ounces)**
- 1-1/8 **teaspoons unflavored gelatin**
- 2 **tablespoons plus 1/4 teaspoon cold water,** *divided*
- 1 **can (21 ounces) raspberry pie filling**
- 3/4 **teaspoon cream of tartar**

1 In a saucepan, combine 1/3 cup sugar and cornstarch. Stir in milk until smooth. Cook and stir over medium heat until thickened and bubbly. Reduce heat; cook and stir 2 minutes longer. Remove from the heat. Stir in a small amount of mixture into egg yolks. Return all to the pan, stirring constantly. Bring to a gentle boil; cook and stir 2 minutes longer. Remove from the heat; stir in butter and extract. Pour hot filling into the crust.

2 Sprinkle gelatin over 2 tablespoons cold water; let stand for 2 minutes. In a saucepan, bring raspberry filling and gelatin mixture to a boil. Reduce heat; simmer, uncovered, for 5 minutes.

3 Meanwhile, in a large bowl, beat egg whites and cream of tartar until soft peaks form. Beat in remaining water. Gradually beat in remaining sugar, 1 tablespoon at a time, on high until stiff, glossy peaks form.

4 Pour hot raspberry filling over custard. Spread meringue evenly over hot filling, sealing edges to crust. Bake at 325° for 15-18 minutes or until meringue is golden brown. Cool on a wire rack for 1 hour. Refrigerate for at least 3 hours before serving. Refrigerate leftovers.

Cheddar Pear Pie

PREP: 10 MIN. BAKE: 25 MIN. + COOLING YIELD: 6-8 SERVINGS

CYNTHIA LABREE ELMER, NEW JERSEY

I take this pie to lots of different gatherings, and I make sure to have copies of the recipe with me since people always ask for it.

- 4 **large ripe pears, peeled and thinly sliced**
- 1/3 **cup sugar**
- 1 **tablespoon cornstarch**
- 1/8 **teaspoon salt**
- 1 **unbaked pastry shell (9 inches)**

TOPPING:
- 1/2 **cup shredded cheddar cheese**
- 1/2 **cup all-purpose flour**
- 1/4 **cup sugar**
- 1/4 **teaspoon salt**
- 1/4 **cup butter, melted**

1 In a large bowl, combine pears, sugar, cornstarch and salt; toss gently to coat. Pour into pastry shell.

2 For topping, combine the cheese, flour, sugar and salt; stir in butter until crumbly. Sprinkle over filling.

3 Bake at 425° for 25-35 minutes or until crust is golden and cheese is melted. Cool on a wire rack for 15-20. Serve warm. Store in the refrigerator.

ELVA ROBERTS
SUMMERSIDE,
PRINCE EDWARD ISLAND

This is the dessert I make when I'm craving something cool and fruity. It's a lovely ending to any meal. The cream cheese adds zing to the fluffy filling.

Peaches and Cream Torte

PREP: 40 MIN. + CHILLING YIELD: 12 SERVINGS

2 cups graham cracker crumbs

1/3 cup packed brown sugar

1/2 cup butter, melted

FILLING:

1 can (29 ounces) sliced peaches

1-1/4 cups sugar, *divided*

2 tablespoons cornstarch

1 package (8 ounces) cream cheese, softened

2 cups heavy whipping cream

1 In a small bowl, combine graham cracker crumbs and brown sugar; stir in butter. Set aside 1/4 cup for topping. Press remaining crumb mixture onto the bottom and 1 in. up the sides of a greased 9-in. springform pan.

2 Place pan on a baking sheet. Bake at 350° for 10 minutes. Cool on a wire rack.

3 Drain peaches, reserving syrup in a 2-cup measuring cup. Add enough water to measure 1-1/2 cups. In a large saucepan, combine 1/4 cup sugar and cornstarch; stir in syrup mixture until smooth. Add peaches. Bring to a boil over medium heat; cook and stir for 2 minutes or until thickened. Cool to room temperature, stirring occasionally.

4 Meanwhile, in a large bowl, beat cream cheese and remaining sugar until smooth. In a small bowl, beat cream until stiff peaks form; fold into cream cheese mixture.

5 Spread half of the cream cheese mixture over crust. Top with half of the peach mixture; repeat layers. Sprinkle with the reserved crumb mixture. Cover and refrigerate for 8 hours or overnight. Remove sides of the pan before slicing.

Sour Cream-Lemon Pie

PREP: 20 MIN. + CHILLING   YIELD: 8 SERVINGS

MARTHA SORENSEN FALLON, NEVADA

I first tasted this delectable pie at a local restaurant and hunted around until I found a similar recipe. This version is a pretty good copy of the one I first tasted. Now, it's my husband's favorite. The sour cream and lemon juice really complement each other.

- 1 cup sugar
- 3 tablespoons plus 1-1/2 teaspoons cornstarch
- 1 tablespoon grated lemon peel
- 1/2 cup lemon juice
- 3 egg yolks, lightly beaten
- 1 cup milk
- 1/4 cup butter, cubed
- 1 cup (8 ounces) sour cream
- 1 pastry shell (9 inches), baked
- 1 cup heavy whipping cream, whipped

Lemon twists for garnish

1 Combine sugar, cornstarch, lemon peel, juice, egg yolks and milk in heavy saucepan; cook over medium heat until thickened. Stir in butter and cool mixture to room temperature.

2 Stir in sour cream and pour filling into pie shell. Spread with whipped cream and garnish with lemon twists. Store in refrigerator.

Royal Raspberry Cake

PREP: 20 MIN. BAKE: 30 MIN. YIELD: 16-20 SERVINGS

GENEVIEVE PRIEWE WHITEWATER, WISCONSIN

My all-time favorite cake recipes include this one. It's easy to make, pretty to look at...and delicious! I never fail to get compliments when I serve this cake to family and friends. The sweet-tart taste is a real treat.

CAKE:

- 2 cups all-purpose flour
- 1/2 teaspoon salt
- 1 tablespoon baking powder
- 1/3 cup butter, room temperature
- 1 cup sugar
- 1 egg, room temperature
- 1 cup milk, room temperature
- 1 teaspoon vanilla extract
- 3-1/2 cups fresh *or* frozen raspberries, thawed

GLAZE:

- 1-1/2 cups confectioners' sugar
- 2 tablespoons cream *or* milk with melted butter
- 1 teaspoon vanilla

Vanilla ice cream, optional

1 In a bowl, whisk together the first three ingredients; set aside. In a bowl, cream butter and sugar until light and fluffy. Beat in egg, milk and vanilla. Add dry ingredients alternately with milk mixture, beating well after each addition. Spread into a greased 13-in. x 9-in. baking dish. Spoon berries over top.

2 Bake at 350° for 30-35 minutes or until center of cake springs back when lightly touched. Cool 5 minutes. Combine glaze ingredients; spread over cake, leaving berries exposed. Serve warm with ice cream.

2. In a large bowl, beat cream cheese until smooth. Stir in the squash until blended. Beat in the sugar, caramel topping, cinnamon, salt, ginger and cloves until blended.

3. In a small bowl, whisk cold milk and pudding mix for two minutes. Let stand for 2 minutes or until soft set. Stir into squash mixture.

4. Spoon into pastry shell. Refrigerate for at least 3 hours. Garnish with whipped cream and coconut.

Chocolate Cake With Fudge Sauce

PREP: 20 MIN. BAKE: 30 MIN. YIELD: 12-15 SERVINGS

LYDIA BRISCOE SCOTT DEPOT, WEST VIRGINIA

My whole family makes sure to leave room for dessert when this wonderful cake is on the menu. We all love chocolate and agree this rich, quick and easy recipe is one of the yummiest ways to enjoy it.

- 1 package (3.4 ounces) cook-and-serve chocolate pudding/pie filling mix
- 2 cups milk
- 1 package (18-1/4 ounces) chocolate cake mix

SAUCE:
- 1/2 cup butter, cubed
- 1 cup (6 ounces) semisweet chocolate chips

Butternut Cream Pie

PREP: 35 MIN. + CHILLING YIELD: 6-8 SERVINGS

SANDRA KREUTER BURNEY, CALIFORNIA

I enjoy making up recipes and began experimenting with squash a couple years ago. Last fall, my garden was loaded with squash, so I came up with this creamy pie. It really went over well at Thanksgiving dinner.

- 1 medium butternut squash (about 2 pounds)
- 1/4 cup hot water
- 1 package (8 ounces) cream cheese, softened
- 1/4 cup sugar
- 2 tablespoons caramel ice cream topping
- 1 teaspoon ground cinnamon
- 1/2 teaspoon salt
- 1/2 teaspoon ground ginger
- 1/4 teaspoon ground cloves
- 3/4 cup plus 2 tablespoons cold milk
- 1 package (5.1 ounces) instant vanilla pudding mix
- 1 pastry shell (9 inches), baked

Whipped cream and toasted flaked coconut

1. Cut squash in half; discard seeds. Place squash cut side down in a microwave-safe dish; add hot water. Cover and microwave for 13-15 minutes or until tender. When cool enough to handle, scoop out pulp and mash. Set aside 1-1/2 cups squash (save remaining squash for another use).

1 can (12 ounces) evaporated milk

2 cups confectioners' sugar

1 teaspoon vanilla extract

Fresh mint, optional

1 In a small saucepan, prepared pudding with milk according to package directions for pudding. Pour into a large bowl; add cake mix and beat until well blended.

2 Spread into a greased 13-in. x 9-in. baking pan. Bake at 350° for 30-35 minutes or until cake springs back when lightly touched and edges pull away from sides of pan. Cool on a wire rack.

3 For sauce, in a large heavy saucepan, melt butter and chocolate over low heat. Stir in evaporated milk and sugar until smooth. Bring to a boil over medium heat; cook and stir for 8 minutes or until thickened. Remove from the heat; stir in vanilla. Serve warm sauce with cake. Serve with mint if desired.

Strawberry Cheesecake Torte

PREP: 30 MIN. + CHILLING BAKE: 25 MIN. + COOLING
YIELD: 12 SERVINGS

KATHY MARTINEZ ENID, OKLAHOMA

After I tasted this dessert at a party, a friend shared the recipe. It originally called for pound cake…and I decided to lighten it up by substituting angel food. The result was this delicious light torte.

1 package (16 ounces) angel food cake mix

1 tablespoon confectioners' sugar

1 package (.3 ounce) sugar-free strawberry gelatin

1/2 cup boiling water

1/4 cup seedless strawberry jam

1 package (8 ounces) reduced-fat cream cheese, cubed

1/3 cup fat-free milk

2 tablespoons lemon juice

3 cups reduced-fat whipped topping

1 package (3.4 ounces) instant cheesecake *or* vanilla pudding mix

1 cup sliced fresh strawberries

1 kiwifruit, peeled, halved and sliced

1-1/2 teaspoons grated lemon peel

1 Line a 15-in. x 10-in. x 1-in. baking pan with ungreased parchment paper. Prepare cake mix according to package directions. Spread the batter evenly in prepared pan. Bake at 350° for 24-26 minutes or until top is lightly browned. Sprinkle sugar over a waxed paper-lined baking sheet. Immediately invert cake onto baking sheet. Gently peel off parchment paper; cool completely.

2 Dissolve gelatin in boiling water. Stir in jam until melted. With a fork, poke cake at 1/2-in. intervals. Brush with gelatin mixture; chill for 10 minutes.

3 In a bowl, beat cream cheese, milk and lemon juice until smooth. Beat in whipped topping and pudding mix. Reserve 1 cup. Cut a small hole in the corner of pastry or plastic bag; insert a large star tip. Fill the bag with pudding mixture.

4 Trim edges of cake. Cut widthwise into three equal rectangles; place one on serving plate. Spread 1/2 cup reserved pudding mixture in center. Pipe pudding mixture around top edge of cake. Repeat layer. Top with third cake layer. Pipe pudding mixture along top edges. Fill center with fruit. Sprinkle with lemon peel. Store in refrigerator.

 There is a quick and simple way to peel kiwifruit with a teaspoon. First, cut off both ends of a kiwi. Then slip a teaspoon just under the skin, matching the spoon's curve to the curve of the fruit. Slide the spoon completely around the kiwi to separate the fruit from the skin. It should easily slip out of the skin in one smooth piece!

1. In a large bowl, cream butter and sugar until light and fluffy. Beat in eggs and vanilla. Combine the flour, cocoa, baking soda and salt; add to creamed mixture alternately with buttermilk, beating well after each addition. Dissolve coffee in water; add to batter. Beat for 2 minutes.

2. Pour into three greased and floured 9-in. round baking pans. Bake at 350° for 16-20 minutes or until a toothpick inserted near the center comes out clean. Cool for 10 minutes before removing from pans to wire racks to cool completely.

3. For topping, dissolve coffee in water in a large bowl; cool. Add cream and brown sugar. Beat until stiff peaks form. Place bottom cake layer on a serving plate; top with 1-1/3 cups of topping. Sprinkle with 1/2 cup of crushed candy bars. Repeat layers twice. Store in the refrigerator.

Toffee-Mocha Cream Torte

PREP: 20 MIN. + COOLING BAKE: 20 MIN. + COOLING
YIELD: 12-14 SERVINGS

LYNN ROGERS RICHFIELD, NORTH CAROLINA

When you really want to impress someone, this scrumptious torte is just the thing to make! Instant coffee granules give the moist chocolate cake a mild mocha flavor...while the fluffy whipped cream layers, blended with brown sugar and crunchy toffee bits, are deliciously rich.

- 1 cup butter, softened
- 2 cups sugar
- 2 eggs
- 1-1/2 teaspoons vanilla extract
- 2-2/3 cups all-purpose flour
- 3/4 cup baking cocoa
- 2 teaspoons baking soda
- 1/4 teaspoon salt
- 1 cup buttermilk
- 2 teaspoons instant coffee granules
- 1 cup boiling water

TOPPING:
- 1/2 teaspoon instant coffee granules
- 1 teaspoon hot water
- 2 cups heavy whipping cream
- 3 tablespoons light brown sugar
- 6 Heath candy bars (1.4 ounces *each*), crushed, *divided*

Frosty Pumpkin Pie

PREP: 15 MIN. + FREEZING YIELD: 8 SERVINGS

JANET JACKSON HOMEDALE, ILLINOIS

This frozen treat is so delightful that no one will guess it's made with reduced-fat ingredients. My gang actually prefers a slice of this layered dessert to traditional pumpkin pie at Christmastime.

- 2 cups frozen reduced-fat vanilla yogurt, softened
- 1 reduced-fat graham cracker crust (9 inches)
- 1 cup canned pumpkin
- 1/2 cup sugar

1 teaspoon pumpkin pie spice

1/2 teaspoon salt

1/2 teaspoon ground ginger

1 carton (8 ounces) frozen reduced-fat whipping topping, thawed

1 Spread yogurt into crust. Freeze for 30 minutes.

2 Meanwhile, in a bowl, combine the pumpkin, sugar, pumpkin pie spice, salt and ginger. Fold in whipped topping. Spoon over frozen yogurt. Freeze for 6 hours or overnight. Remove from the freezer 20 minutes before cutting.

Coconut Cream Dream Cake

PREP: 30 MIN. BAKE: 20 MIN. + COOLING YIELD: 6 SERVINGS

PAMELA SHANK PARKERSBURG, WEST VIRGINIA

This pretty four-layer cake is easy to make with an instant pudding filling and 7-minute frosting. It tastes like coconut cream pie, so it's like getting the best of two desserts in one.

3/4 cup sugar

2 tablespoons shortening

2 tablespoons butter, softened

1 egg

1 egg yolk

3/4 teaspoon vanilla extract

1 cup all-purpose flour

1 teaspoon baking powder

1/2 teaspoon salt

1/2 cup 2% milk

FROSTING/FILLING:

1/2 cup sugar

4 teaspoons water

2 teaspoons light corn syrup

1 egg white

1/4 teaspoon cream of tartar

1/4 teaspoon vanilla extract

1 cup cold 2% milk

1/2 teaspoon coconut extract

1/2 cup instant vanilla pudding mix

6 tablespoons flaked coconut, *divided*

1 In a small bowl, cream the sugar, shortening and butter until light and fluffy. Beat in egg and yolk. Add the vanilla. Combine the flour, baking powder and salt; add to creamed mixture alternately with milk. Beat just until combined.

2 Pour into two 6-in. round baking pans coated with cooking spray. Bake at 350° for 20-25 minutes or until a toothpick comes out clean. Cool for 10 minutes; remove from pans to wire racks. Cool completely.

3 For frosting, in a double boiler over simmering water, combine the sugar, water, corn syrup, egg white and cream of tartar. With a portable mixer, beat on low speed for 1 minute. Continue beating on low over low heat until frosting reaches 160°, about 5 minutes. Pour into a small bowl; add vanilla. Beat on high until stiff peaks form, about 7 minutes.

4 For filling, in a bowl, whisk the milk, extract and pudding mix for 2 minutes. Let stand for 2 minutes or until soft-set. Finely chop 1/4 cup coconut; fold into pudding mix.

5 Split each cake into two horizontal layers. Spread a third of the pudding over one cake layer; repeat layers twice. Top with remaining cake. Frost top and sides. Toast remaining coconut; sprinkle over top. Store in the refrigerator.

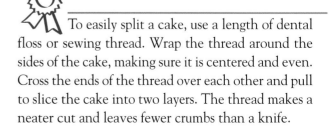

To easily split a cake, use a length of dental floss or sewing thread. Wrap the thread around the sides of the cake, making sure it is centered and even. Cross the ends of the thread over each other and pull to slice the cake into two layers. The thread makes a neater cut and leaves fewer crumbs than a knife.

chocolate velvet dessert, p. 222

Decadent desserts make a perfect finale to a winning meal. Here, you'll find luscious cobblers, custards, frozen treats, showstopping cheesecakes and more!

just desserts

Chocolate Chip Cookie Dough Cheesecake

PREP: 25 MIN. BAKE: 45 MIN. + CHILLING YIELD: 12-14 SERVINGS

JULIE CRAIG JACKSON, WISCONSIN

I created this recipe to combine two of my favorites—cheesecake for the grown-up in me and chocolate chip cookie dough for the little girl in me. Sour cream offsets the sweetness and adds a nice tang. Everyone who tries this scrumptious treat loves it.

1-3/4 cups crushed chocolate chip cookies *or* chocolate wafer crumbs
1/4 cup sugar
1/3 cup butter, melted

FILLING:
3 packages (8 ounces *each*) cream cheese, softened
1 cup sugar
3 eggs, lightly beaten
1 cup (8 ounces) sour cream
1/2 teaspoon vanilla extract

COOKIE DOUGH:
1/4 cup butter, softened
1/4 cup sugar
1/4 cup packed brown sugar
1 tablespoon water
1 teaspoon vanilla extract
1/2 cup all-purpose flour
1-1/2 cups miniature semisweet chocolate chips, *divided*

1 In a small bowl, combine cookie crumbs and sugar; stir in butter. Press onto the bottom and 1 in. up the sides of a greased 9-in. pan. Place pan on a baking sheet; set aside.

2 For filling, in a large bowl, beat cream cheese and sugar until smooth. Add eggs; beat on low just until combined. Add sour cream and vanilla; beat just until blended. Pour over crust; set aside.

3 For cookie dough, in another bowl, cream butter and sugars on medium speed until light and fluffy. Add water and vanilla. Gradually add flour. Stir in 1 cup chocolate chips. Drop dough by teaspoonfuls over filling, gently pushing dough below surface (dough should be completely covered by filling). Place pan on a baking sheet.

4 Bake at 350° for 45-55 minutes or until center is almost set. Cool on a wire rack for 10 minutes. Carefully run a knife around edge of pan to loosen; cool 1 hour longer. Refrigerate overnight.

5 Remove sides of pan. Sprinkle with remaining chips. Refrigerate leftovers.

Creamy Caramel Flan

PREP: 25 MIN. + STANDING BAKE: 50 MIN. + CHILLING
YIELD: 8-10 SERVINGS

PAT FORETE MIAMI, FLORIDA

If you're unfamiliar with flan, think of it as a tasty variation on custard. One warning, though—it's very filling. A small slice goes a long way!

3/4 cup sugar

1 package (8 ounces) cream cheese, softened

5 eggs

1 can (14 ounces) sweetened condensed milk

1 can (12 ounces) evaporated milk

1 teaspoon vanilla extract

1. In a heavy saucepan, cook and stir sugar over medium-low heat until melted and golden, about 15 minutes. Quickly pour into an ungreased 2-qt. round baking or souffle dish, tilting to coat the bottom; let stand for 10 minutes.

2. In a bowl, beat the cream cheese until smooth. Beat in eggs, one at a time, until thoroughly combined. Add remaining ingredients; mix well. Pour mixture over caramelized sugar.

3. Place the dish in a larger baking pan. Pour boiling water into larger pan to a depth of 1 in. Bake at 350° for 50-60 minutes or until center is just set (mixture will jiggle).

4. Remove dish from a larger pan to a wire rack; cool for 1 hour. Refrigerate overnight.

5. To unmold, run a knife around edges and invert onto a large rimmed serving platter. Cut into wedges or spoon onto dessert plates; spoon sauce over each serving.

Old-Fashioned Pear Dessert

PREP: 20 MIN. BAKE: 35 MIN. + COOLING YIELD: 9 SERVINGS

EILEEN UEBERROTH TOLEDO, OHIO

This no-fail pear recipe turns out moist, firm and fruity every time. Some members of our family request these rich squares instead of cake for their birthdays.

2-1/4 cups all-purpose flour

5 tablespoons sugar, *divided*

3/4 teaspoon salt

3/4 cup cold butter

3 egg yolks

4-1/2 teaspoons lemon juice

FILLING:

1/2 cup sugar

4 tablespoons cornstarch, *divided*

1/2 teaspoon salt

1/2 teaspoon ground cinnamon

3/4 cup water

2 tablespoons plus 1-1/2 teaspoons lemon juice

2 tablespoons butter

1 teaspoon vanilla extract

5 cups chopped peeled ripe pears

1. In a large bowl, combine the flour, 3 tablespoons sugar and salt; cut in butter until crumbly. In a small bowl, whisk egg yolks and lemon juice; stir into dry ingredients with a fork. Remove 1 cup to another bowl; stir in the remaining sugar and set aside for the topping.

2. Press remaining crumb mixture onto the bottom and up the sides of a greased 8-in. square baking dish. Bake at 375° for 10-12 minutes or until edges are lightly browned.

3. Meanwhile, for filling, combine the sugar, 2 tablespoons cornstarch, salt and cinnamon in a small saucepan; slowly stir in water and lemon juice until smooth. Bring to a boil over medium heat; cook and stir for 1 minute or until thickened. Remove from the heat; stir in butter and vanilla.

4. Toss pears with remaining cornstarch; spoon over crust. Top with filling. Sprinkle with reserved topping. Bake for 35-40 minutes or until filling is bubbly and topping is lightly browned. Cool on a wire rack.

There's no need to discard leftover egg whites. Freeze them by double-bagging in resealable plastic bags, or freeze in ice cube trays reserved just for that purpose. Transfer to bags. Frozen egg whites can keep from 1-6 months. Just remember to label them.

Chocolate Peanut Butter Dessert

PREP: 40 MIN. + FREEZING YIELD: 10-12 SERVINGS

CHRISTINE MONTALVO WINDSOR HEIGHTS, IOWA

When I want to splurge on a rich treat, I whip up this chocolate-glazed frozen peanut butter mousse. It's so luscious, even a thin piece will satisfy. It tastes like a peanut butter cup. When plating individual servings, I place a slice on a dessert plate, then top it with freshly whipped cream and chocolate shavings.

- 1-1/4 cups packed dark brown sugar
- 1 cup heavy whipping cream, *divided*
- 3 egg yolks
- 1-1/4 cups creamy peanut butter
- 6 tablespoons butter, softened

GLAZE:
- 1-1/2 cups heavy whipping cream
- 2 tablespoons butter
- 4 teaspoons dark corn syrup
- 12 squares (1 ounce *each*) bittersweet chocolate, chopped
- 1/4 cup coarsely chopped dry roasted peanuts

1 In a small saucepan, combine the brown sugar, 1/2 cup cream and yolks. Cook and stir over medium heat until mixture reaches 160° and is thick enough to coat the back of a metal spoon. Cover and refrigerate for 3 hours or until thickened.

2 Line an 8-in. x 4-in. loaf pan with plastic wrap; set aside. In a large bowl, cream the peanut butter and butter until light and fluffy. Add the brown sugar mixture; beat until smooth. In small bowl, beat remaining cream until stiff peaks form. Fold into peanut butter mixture. Spoon into prepared pan. Cover and refrigerate.

3 For glaze, in a large heavy saucepan, bring the cream, butter and corn syrup to a boil, stirring frequently. Remove from the heat. Add chocolate; whisk until smooth. Set aside 1/3 cup glaze to cool. Place remaining glaze in a microwave-safe bowl; cover and refrigerate overnight. Spread cooled glaze over loaf; cover and freeze overnight.

4 Using plastic wrap, lift loaf out of pan. Place chocolate side down on a wire rack; place on a 15-in. x 10-in. x 1-in. pan. Discard plastic wrap.

5 In microwave, warm refrigerated glaze; stir until smooth. Pour over loaf; spread with a metal spatula to completely cover top and sides. Sprinkle with peanuts. Freeze for 1 hour or until glaze is set.

Mocha Truffle Cheesecake

PREP: 20 MIN. BAKE: 50 MIN. + CHILLING YIELD: 12-16 SERVINGS

SHANNON DORMADY GREAT FALLS, MONTANA

I went through a phase when I couldn't get enough coffee or cheesecake, so I created this dessert that combines the two.

- 1 package (18-1/4 ounces) devil's food cake mix
- 6 tablespoons butter, melted
- 1 egg
- 1 to 3 tablespoons instant coffee granules

FILLING/TOPPING:
- 2 packages (8 ounces *each*) cream cheese, softened
- 1 can (14 ounces) sweetened condensed milk
- 2 cups (12 ounces) semisweet chocolate chips, melted and cooled
- 3 to 6 tablespoons instant coffee granules
- 1/4 cup hot water
- 3 eggs, lightly beaten
- 1 cup heavy whipping cream
- 1/4 cup confectioners' sugar
- 1/2 teaspoon almond extract

1 In a large bowl, combine the cake mix, butter, egg and coffee granules until well blended. Press onto the bottom and 2 in. up the sides of a greased 10-in. springform pan.

1 teaspoon vanilla extract

3/4 cup semisweet chocolate chips, melted

3/4 cup slivered almonds, toasted

1/3 cup milk chocolate toffee bits

1 In a large saucepan, heat milk to 175°; stir in 1/2 cup sugar until dissolved. In a small bowl, whisk egg yolks and remaining sugar. Stir in coffee granules and bittersweet chocolate. Whisk in a small amount of hot milk mixture. Return all to the pan, whisking constantly.

2 Cook and stir over low heat until mixture reaches at least 160° and coats the back of a metal spoon. Remove from the heat. Cool quickly by placing the pan in a bowl of ice water; let stand for 30 minutes, stirring frequently.

3 Transfer to a large bowl; stir in cream and vanilla. Press plastic wrap onto surface of custard. Refrigerate for several hours or overnight.

4 Line a baking sheet with waxed paper; spread melted semisweet chocolate to 1/8-in. thickness. Refrigerate for 20 minutes; chop coarsely.

5 Fill cylinder of ice cream freezer two-thirds full with the custard; freeze according to manufacturer's directions. Stir in some of the chopped chocolate, almonds and toffee bits. Refrigerate remaining custard until ready to freeze. Stir in the remaining chocolate, almonds and toffee bits. Allow to ripen in ice cream freezer or firm up in the refrigerator freezer for 2-4 hours before serving.

2 For filling, in another large bowl, beat cream cheese until smooth. Beat in milk and melted chips. Dissolve coffee granules in water. Add the coffee and eggs to the cream cheese mixture; beat on low speed just until combined.

3 Pour into crust. Place pan on a baking sheet. Bake at 325° for 50-55 minutes or until center is almost set. Cool on a wire rack for 10 minutes. Carefully run a knife around edge of pan to loosen; cool 1 hour longer. Chill overnight.

4 Remove sides of pan. Just before serving, in a large bowl, beat cream until soft peaks form. Beat in sugar and extract until stiff peaks form. Spread over top of cheesecake. Refrigerate leftovers.

Chocolate Crunch Ice Cream

PREP: 30 MIN. + CHILLING **PROCESS:** 20 MIN./BATCH + FREEZING
YIELD: 1-1/2 QUARTS

ROSALIE PETERS CALDWELL, TEXAS

Making ice cream goes smoothly when you do prep work in advance. I make the custard ahead and refrigerate it overnight. Plus, I toast the almonds beforehand and separate my add-ins into labeled containers.

1-1/2 cups milk

3/4 cup sugar, *divided*

4 egg yolks

2-1/2 teaspoons instant coffee granules

2 cups 60% cocoa bittersweet chocolate baking chips, melted and cooled

1-1/2 cups heavy whipping cream

Hazelnut Cheesecake Parfaits

PREP: 25 MIN. + CHILLING YIELD: 2 SERVINGS

SHELLY PLATTEN AMHERST, WISCONSIN

These parfaits are rich and impressive-looking, but light and not too sweet–the perfect finale for a romantic dinner. Sugared-toasted hazelnuts add gourmet flavor.

> 1/4 **cup chopped hazelnuts**
> 1/2 **teaspoon sugar**
> 1/3 **cup semisweet chocolate chips**
> 2 **tablespoons half-and-half cream**
> 2 **tablespoons whipped cream cheese**
> 2 **teaspoons brown sugar**
> 1/2 **cup coffee yogurt**
> 1/4 **teaspoon vanilla extract**
> 2/3 **cup whipped topping**
> 2 **whole chocolate graham crackers, crushed**
> **Chocolate curls and additional whipped topping, optional**

1 In a small heavy skillet, cook and stir the hazelnuts over medium heat until toasted, about 4 minutes. Sprinkle with sugar; cook and stir for 2-4 minutes or until sugar is melted. Spread on foil to cool.

2 In a small saucepan, melt chocolate chips with cream over low heat; stir until smooth. Remove from the heat; cool to room temperature. In a small bowl, beat cream cheese and brown sugar until blended. Beat in yogurt and vanilla; fold in whipped topping.

3 In two parfait glasses, layer the graham crackers, yogurt mixture, chocolate mixture and hazelnuts. Refrigerate until chilled. Garnish with chocolate curls and whipped topping if desired.

Cherry Cheesecake Tarts

PREP: 15 MIN. BAKE: 20 MIN. + COOLING YIELD: 6 SERVINGS

MARY LINDELL SANFORD, MICHIGAN

If your children or grandchildren are looking for a perfect gift to give their teachers, these may be the answer. Dress up each tart with a paper doily, place on a colorful plastic or paper plate and cover with clear wrap. Secure with a festive bow or a gift card and tag. And don't forget to include the recipe for the tart. When I gave this as a gift to each of the secretaries at the high school where I work, it soon became a hit with their families, too!

> 1 **package (10 ounces) frozen puff pastry shells**
> 2 **packages (3 ounces *each*) cream cheese, softened**
> 1/4 **cup confectioners' sugar**
> 1/2 **teaspoon almond extract**
> 1 **can (21 ounces) cherry pie filling**
> **Additional confectioners' sugar**

1 Bake pastry shells according to package directions. In a small bowl, beat cream cheese, sugar and extract. With a fork, carefully remove the circular top of each baked shell and set aside. Remove any soft layers of pastry inside shells and discard.

2 Spoon the cream cheese filling into shells; place on a baking sheet. Bake at 400° for 5 minutes. Cool for 1 hour. Refrigerate until serving.

3 Just before serving, spoon pie filling into shells. Top with reserved pastry circles. Dust with confectioners' sugar. Refrigerate leftovers.

MARGUERITE SHAEFFER
SEWELL, NEW JERSEY

This is great for a large family gathering or church dinner during peach season. The rest of the year canned peaches are fine, but, of course, fresh is best.

Peach Blackberry Cobbler

PREP: 40 MIN. BAKE: 40 MIN. YIELD: 12 SERVINGS

12 medium peaches, peeled and sliced

1/3 cup all-purpose flour

1/4 cup honey

3 tablespoons lemon juice

1/4 teaspoon salt

3 cups fresh blackberries

TOPPING:

2 cups all-purpose flour

1/2 cup sugar

1 teaspoon baking powder

1/2 teaspoon salt

1/4 teaspoon baking soda

1/3 cup cold butter

1-1/4 cups buttermilk

1 tablespoon coarse sugar

1 In a large bowl, combine the peaches, flour, honey, lemon juice and salt; let stand for 15 minutes. Fold in blackberries. Transfer to a 13-in. x 9-in. baking dish coated with cooking spray.

2 For topping, in a large bowl, combine the flour, sugar, baking powder, salt and baking soda. Cut in butter until crumbly. Make a well in the center; pour in buttermilk. Stir just until a soft dough forms. Drop by tablespoonfuls over fruit mixture; sprinkle with coarse sugar.

3 Bake at 400° for 40-45 minutes or until filling is bubbly and a toothpick inserted in topping comes out clean. Serve warm.

To peel peaches, place in a large pot of boiling water for 10-20 seconds or until the skin splits. Use a slotted spoon to transfer to an ice water bath to cool. Use a paring knife to peel the skin. If stubborn areas of skin won't peel off, just return the fruit to the boiling water for a few more seconds.

Apple Turnovers

PREP: 50 MIN. + CHILLING BAKE: 20 MIN. YIELD: 4 SERVINGS

DOROTHY BAYES SARDIS, OHIO

These traditional turnovers are tender and flaky, with an apple pie-like filling and a thin, white glaze. I freeze the extras and warm them up in the microwave. They're great with coffee.

- 1 **cup all-purpose flour**
- 1/2 **teaspoon salt**
- 1/2 **cup cold butter,** *divided*
- 1/4 **cup ice water**

FILLING:
- 1/3 **cup sugar**
- 2 **teaspoons cornstarch**
- 1/8 **teaspoon ground cinnamon**
- 2 **medium tart apples, peeled and thinly sliced**
- 1 **teaspoon lemon juice**
- 2 **tablespoons beaten egg**
- 1-1/2 **teaspoons water**

GLAZE:
- 1/4 **cup confectioners' sugar**
- 1 **teaspoon water**

1 Combine flour and salt; cut in 1/4 cup butter until crumbly. Gradually add water, tossing with a fork until a ball forms. On a lightly floured surface, roll dough into a 12-in. x 6-in. rectangle.

2 Cut remaining butter into thin slices. Starting at a short side of dough, arrange half of the butter slices over two-thirds of rectangle to within 1/2 in. of edges. Fold unbuttered third of dough over middle third. Fold remaining third over the middle, forming a 6-in. x 4-in. rectangle. Roll dough into a 12-in. x 6-in. rectangle.

3 Repeat steps of butter layering and dough folding, ending with a 6-in. x 4-in. rectangle. Wrap in plastic wrap; refrigerate for 15 minutes. Roll dough into a 12-in. x 6-in. rectangle. Fold in half lengthwise, then widthwise. Wrap in plastic wrap; refrigerate for 1 hour.

4 Meanwhile, for filling, in a small saucepan, combine the sugar, cornstarch and cinnamon. Add apples and lemon juice; toss to coat. Bring to a boil over medium heat, stirring constantly. Reduce heat; simmer, uncovered, for 5-10 minutes or until apples are tender, stirring often. Remove from the heat.

5 In a small bowl, combine egg and water. Roll dough into a 12-in. square; cut into four squares. Brush with half of the egg mixture. Spoon about 1/4 cup filling on half of each square; fold dough over filling. Press edges with a fork to seal. Place on an ungreased baking sheet. Brush with remaining egg mixture. With a sharp knife, cut three small slits in the top of each turnover.

6 Bake at 450° for 17-22 minutes or until golden brown. Remove to a wire rack. Combine glaze ingredients; drizzle over turnovers. Serve warm.

Chocolate and Fruit Trifle

PREP: 20 MIN. + CHILLING BAKE: 20 MIN. + COOLING
YIELD: 12-16 SERVINGS

ANGIE DIERIKX STATE CENTER, IOWA

This refreshing dessert layered with devil's food cake, a creamy pudding mixture, red berries and green kiwi is perfect for the holidays.

- 1 **package (18-1/4 ounces) devil's food cake mix**
- 1 **can (14 ounces) sweetened condensed milk**
- 1 **cup cold water**
- 1 **package (3.4 ounces) instant vanilla pudding mix**
- 2 **cups heavy whipping cream, whipped**
- 2 **tablespoons orange juice**
- 2 **cups fresh strawberries, chopped**
- 2 **cups fresh raspberries**
- 2 **kiwifruit, peeled and chopped**

1 Prepare cake batter according to package directions; pour into a greased 15-in. x 10-in. x 1-in. baking pan. Bake at 350° for 20 minutes or until a toothpick inserted near the center comes out clean. Cool completely on a wire rack. Crumble enough cake to measure 8 cups; set aside. (Save remaining cake for another use.)

2   In a large bowl, whisk the milk, water and pudding mix for 2 minutes. Let stand for two minutes or until soft-set. Fold in the whipped cream.

3   To assemble, spread 2-1/2 cups pudding mixture in a 4-qt. glass bowl. Top with half of the crumbled cake; sprinkle with 1 tablespoon orange juice. Arrange half of the berries and kiwi over cake.

4   Repeat pudding and cake layers; sprinkle with remaining orange juice. Top with remaining pudding mixture. Spoon remaining fruit around edge of bowl. Cover and refrigerate until serving.

Strawberry Crepes

PREP: 25 MIN. + CHILLING COOK: 1 HOUR YIELD: 22 CREPES

DEBRA LATTA PORT MATILDA, PENNSYLVANIA

I always feel like a French chef when I serve these pretty crepes. Although they take a little time to prepare, they're well worth the effort. My guests are always impressed.

1-1/2 cups milk
   3   eggs
   2   tablespoons butter, melted
1/2   teaspoon lemon extract
1-1/4 cups all-purpose flour
   2   tablespoons sugar
Dash salt
TOPPING:
1/2   cup sugar
   2   tablespoons cornstarch
3/4   cup water

   1   tablespoon lemon juice
   1   teaspoon strawberry extract
1/4   teaspoon red food coloring, optional
   4   cups sliced fresh strawberries
FILLING:
   1   cup heavy whipping cream
   1   package (8 ounces) cream cheese, softened
   2   cups confectioners' sugar
   1   teaspoon vanilla extract

1   In a large bowl, combine milk, eggs, butter and extract. Combine flour, sugar and salt; add to milk mixture and beat until smooth. Cover and refrigerate for 1 hour.

2   Heat a lightly greased 8-in. nonstick skillet. Stir batter; pour 2 tablespoons into center of skillet. Lift and tilt pan to evenly coat bottom. Cook until top appears dry; turn and cook 15-20 seconds longer. Remove to a wire rack. Repeat with remaining batter, greasing skillet as needed. When cool, stack crepes with waxed paper or paper towels in between.

3   For topping, in a small saucepan, combine sugar and cornstarch; stir in water and lemon juice until smooth. Bring to a boil over medium heat; cook and stir for 1 minute or until thickened. Stir in extract and food coloring if desired. Cool. Add strawberries.

4   For filling, in a small bowl, beat the cream until stiff peaks form; set aside. In a large bowl, beat the cream cheese, confectioners' sugar and vanilla until smooth; fold in whipped cream. Spoon 2 rounded tablespoons of filling down the center of each crepe; roll up. Top with strawberry topping.

Golden Lemon Glazed Cheesecake

PREP: 20 MIN. + COOLING BAKE: 40 MIN. + CHILLING
YIELD: 16 SERVINGS

BETTY JACQUES HEMET, CALIFORNIA

We give performances of A Living Christmas Tree every holiday season at our church, then hold an open house after each one. I've served this cheesecake for years.

  2-1/2 **cups graham cracker crumbs**
    1/4 **cup sugar**
    2/3 **cup butter, melted**

FILLING:
      3 **packages (8 ounces *each*) cream cheese, softened**
  1-1/4 **cups sugar**
      3 **eggs, lightly beaten**
      3 **tablespoons lemon juice**
      1 **tablespoon grated lemon peel**
      1 **teaspoon vanilla extract**

GLAZE:
      1 **small lemon, thinly sliced, *divided***
      3 **cups water, *divided***
      1 **cup sugar**
      3 **tablespoons cornstarch**
    1/3 **cup lemon juice**

1 In a large bowl, combine crumbs, sugar and butter. Press onto bottom and 2 inches up sides of a greased 9-in. springform pan. Place pan on a baking sheet. Bake at 350° for 10 minutes. Cool on a wire rack.

2 For filling, in a large bowl, beat cream cheese and sugar until smooth. Add eggs; beat on low speed until combined. Stir in the lemon juice, lemon peel and vanilla just until blended. Pour into the crust. Return pan to baking sheet.

3 Bake for 40-45 minutes or until center is almost set. Cool pan on wire rack for 10 minutes. Carefully run a knife around edge of pan to loosen; cool 1 hour longer. Refrigerate overnight.

4 Set aside 1 lemon slice; coarsely chop the remaining lemon slices. In a small saucepan, combine the chopped lemon and 2 cups water; bring to a boil. Reduce heat; simmer, uncovered, for 15 minutes. Drain and discard liquid.

5 In another saucepan, combine the sugar and cornstarch; stir in the remaining water until smooth. Add lemon juice and lemon pulp. Bring to a boil; cook and stir for 3 minutes or until thickened. Refrigerate until cooled, stirring occasionally.

6 Pour the lemon glaze over the top of the cheesecake; garnish with the reserved lemon slice. Refrigerate any leftovers.

Cran-Apple Cobbler

PREP: 20 MIN. BAKE: 30 MIN. YIELD: 6-8 SERVINGS

JO ANN SHEEHAN RUTHER GLEN, VIRGINIA

My cranberry-packed cobbler is the crowning glory of many of our late fall and winter meals. My family isn't big on pies, so this favorite is preferred at our Thanksgiving and Christmas celebrations. The aroma of cinnamon and fruit is irresistible.

2-1/2 cups sliced peeled apples

2-1/2 cups sliced peeled firm pears

1 to 1-1/4 cups sugar

1 cup fresh *or* frozen cranberries, thawed

1 cup water

3 tablespoons quick-cooking tapioca

3 tablespoons red-hot candies

1/2 teaspoon ground cinnamon

2 tablespoons butter

TOPPING:

3/4 cup all-purpose flour

2 tablespoons sugar

1 teaspoon baking powder

1/4 teaspoon salt

1/4 cup cold butter, cubed

3 tablespoons milk

Vanilla ice cream

1 In a large saucepan, combine the first eight ingredients; let stand for 5 minutes. Cook and stir over medium heat until mixture comes to a full rolling boil, about 18 minutes. Transfer cran-apple mixture to a greased 2-qt. baking dish; dot with butter.

2 For topping, in a small bowl, combine the flour, sugar, baking powder and salt in a bowl. Cut in butter until mixture resembles coarse crumbs. Stir in milk until a soft dough forms.

3 Drop topping by heaping tablespoonfuls onto hot fruit. Bake at 375° for 30-35 minutes or until golden brown. Serve warm with ice cream.

Rich Truffle Wedges

PREP: 30 MIN. + COOLING BAKE: 25 MIN. + COOLING
YIELD: 12 SERVINGS

PATRICIA VATTA NORWOOD, ONTARIO

I've made and served this decadent dessert numerous times, to the delight of guests and family. It has a fudgy consistency and a big chocolate taste. The tart raspberry sauce complements the flavor and looks lovely spooned over each slice.

1/2 cup butter

6 ounces semisweet chocolate, chopped

3 eggs

2/3 cup sugar

1 teaspoon vanilla extract

1/4 teaspoon salt

2/3 cup all-purpose flour

GLAZE:

1/4 cup butter

2 ounces semisweet chocolate, chopped

2 teaspoons honey

SAUCE:

2 cups fresh *or* frozen unsweetened raspberries

2 tablespoons sugar

Whipped cream, fresh raspberries and mint, optional

1 In a microwave or double boiler, melt butter and chocolate; stir until smooth. Cool for 10 minutes. In a bowl, beat eggs, sugar, vanilla and salt until thickened, about 4 minutes. Blend in chocolate mixture. Stir in flour; mix well.

2 Pour into a greased and floured 9-in. springform pan. Bake at 350° for 25-30 minutes or until a toothpick inserted near the center comes out clean. Cool completely on a wire rack.

3 Combine the glaze ingredients in a small saucepan; cook and stir over low heat until melted and smooth. Cool slightly. Run a knife around the edge of springform pan to loosen; remove cake to serving plate. Spread glaze over the top and sides; set aside.

4 For sauce, puree raspberries in a blender or food processor. Press through a sieve if desired; discard seeds. Stir in sugar; chill until serving.

5 Spoon sauce over individual servings. Garnish with whipped cream, raspberries and mint if desired.

Apricot Rice Custard

PREP: 35 MIN. COOK: 15 MIN. YIELD: 8-10 SERVINGS

ELIZABETH MONTGOMERY TAYLORVILLE, ILLINOIS

Creamy rice custard drizzled with apricot sauce makes a comforting dessert or a refreshingly different breakfast. I haven't been cooking all that long, but it's easy to impress people with this recipe since it's simple and delicious.

- 1 cup uncooked long grain rice
- 3 cups milk
- 1/2 cup sugar
- 1/2 teaspoon salt
- 2 eggs, lightly beaten
- 1/2 teaspoon vanilla extract
- 1/4 teaspoon almond extract

Dash ground cinnamon

SAUCE:
- 1 can (8-1/2 ounces) apricot halves
- 1 can (8 ounces) crushed pineapple, undrained
- 1/3 cup packed brown sugar
- 2 tablespoons lemon juice
- 1 tablespoon cornstarch

1   In a large saucepan, cook rice according to package directions. Stir in milk, sugar and salt; bring to a boil. Reduce heat to low. Stir 1/2 cup into eggs; return all to the pan, stirring constantly. Cook and stir for 15 minutes or until mixture reaches 160° or coats the back of a metal spoon (do not boil).

2   Remove the saucepan from the heat; stir in the extracts and cinnamon.

3   For sauce, drain apricot syrup into a small saucepan. Chop apricots; add to syrup. Stir in remaining sauce ingredients; bring to a boil. Boil for 2 minutes, stirring occasionally. Serve sauce and custard warm or chilled.

Berry Nectarine Buckle

PREP: 25 MIN. BAKE: 35 MIN. YIELD: 20 SERVINGS

LISA SJURSEN-DARLING SCOTTSVILLE, NEW YORK

I found this recipe a long time ago, but modified it over the years. We enjoy its combination of blueberries, raspberries, blackberries and nectarines, particularly when the cake is served warm with low-fat frozen yogurt.

- 1/3 cup all-purpose flour
- 1/3 cup packed brown sugar
- 1 teaspoon ground cinnamon
- 3 tablespoons cold butter

BATTER:
- 6 tablespoons butter, softened
- 3/4 cup plus 1 tablespoon sugar, *divided*
- 2 eggs
- 1-1/2 teaspoons vanilla extract
- 2-1/4 cups all-purpose flour
- 2-1/2 teaspoons baking powder
- 1/2 teaspoon salt
- 1/2 cup fat-free milk
- 1 cup fresh blueberries
- 1 pound medium nectarines, peeled, sliced and patted dry *or* 1 package (16 ounces) frozen unsweetened sliced peaches, thawed and patted dry
- 1/2 cup fresh raspberries
- 1/2 cup fresh blackberries

1. For topping, in a small bowl, combine flour, brown sugar and cinnamon; cut in butter until crumbly. Set aside.

2. For batter, in a large bowl, cream the butter and 3/4 cup sugar until light and fluffy. Add eggs, one at a time, beating well after each addition. Beat in vanilla. Combine the flour, baking powder and salt; add to creamed mixture alternately with milk, beating well after each addition. Set aside 3/4 cup batter. Fold blueberries into remaining batter.

3. Spoon into a 13-in. x 9-in. baking dish coated with cooking spray. Arrange nectarines on top; sprinkle with remaining sugar. Drop reserved batter by teaspoonfuls over nectarines. Sprinkle with raspberries, blackberries and reserved topping.

4. Bake at 350° for 35-40 minutes or until a toothpick inserted near the center comes out clean. Serve warm.

Orange Cream Cheesecake

PREP: 25 MIN. + CHILLING **YIELD:** 10-12 SERVINGS

MADONNA FAUNCE BOISE, IDAHO

I love serving this impressive-looking cheesecake with its pretty layers and smooth texture. The combination of orange, cream cheese and whipped topping is simply irresistible.

- 2 cups graham cracker crumbs
- 1 teaspoon ground cinnamon
- 1 teaspoon grated orange peel
- 1/2 cup butter, melted

FILLING:
- 1 package (3 ounces) orange gelatin
- 3 packages (8 ounces *each*) cream cheese, softened
- 1-1/4 cups sugar
- 1 can (5 ounces) evaporated milk
- 1 teaspoon lemon juice
- 1/3 cup thawed orange juice concentrate
- 1 teaspoon vanilla extract
- 1 envelope unflavored gelatin
- 2 tablespoons cold water
- 2 tablespoons boiling water
- 1 carton (8 ounces) frozen whipped topping, thawed

TOPPING:
- 2 cups whipped topping
- 1/4 cup sugar
Lemon slices, orange peel strips, kumquats and lemon balm for garnish, optional

1. In a large bowl, combine the cracker crumbs, cinnamon, orange peel and butter. Press into the bottom of a greased 10-in. springform pan. Refrigerate for at least 30 minutes.

2. For filling, prepare orange gelatin according to package directions. Set aside 1/2 cup at room temperature. Chill remaining gelatin until slightly thickened, 40-60 minutes.

3. In a large bowl, beat cream cheese and sugar for 2 minutes. Gradually beat in milk and lemon juice. Beat on medium-high speed 2 minutes longer. Gradually beat in orange juice concentrate and vanilla.

4. In a small bowl, sprinkle unflavored gelatin over cold water; let stand for 2 minutes. Stir in boiling water until gelatin is completely dissolved. Stir into room temperature orange gelatin. Stir into cream cheese mixture, then fold in whipped topping. Pour into crust.

5. For topping, in a large bowl, beat whipped topping and sugar. Beat in refrigerated orange gelatin (mixture will be thin). Chill for 30 minutes. Gently spoon over filling (pan will be full). Refrigerate for 8 hours or overnight. Garnish with lemon slices, orange peel strips, kumquats and lemon balm if desired.

To add a special finishing touch to a variety of desserts, make sugared cranberries and orange peel. Combine several orange peel strips, 1/3 cup fresh cranberries and 1/2 cup sugar. Stir gently to combine. Cover and refrigerate for 1 hour.

Gingered Apricot and Apple Crumble

PREP: 15 MIN. BAKE: 50 MIN. YIELD: 12 SERVINGS

SYLVIA RICE DIDSBURY, ALBERTA

Hot or cold, plain or topped with ice cream, this crumble is tasty. For variety, leave out the apricots and make traditional apple crisp if you like.

- 1 cup apricot nectar
- 3/4 cup finely chopped dried apricots
- 1/3 cup honey
- 1/4 cup maple syrup
- 2 tablespoons lemon juice
- 8 cups sliced peeled tart apples (about 8 large)
- 3 tablespoons all-purpose flour
- 1 teaspoon ground cinnamon
- 1/2 teaspoon ground ginger
- 1/2 teaspoon ground cardamom

TOPPING:
- 3/4 cup all-purpose flour
- 1/2 cup quick-cooking oats
- 1/2 cup chopped pecans, optional
- 1/4 cup canola oil
- 1/4 cup maple syrup

1 In a large bowl, combine the first five ingredients; set aside. Arrange apples in an ungreased 13-in. x 9-in. baking dish.

2 Combine flour, cinnamon, ginger and cardamom; stir into the apricot mixture. Spoon over apples.

3 Combine topping ingredients; sprinkle over fruit. Bake at 350° for 50-60 minutes or until topping is golden brown and fruit is tender.

Blackberry Cobbler

PREP: 15 MIN. + STANDING BAKE: 45 MIN. YIELD: 10 SERVINGS

LESLIE BROWNING LEBANON, KENTUCKY

This sweet delight has helped my family stay healthy, lose weight and still be able to enjoy dessert! Other kinds of berries or even fresh peaches are just as delicious in this fruit-filled cobbler.

- 1/2 cup sugar
- 4-1/2 teaspoons quick-cooking tapioca
- 1/4 teaspoon ground allspice
- 5 cups fresh *or* frozen blackberries, thawed
- 2 tablespoons orange juice

DOUGH:
- 1 cup all-purpose flour
- 1/3 cup plus 1 tablespoon sugar, *divided*
- 1/4 teaspoon baking soda
- 1/4 teaspoon salt
- 1/3 cup reduced-fat vanilla yogurt
- 1/3 cup fat-free milk
- 3 tablespoons butter, melted

1 In a large bowl, combine the sugar, tapioca and allspice. Add blackberries and orange juice; toss to coat. Let stand for 15 minutes. Spoon into a 2-qt. baking dish coated with cooking spray.

2 For dough, in a large bowl, combine the flour, 1/3 cup sugar, baking soda and salt. Combine the yogurt, milk and butter; stir into dry ingredients until smooth. Spread over the berry mixture.

3 Bake at 350° for 20 minutes. Sprinkle with remaining sugar. Bake 25-30 minutes longer or until golden brown. Serve warm.

Pretty Plum Parfaits

PREP: 30 MIN. + CHILLING YIELD: 4 SERVINGS

NORMA REYNOLDS YORK, PENNSYLVANIA

With a plum tree in our backyard, I'm always eager to try new plum recipes. But none are as good as this wonderful dessert! Light, refreshing and easy to whip up, these fruit parfaits are an ideal summer treat.

- 9 to 12 medium medium-ripe red *or* purple plums (2 pounds), sliced
- 1/2 cup red currant jelly
- 1/2 cup packed brown sugar
- 1 orange peel strip (1 to 3 inches)
- 1 cinnamon stick (3 inches)
- 1 cup heavy whipping cream
- 1 tablespoon confectioners' sugar
- 1/2 teaspoon vanilla extract

Fancy cookies and additional whipped cream and plum slices, optional

1 In a large heavy saucepan, combine the plums, jelly, brown sugar, orange peel and cinnamon stick. Bring to a boil. Reduce heat; simmer, uncovered, for 10-15 minutes or until plums are tender, stirring occasionally. Remove from the heat; cool slightly. Discard orange peel and cinnamon stick; coarsely mash plums. Cover and refrigerate.

2 Just before serving, beat cream until it begins to thicken. Add sugar and vanilla; beat until soft peaks form. Place about 1/4 cup plum mixture each in four chilled parfait glasses; top with 1/4 cup whipped cream. Repeat layers. Top with remaining plum mixture. Garnish with a cookie, dollop of whipped cream and plum slice if desired.

Valentine Berries and Cream

PREP: 30 MIN. + CHILLING YIELD: 8-10 SERVINGS

TAMERA O'SULLIVAN APPLE VALLEY, MINNESOTA

Everyone was impressed with this scrumptious chocolate heart served at our adult Sunday school class potluck.

- 8 ounces semisweet chocolate, chopped
- 1 tablespoon shortening
- 2 packages (3 ounces *each*) cream cheese, softened
- 1/4 cup butter, softened
- 1-1/2 cups confectioners' sugar
- 1/3 cup baking cocoa
- 2 tablespoons milk
- 1 teaspoon vanilla extract
- 2-1/2 cups heavy whipping cream, whipped, *divided*
- 1-1/2 cups fresh strawberries, halved

1 Line a 9-in. heart-shaped or square pan with foil; set aside. In a large heavy saucepan over low heat, melt chocolate and shortening; stir until smooth. Pour into prepared pan, swirling to coat the bottom and 1-1/2 in. up the sides.

2 Refrigerate for 1 minute, then swirl the chocolate to reinforce sides of heart or box. Refrigerate for 30 minutes or until firm. Using foil, lift from pan; remove foil and place chocolate heart on a serving plate.

3 Beat cream cheese and butter until smooth. Combine confectioners' sugar and cocoa; add to creamed mixture with milk and vanilla. Beat until smooth.

4 Gently fold two-thirds of the whipped cream into cream cheese mixture. Spoon into heart. Insert star tip #32 into a pastry or plastic bag; fill with the remaining whipped cream. Pipe around the edge of heart. Garnish with strawberries.

2. For ice cream, in a large saucepan, heat the milk to 175°. Combine sugars and cornstarch; gradually stir into milk. Bring to a boil; cook and stir for 2 minutes or until thickened. Whisk a small amount of the hot mixture into the eggs. Return all to the pan, whisking constantly. Cook and stir over low heat until mixture reaches at least 160° and coats the back of a metal spoon. Remove from the heat.

3. Cool quickly by placing pan in a bowl of ice water; stir for 2 minutes. Stir in the cream, syrup and vanilla. Press waxed paper onto surface of custard. Refrigerate for several hours or overnight.

4. Stir in the nuts. Place in ice cream freezer and freeze according to manufacturer's directions. Allow to ripen in ice cream freezer or firm up in your refrigerator freezer an hour before serving.

Chocolate Velvet Dessert

PREP: 20 MIN. + CHILLING BAKE: 45 MIN. + COOLING
YIELD: 12-16 SERVINGS

MOLLY SEIDEL EDGEWOOD, NEW MEXICO

This creamy concoction is the result of several attempts to duplicate a dessert I had on vacation. It looks so beautiful on a buffet table that many folks are tempted to forgo the main course in favor of this chocolaty treat.

1-1/2 cups chocolate wafer crumbs
   2 tablespoons sugar

Butter Pecan Ice Cream

PREP: 45 MIN. + CHILLING FREEZE: 30 MIN. + FREEZING
YIELD: ABOUT 2 QUARTS

PATRICIA SIMMS DALLAS, TEXAS

I like to make this very rich ice cream at home, then take it to parties or dinners. It's so convenient. If I pour it in the freezer right before we leave, it's done when we arrive—and it "ripens" by the time that it's served!

TOASTED NUTS:
   3 tablespoons butter, melted
3/4 cup chopped pecans
1/8 teaspoon salt
   1 tablespoon sugar

ICE CREAM:
2-1/2 cups milk
1/2 cup packed brown sugar
1/4 cup sugar
   2 tablespoons cornstarch
   2 eggs, lightly beaten
   1 cup heavy whipping cream
1/3 cup maple-flavored pancake syrup
   2 teaspoons vanilla extract

1. On a baking sheet, combine the butter, pecans, salt and 1 tablespoon sugar and spread into a single layer. Roast at 350° for 15 minutes. Stir and roast 15 minutes longer. Cool.

1/4 cup butter, melted

2 cups (12 ounces) semisweet chocolate chips

6 egg yolks

1-3/4 cups heavy whipping cream

1 teaspoon vanilla extract

CHOCOLATE BUTTERCREAM FROSTING:

1/2 cup butter, softened

3 cups confectioners' sugar

3 tablespoons baking cocoa

3 to 4 tablespoons milk

1 In a small bowl, combine wafer crumbs and sugar; stir in butter. Press onto the bottom and 1-1/2 in. up the sides of a greased 9-in. springform pan. Place on a baking sheet. Bake at 350° for 10 minutes. Cool on a wire rack.

2 In a microwave, melt chocolate chips; stir until smooth. Cool. In a small bowl, combine the egg yolks, cream and vanilla. Gradually stir a third of the cream mixture into melted chocolate until blended. Fold in remaining cream mixture just until blended. Pour into crust.

3 Place pan on a baking sheet. Bake at 350° for 45-50 minutes or until center is almost set. Cool on a wire rack for 10 minutes. Carefully run a knife around edge of pan to loosen; cool 1 hour longer. Refrigerate dessert overnight.

4 For frosting, in a small bowl, combine the butter, confectioners' sugar, cocoa and enough milk to achieve a piping consistency. Using a large star tip, pipe frosting on dessert.

Macadamia Berry Dessert

PREP: 30 MIN. + FREEZING YIELD: 12 SERVINGS

LOUISE WATKINS SPARTA, WISCONSIN

My family and friends love this sensation, and I've shared the recipe several times. The crunchy nut crust and colorful raspberry filling make it special enough for guests. During the holidays, I substitute a can of whole-berry cranberry sauce for the raspberries.

1 cup crushed vanilla wafers (about 30 wafers)

1/2 cup finely chopped macadamia nuts

1/4 cup butter, melted

1 can (14 ounces) sweetened condensed milk

3 tablespoons orange juice

3 tablespoons lemon juice

1 package (10 ounces) frozen sweetened raspberries, thawed

1 carton (8 ounces) frozen whipped topping, thawed

Fresh raspberries and additional whipped topping, optional

1 Combine the wafer crumbs, nuts and butter. Press onto the bottom of a greased 9-in. springform pan. Bake at 375° for 8-10 minutes or until golden brown. Cool completely.

2 In a large bowl, beat the milk, orange juice and lemon juice on low speed until well blended. Stir in raspberries. Fold in whipped topping. Pour over crust. Cover and freeze for 3 hours or until firm. May be frozen for up to 3 months.

3 Remove from the freezer 15 minutes before serving. Carefully run a knife around edge of pan to loosen. Remove sides of pan. Garnish with raspberries and whipped topping if desired.

The macadamia nut tree originated in Queensland, Australia and was brought to Hawaii in 1882, where today most of the world's macadamias are grown. It takes about 7 years for a macadamia tree to bear fruit, making the nut a delicacy. Because the macadamia is one of the hardest nuts to crack open, the nuts are mostly sold shelled.

2. For filling, in a large bowl, beat cream cheese and sugar until smooth. Beat in egg and vanilla just until combined. Spread over crust.

3. In another bowl, toss the apples, sugar and cinnamon; arrange over filling. Bake at 400° for 40 minutes or until apples are tender and crust is golden brown. Cool on a wire rack. Store in the refrigerator.

Strawberry Cheesecake Ice Cream

PREP: 20 MIN. + COOLING FREEZE: 2 HOURS YIELD: 1 GALLON

IRENE YODER FILLMORE, NEW YORK

The custard-like ice cream is so rich and velvety that it tastes like you fussed for hours. But it's easy to make…and attractive, too. I like to serve it with chocolate fudge sauce.

> 3 cups sugar
> 3 tablespoons all-purpose flour
>
> Pinch salt
>
> 8 cups milk
> 4 eggs, lightly beaten
> 1 package (8 ounces) cream cheese, cubed
> 1 teaspoon vanilla extract
> 3 cups fresh *or* frozen unsweetened strawberries, thawed
> 2 cups heavy whipping cream

Bavarian Apple Tart

PREP: 25 MIN. BAKE: 40 MIN. + COOLING YIELD: 12 SERVINGS

MARY ANNE ENGEL WEST ALLIS, WISCONSIN

Everyone in my card club had something to say about this tart's wonderful taste. The delicate crust, smooth filling and sweet topping are delicious. There wasn't a leftover in sight when I served this.

> 1/3 cup butter, softened
> 1/3 cup sugar
> 1/2 teaspoon vanilla extract
> 1 cup all-purpose flour
> 1/8 teaspoon ground cinnamon

FILLING:
> 1 package (8 ounces) reduced-fat cream cheese
> 1/4 cup sugar
> 1 egg
> 1-1/2 teaspoons vanilla extract

TOPPING:
> 4 cups thinly sliced peeled tart apples (about 2 medium)
> 1/3 cup sugar
> 3/4 teaspoon ground cinnamon

1. In a large bowl, cream butter and sugar until light and fluffy. Stir in the vanilla, flour and cinnamon. Press onto the bottom and 1 in. up the sides of a 9-in. springform pan coated with cooking spray.

1. In a heavy saucepan, combine the sugar, flour and salt. Gradually add milk until smooth. Bring to a boil over medium heat; cook and stir for 2 minutes or until thickened. Remove from the heat; cool slightly.

2. Whisk a small amount of hot milk mixture into the eggs; return all to the pan, whisking constantly. Cook and stir over low heat until mixture reaches at least 160° and coats the back of a metal spoon. Stir in the cream cheese until melted.

3. Remove from the heat. Cool quickly by placing pan in a bowl of ice water; stir for 2 minutes. Stir in vanilla. Press plastic wrap onto surface of custard. Refrigerate for several hours or overnight.

4. Stir strawberries and cream into custard. Fill cylinder of ice cream freezer two-thirds full; freeze according to the manufacturer's directions. Refrigerate remaining mixture until ready to freeze. When ice cream is frozen, transfer to a freezer container; freeze for 2-4 hours before serving.

Blueberry and Kiwi Flan

PREP: 45 MIN. + CHILLING **YIELD:** 16-20 SERVINGS

POLLIE MALONE AMES, IOWA

This is a recipe that's fun to make, pretty to serve and tastes good, too. It's also versatile—you can use whatever fruits are your favorites.

CRUST:
- 1/2 **cup sugar**
- 1/2 **cup confectioners' sugar**
- 1/2 **cup butter**
- 1/2 **cup canola oil**
- 1 **egg**
- 2 **cups plus 2 tablespoons all-purpose flour**
- 1/2 **teaspoon cream of tartar**
- 1/2 **teaspoon baking soda**
- 1/2 **teaspoon vanilla extract**

CREAM CHEESE FILLING:
- 1 **package (8 ounces) cream cheese**
- 1/3 **cup sugar**
- 1 **teaspoon vanilla extract**

FRUIT LAYER:
- 3 **cups fresh blueberries**
- 2 **medium kiwifruit, peeled and thinly sliced**

CITRUS GLAZE:
- 1/2 **cup water**
- 1/2 **cup orange juice**
- 2 **tablespoons lemon juice**
- 1/4 **cup sugar**
- 1 **tablespoon cornstarch**

1. In a large bowl, combine the crust ingredients together until blended. Divide dough in half; press onto the bottom and up the sides of greased two 12-in. pizza pans or tart pans with removable bottoms.

2. Bake at 350° for 10-12 minutes or until crust is golden brown. Cool. Carefully remove one crust to round platter. Freeze the other crust for later use (may be frozen for up to 3 months).

3. In a large bowl, cream together cream cheese filling ingredients; spread on crust. Spread blueberries and kiwi on top of cheese layer in decorative pattern. Refrigerate.

4. For glaze, in a small saucepan, combining all the glaze ingredients; bring to a boil. Cook and stir for 1 minute or until thickened; cool. Spread over fruit layer; refrigerate until serving time.

 To freeze fresh berries, place on a cookie sheet and freeze for about 1-1/2 hours; transfer to freezer bags. The berries won't stick together, so you can pour out the amount you need.

Banana Bread Pudding

PREP: 10 MIN. BAKE: 40 MIN. YIELD: 6 SERVINGS

MARY DETWEILER MIDDLEFIELD, OHIO

When I visited my grandmother in summer, I always looked forward to the comforting pudding she'd make. With its crusty golden top, custard-like inside and smooth vanilla sauce, this bread pudding is a real homespun delight. Now I make it for my grandchildren.

- 4 cups cubed day-old French *or* sourdough bread (1-inch pieces)
- 1/4 cup butter, melted
- 3 eggs
- 2 cups milk
- 1/2 cup sugar
- 2 teaspoons vanilla extract
- 1/2 teaspoon ground cinnamon
- 1/2 teaspoon ground nutmeg
- 1/2 teaspoon salt
- 1 cup sliced firm bananas (1/4-inch pieces)

SAUCE:
- 3 tablespoons butter
- 2 tablespoons sugar
- 1 tablespoon cornstarch
- 3/4 cup milk
- 1/4 cup light corn syrup
- 1 teaspoon vanilla extract

1 Place bread cubes in a greased 2-qt. casserole dish; pour butter over and toss to coat. In a medium bowl, lightly beat eggs; add milk, sugar, vanilla, cinnamon, nutmeg and salt. Stir in bananas.

2 Pour over bread cubes and stir to coat. Bake, uncovered, at 375° for 40 minutes or until a knife inserted near the center comes out clean.

3 Meanwhile, for sauce, melt butter in a small saucepan. Combine sugar and cornstarch; add to butter. Stir in milk and corn syrup. Cook and stir over medium heat until the mixture comes to a full boil. Boil for 1 minute. Remove from the heat; stir in the vanilla. Serve warm sauce over warm pudding.

Tuxedo Cream Dessert

PREP: 40 MIN. + CHILLING YIELD: 6-8 SERVINGS

CAMILLA SAULSBURY NACOGDOCHES, TEXAS

My adaptation of my grandmother's signature dessert always garners oohs and aahs. It's pretty, deliciously rich and creamy. Gran and I have both considered it a favorite for entertaining because it can be made a day ahead.

- 1-3/4 teaspoons unflavored gelatin
- 2 tablespoons cold water
- 1-1/2 cups heavy whipping cream, *divided*
- 3/4 cup semisweet chocolate chips

VANILLA LAYER:
- 1-3/4 teaspoons unflavored gelatin
- 2 tablespoons cold water
- 1-2/3 cups heavy whipping cream, *divided*
- 1/4 cup sugar
- 2 teaspoons vanilla extract

STRAWBERRY SAUCE:
- 2 cups sliced fresh strawberries
- 2 to 3 tablespoons sugar

1 In a small bowl, sprinkle gelatin over cold water; let stand for 1 minute. In a small saucepan, bring 1 cup cream to a simmer. Stir 1/2 cup into gelatin mixture until gelatin is completely dissolved. Stir chocolate chips into remaining warm cream until melted. Stir in gelatin mixture and remaining cream.

2 Transfer to an 8-in. x 4-in. loaf pan coated with cooking spray. Cover and refrigerate for 30 minutes or until firm.

3 For vanilla layer, in a small bowl, sprinkle gelatin over cold water; let stand for 1 minute. In a small saucepan, bring 1 cup cream and sugar to a simmer. Stir in gelatin mixture until gelatin is completely dissolved. Stir in

3 eggs, lightly beaten

8 squares (1 ounce *each*) white baking chocolate, melted

1. In a large saucepan, bring rhubarb, 1/3 cup sugar and orange juice to a boil. Reduce heat; cook and stir until thickened and rhubarb is tender. Set aside.

2. In a small bowl, combine cracker crumbs and butter. Press onto the bottom of a greased 9-in. springform pan. Place on a baking sheet. Bake at 350° for 7-9 minutes or until lightly browned. Cool on a wire rack.

3. In a large bowl, beat the cream cheese, sour cream, cornstarch, vanilla, salt and remaining sugar until smooth. Add eggs; beat just until combined. Fold in white chocolate.

4. Pour half of the filling into crust. Top with half of the rhubarb sauce; cut through batter with a knife to gently swirl rhubarb. Layer with remaining filling and rhubarb sauce; cut through top layers with a knife to gently swirl rhubarb.

5. Place pan on a double thickness of heavy-duty foil (about 16 in. square). Securely wrap foil around pan. Place in a large baking pan; add 1 in. of hot water to larger pan. Bake at 350° for 60-70 minutes or until center is almost set.

6. Cool on a wire rack for 10 minutes. Carefully run a knife around edge of pan to loosen; cool 1 hour longer. Cover and chill overnight. Refrigerate leftovers.

Editor's Note: If using frozen rhubarb, measure rhubarb while still frozen, then thaw completely. Drain in a colander, but do not press liquid out.

vanilla and remaining cream. Carefully spoon over chocolate layer. Cover and refrigerate for at least 2 hours or until firm.

4. For sauce, in a blender, puree strawberries and sugar. Transfer to a bowl; cover and refrigerate until serving.

5. Just before serving, unmold dessert and cut into slices. Serve with strawberry sauce.

Rhubarb Swirl Cheesecake

PREP: 40 MIN. BAKE: 1 HOUR + CHILLING YIELD: 12-14 SERVINGS

CAROL WITCZAK TINLEY PARK, ILLINOIS

I love cheesecake and my husband loves chocolate, so this is a favorite treat of ours. The rhubarb adds a tartness that complements the sweet flavors so well.

2-1/2 cups thinly sliced fresh *or* frozen rhubarb

1/3 cup plus 1/2 cup sugar, *divided*

2 tablespoons orange juice

1-1/4 cups graham cracker crumbs

1/4 cup butter, melted

3 packages (8 ounces *each*) cream cheese, softened

2 cups (16 ounces) sour cream

1 tablespoon cornstarch

2 teaspoons vanilla extract

1/2 teaspoon salt

Special Pleasure Chocolate Cheesecake

PREP: 20 MIN. BAKE: 40 MIN. + CHILLING YIELD: 24 SERVINGS

BENJAMIN & SUE ELLEN CLARK WARSAW, NEW YORK

When I have time, I enjoy making cheesecakes. In fact, I've come up with a couple of my own recipes, and thought this one stood above the rest. I like this fail-proof dessert because it's so easy to prepare and has just the right mix of ingredients to make it a "special pleasure" for any palate!

- 1 package (18 ounces) ready-to-bake refrigerated triple-chocolate cookie dough
- 1 package (8 ounces) milk chocolate toffee bits
- 1 package (9-1/2 ounces) Dove dark chocolate candies
- 3 packages (8 ounces *each*) cream cheese, softened
- 1 can (14 ounces) sweetened condensed milk
- 1 carton (6 ounces) vanilla yogurt
- 4 eggs, lightly beaten
- 1 teaspoon vanilla extract

Whipped cream

1 Let dough stand at room temperature for 5-10 minutes to soften. Press nine portions of dough into an ungreased 13-in. x 9-in. baking dish (save remaining dough for another use). Set aside 2 tablespoons toffee bits for garnish; sprinkle remaining toffee bits over dough.

2 In a small microwave-safe bowl, heat chocolate candies at 70% power for 15 seconds; stir. Microwave in 5-second intervals until melted; stir until smooth.

3 In a large bowl, beat the cream cheese, milk and yogurt until smooth. Add eggs; beat on low speed just until combined. Fold in vanilla and melted chocolate. Pour over crust.

4 Bake at 350° for 40-45 minutes or until center is almost set. Cool on a wire rack. Refrigerate for 4 hours or overnight. Garnish with whipped cream and reserved toffee bits. Refrigerate leftovers.

Rocky Road Freeze

PREP: 15 MIN. + FREEZING YIELD: ABOUT 1-1/2 QUARTS

SHELIA BERRY CARRING PLACE, ONTARIO

Vary my recipe if you like. In place of peanuts, try using walnuts, pecans or cashews on occasion. Or substitute peanut butter chips for the chocolate chips. For a luscious treat-on-the-go, put a double scoop into a cone. You can also serve this for fancy events…it looks luxurious in a clear-glass sauce dish.

- 1 can (14 ounces) sweetened condensed milk
- 1/2 cup chocolate syrup
- 2 cups heavy whipping cream
- 1 cup miniature marshmallows
- 1/2 cup miniature chocolate chips
- 1/2 cup chopped salted peanuts

1 In a small bowl, combine the milk and chocolate syrup; set aside. In a large bowl, beat cream until stiff peaks form. Fold in chocolate mixture, marshmallows, chocolate chips and peanuts.

2 Transfer to a freezer-proof container; cover and freeze for 5 hours or until firm. Remove from freezer 10 minutes before serving.

Peanut Butter Chocolate Dessert

PREP: 20 MIN. + CHILLING YIELD: 12-16 SERVINGS

DEBBIE PRICE LARUE, OHIO

This classic recipe combines chocolate and peanut butter. It's a cinch to make because it doesn't require any baking.

- 20 chocolate cream-filled chocolate sandwich cookies, *divided*
- 2 tablespoons butter, softened
- 1 package (8 ounces) cream cheese, softened
- 1/2 cup peanut butter
- 1-1/2 cups confectioners' sugar, *divided*
- 1 carton (16 ounces) frozen whipped topping, thawed, *divided*
- 15 miniature peanut butter cups, chopped
- 1 cup cold milk
- 1 package (3.9 ounces) instant chocolate fudge pudding mix

1 Crush 16 cookies; toss with the butter. Press into an ungreased 9-in. square dish; set aside.

2 In a large bowl, beat the cream cheese, peanut butter and 1 cup confectioners' sugar until smooth. Fold in half of the whipped topping. Spread over crust. Sprinkle with peanut butter cups.

3 In another large bowl, beat milk, pudding mix and remaining confectioners' sugar on low speed for 2 minutes. Let stand for 2 minutes or until soft-set. Fold in remaining whipped topping; spread over peanut butter cups.

4 Crush remaining cookies; sprinkle over top. Cover and chill for at least 3 hours.

Apple Crumble

PREP: 30 MIN. BAKE: 40 MIN. + COOLING YIELD: 9 SERVINGS

CAROL SIMPKINS SANTA CRUZ, CALIFORNIA

While visiting friends in New Zealand, I watched someone make this dessert. At home, I came up with my own version.

- 8 sheets phyllo dough (14 inches x 9 inches)
- Butter-flavored cooking spray
- 1/2 cup packed brown sugar
- 2 tablespoons all-purpose flour
- 1/2 teaspoon ground cinnamon
- 1/2 teaspoon ground ginger
- 4 medium tart apples, peeled and sliced

TOPPING:
- 1/2 cup all-purpose flour
- 1/2 cup packed brown sugar
- 1/2 cup soft whole wheat bread crumbs
- 1/4 teaspoon ground ginger
- 1/4 teaspoon ground cinnamon
- 1/2 cup cold butter
- 1/4 cup slivered almonds

1 Cut phyllo sheets in half; spritz with cooking spray. Layer phyllo, sprayed side up, in a greased 8-in. square baking dish.

2 In a bowl, combine brown sugar, flour, cinnamon and ginger. Add apples; toss to coat. Spoon over dough.

3 For topping, in another large bowl, combine the flour, brown sugar, bread crumbs, ginger and cinnamon; cut in butter until mixture resembles coarse crumbs. Add almonds; sprinkle over apple mixture.

4 Bake at 350° for 40-45 minutes or until filling is bubbly and topping is golden. Cool for 10 minutes before serving.

general recipe index

CHEESE

Bacon-Cheese Appetizer Pie, 16
Bacon Cheeseburger Balls, 17
Beef 'n' Cheese Dip, 17
Beef Stew with Cheddar
    Dumplings, 54
Berry Cheesecake Muffins, 130
Cheddar Pear Pie, 199
Cherry Cheesecake Tarts, 212
Chocolate Chip Cookie Dough
    Cheesecake, 208
Chunky Blue Cheese Dip, 8
Cream Cheese Coils, 136
Creamy Swiss Onion Soup, 47
Four-Cheese Baked Ziti, 124
Four-Cheese Spinach Pizza, 108
Garlic Parmesan Breadsticks, 146
Golden Lemon Glazed
    Cheesecake, 216
Gorgonzola Figs with Balsamic
    Glaze, 16
Hazelnut Cheesecake
    Parfaits, 212
Italian Parmesan Bread, 141
Lemon Cheese Braid Bread, 131
Mocha Truffle Cheesecake, 210
Orange Cream Cheesecake, 219
Parmesan Chicken, 88
Parmesan Herb Loaf, 140
Pineapple Pecan Cheese Ball, 14
Rhubarb Swirl Cheesecake, 227
Rich 'n' Cheesy Macaroni, 116
Savory Cheese Soup, 59
Special Pleasure Chocolate
    Cheesecake, 228
Strawberry Cheesecake
    Ice Cream, 224
Strawberry Cheesecake Torte, 203
Swiss Potato Squares, 116
The Ultimate Grilled Cheese, 107
Three Cheese Enchiladas, 125

CHERRIES

Cherry Cheesecake Tarts, 212
Cherry Chip Scones, 154
Chocolate-Cherry Ice Cream
    Pie, 198
White Chocolate Mousse Cherry
    Pie, 196

CHICKEN

Almond Chicken Salad, 36
Apricot Chicken, 86
Baked Chicken and Acorn
    Squash, 80
Bombay Chicken, 79
Broccoli Chicken Cups, 10
Brown Rice Salad with Grilled
    Chicken, 36
Buffalo Wing Poppers, 9
Chickaritos, 19
Chicken and Asparagus Kabobs, 76
Chicken and Dumpling
    Casserole, 124
Chicken and Stuffing Pie, 117
Chicken Barley Soup, 59
Chicken in Basil Cream, 80
Chicken in Lime Butter, 91
Chicken in Potato Baskets, 123
Chicken Pear Mixed Greens
    Salad, 37
Chicken Pesto Pizza, 78
Chicken Pizza Packets, 89
Chicken Salad Panini, 39
Chicken Stew with Gnocchi, 48
Chicken with Spicy Fruit, 82
Colorful Chicken 'n' Squash Soup, 45
Corsican Chicken, 83
Creamy Chicken Lasagna, 113
Curried Chicken Salad
    Sandwiches, 31
Easy Chicken Potpie, 120
Fiery Chicken Spinach Salad, 24
Grilled Jerk Chicken Wings, 13
Honey Rosemary Chicken, 75
Italian Peasant Soup, 56
Marvelous Chicken Enchiladas, 120
Mexican Chicken Corn Chowder, 58
Mexican Chicken Manicotti, 112
Nutty Oven-Fried Chicken, 83
Orange Walnut Chicken, 84
Parmesan Chicken, 88
Pasta with Chicken and Squash, 74
Roasted Chicken with Garlic-Sherry
    Sauce, 87
Savory Chicken Dinner, 81
Sesame Chicken with Mustard
    Sauce, 84
Smothered Chicken Breasts, 79

Southern Barbecued Chicken, 81
Spinach Crab Chicken, 91
Squash-Stuffed Chicken, 82
Sunday Chicken Stew, 60
Sweet 'n' Spicy Chicken, 74
Tempura Chicken Wings, 18

CHOCOLATE

Chocolate and Fruit Trifle, 214
Chocolate Cake with Fudge
    Sauce, 202
Chocolate Caramel Fondue, 11
Chocolate-Cherry Ice Cream
    Pie, 198
Chocolate Chip Banana Cream
    Pie, 187
Chocolate Chip Cookie Dough
    Cheesecake, 208
Chocolate Coconut Candies, 171
Chocolate Crunch Ice Cream, 211
Chocolate Malted Cookies, 177
Chocolate Mocha Torte, 188
Chocolate Peanut Butter
    Dessert, 210
Chocolate Pretzel Cookies, 183
Chocolate Velvet Dessert, 222
Chocolate Whipping Cream
    Torte, 194
Coffee Shop Fudge, 182
Cookie Dough Truffles, 170
Frosted Fudge Brownies, 178
Maple Peanut Delights, 168
Mocha Truffles, 176
Peanut Butter Chocolate
    Dessert, 229
Pumpkin Chip Muffins, 142
Rich Truffle Wedges, 217
Rocky Road Freeze, 228
Special Mocha Cupcakes, 186
Special Pleasure Chocolate
    Cheesecake, 228
Toffee-Mocha Cream Torte, 204
Ultimate Double Chocolate
    Brownies, 170
Valentine Berries and Cream, 221
Very Chocolate Brownies, 169
White Chocolate Banana Cake, 193
White Chocolate Mousse Cherry
    Pie, 196

Pork with Pineapple Salsa, 101
Pork with Tangy Mustard Sauce, 100
Spicy Pork Tenderloin Salad, 33
Spicy Pork with Ginger-Maple
   Sauce, 95
Sweet 'n' Sour Ribs, 92
Tangy Pork Chops, 96
Teriyaki Pork Roast, 92

POTATOES & SWEET POTATOES

Chicken in Potato Baskets, 123
Chicken Stew with Gnocchi, 48
Creamy Chive Mashed Potatoes, 25
Duo Tater Bake, 27
Pleasing Potato Pizza, 107
Pork Chop Potato Dinner, 101
Southwestern Spuds, 37
Sweet Potato Fries, 30
Sweet Potatoes and Apples
   Au Gratin, 32
Swirled Potato Bake, 38
Swiss Potato Squares, 116
Tangy Potato Salad, 22
Warm Mustard Potato Salad, 41

PUMPKIN

Butter Pecan Pumpkin Pie, 194
Cream-Filled Pumpkin
   Cupcakes, 192
Curried Pumpkin Soup, 44
Frosty Pumpkin Pie, 204
Pumpkin Chip Muffins, 142
Pumpkin Scones with Berry
   Butter, 150

RASPBERRIES

Berry Cheesecake Muffins, 130
Berry Nectarine Buckle, 218
Croissant French Toast, 158
Macadamia Berry Dessert, 223
Raspberry Meringue Pie, 199
Raspberry Streusel Coffee Cake, 156
Royal Raspberry Cake, 201
Special Summer Berry Medley, 23

RHUBARB

Creamy Rhubarb Crepes, 159
Rhubarb Corn Bread Stuffing, 40

Rhubarb Swirl Cheesecake, 227
Strawberry Rhubarb Coffee
   Cake, 151

RICE

Apricot Rice Custard, 218
Brown Rice Salad with Grilled
   Chicken, 36
Cranberry Rice with Caramelized
   Onions, 30
Wild Rice Seafood Salad, 25

SALADS

Almond Chicken Salad, 36
Brown Rice Salad with Grilled
   Chicken, 36
Chicken Pear Mixed Greens
   Salad, 37
Chicken Salad Panini, 39
Crunchy Romaine Strawberry
   Salad, 32
Curried Chicken Salad
   Sandwiches, 31
Festive Fruit Salad, 40
Fiery Chicken Spinach Salad, 24
Fresh Broccoli and Mandarin
   Salad, 26
Fresh Corn Salad, 31
Orange Avocado Salad, 41
Sesame Cucumber Salad, 24
Shrimp 'n' Scallops Tropical Salad, 22
Smoked Turkey Pasta Salad, 34
Special Summer Berry Medley, 23
Spicy Pork Tenderloin Salad, 33
Summer Salad with Citrus
   Vinaigrette, 28
Summer Spinach Salad, 38
Tangy Potato Salad, 22
Tomato Corn Salad, 28
Warm Mustard Potato Salad, 41
Wild Rice Seafood Salad, 25

SANDWICHES

Chicken Salad Panini, 39
Curried Chicken Salad
   Sandwiches, 31
Garden Turkey Burgers, 77
Grilled Ham and Egg Salad
   Sandwiches, 162

Melt-in-Your-Mouth Sausages, 96
Onion Beef au Jus, 66
Onion Italian Sausage, 97
Pineapple-Stuffed Burgers, 67
Spicy Pork with Ginger-Maple
   Sauce, 95
Sweet Pepper Sandwiches, 109
Taco Puffs, 68
Terrific Teriyaki Burgers, 64
The Ultimate Grilled Cheese, 107
Zesty Turkey Burgers, 90

SAUSAGE

Asparagus Sausage Crepes, 152
Breakfast Pockets, 164
Chicago-Style Pan Pizza, 93
Creamy Sausage Stew, 52
Florentine Spaghetti Bake, 123
Italian Peasant Soup, 56
Italian Sausage and Zucchini
   Stir-Fry, 94
Italian Sausage Strata, 163
Meaty Three-Bean Chili, 61
Melt-in-Your-Mouth Sausages, 96
Onion Italian Sausage, 97
Pepperoni Pizza Chili, 54
Pepperoni Spinach Quiche, 160
Pizza Loaf, 146
Sausage Spinach Bake, 153
Southwest Sausage Bake, 161
Spicy Pork with Ginger-Maple
   Sauce, 95
Surprise Sausage Bundles, 142
Traditional Lasagna, 126

SEAFOOD

Broccoli Shrimp Alfredo, 104
Deviled Crab Dip, 12
Marinated Shrimp, 11
Mexican Shrimp Bisque, 46
New England Clam Chowder, 55
Seafood Lasagna, 114
Shrimp 'n' Noodle Bowls, 108
Shrimp 'n' Scallops Tropical
   Salad, 22
Southwestern Scallops, 105
Spinach Crab Chicken, 91
Veggie Shrimp Egg Rolls, 15
Wild Rice Seafood Salad, 25

alphabetical index